ALLIANCE
ADVANTAGE

❖

Yves L. Doz
Gary Hamel

ALLIANCE ADVANTAGE

❖

The Art of
Creating Value
through
Partnering

HARVARD BUSINESS SCHOOL PRESS
BOSTON, MASSACHUSETTS

Library of Congress Cataloging-in-Publication Data
Doz, Yves L.
    Alliance advantage: the art of creating value through
    partnering / Yves L. Doz, Gary Hamel.
        p.   cm.
    Includes bibliographical references and index.
    ISBN 0-87584-616-5
    1. Strategic alliances (Business)   2. Partnership.
    3. Interorganizational relations.   4. Competition.
I. Hamel, Gary.
    II. Title.
    HD69.S8D69   1998
    658.1'6—dc21   97-51446
                                                                 CIP

The paper used in this publication meets the requirements of the American
National Standard for Permanence of Paper for Printed Library Materials
Z39.49-1984.

Contents

ALLIANCE
ADVANTAGE

❖

❖
PREFACE

N O COMPANY can go it alone. For industry giants and ambitious start-ups alike, strategic partnerships have become central to competitive success in fast-changing global markets. More than ever, many of the skills and resources essential to a company's future prosperity lie outside the firm's boundaries, and outside management's direct control. In this new world of networks, coalitions, and alliances, strategic partnerships are not an option but a necessity—be it Toyota's network of suppliers, Microsoft's extended family of independent software developers, the member airlines in the Star Alliance, or the disparate group of companies cooperating with Motorola in launching dozens of communication satellites. To fully exploit the opportunities open to it, a company today must have an ability to conceive, shape, and sustain a wide variety of strategic partnerships. Indeed, right now, a plethora of new and imaginative strategic alliances is transforming industries from transportation to communication, health care, life sciences, media and entertainment, information technology, aerospace, and beyond. Hence the challenge: if the "capacity to collaborate" is not already a core competence in your organization, you had better get busy making it so.

We decided to write this book because, while we observed some executives making shrewd strategic use of alliances, we saw many more whose approach to forming and managing alliances seemed to destroy more value than it created. While alliances can create enormous wealth, they can also become black holes for management time and resources. In our experience, few executives have more than a superficial understanding of what drives the economic and competitive consequences of strategic alliances. Few understand how to move beyond the "deal" and the "structural" aspects of alliance making to the active management of alliances for robust value creation. Thus, while alliances have become inevitable, few live up to their early billing.

Typically, managers devote much attention to the formal design of an alliance at its inception. The legal structure, governance structure, gain-sharing terms, and exit clauses are the subjects of protracted bargaining and detailed scrutiny. Yet, all too often, the underlying assumptions about the strategic logic of the alliance have been poorly tested and are more fantasy than reality. Worse still, senior management often disengages once the deal is done, naively hoping that the alliance will fly along on autopilot. The challenge of sustaining the ongoing process of collaboration attracts little top management attention. No wonder the majority of alliances fall woefully short of original objectives. Clever deal making and grand visions are not enough. This book, therefore, is designed to focus executive attention on the process of value creation within alliances over time. It is not the deal per se that creates value, but the capacity of two partners to dynamically and creatively maneuver their alliance through a thicket of uncertainties, changing priorities, organizational frictions, and competitive surprises.

This book itself is the product of a strategic alliance. Each of us approached the alliance phenomenon from a different perspective but with a common interest in illuminating the longer-term competitive consequences of alliances. Gary's starting point was the role of alliances in global competition. Yves's initial interest was in the role of alliances in innovation and new business development. We were both intrigued by the processes of learning and evolution within alliances over time, and how these processes drove gains or losses in the competitiveness of partners.

Understanding the long-term competitive consequences of alliances requires a long-term vantage point: one has to observe the unfolding of alliances over time, assess their consequences, and analyze how managers perceived those consequences and factored them into their decisions. Today's breathless headlines about the latest grand partnership are of little help if the goal is to delve deeply into the subtle but important nuances that separate wealth-creating alliances from wealth-destroying alliances. Instead, one must take a longitudinal view, understanding how value creation and the competition position of each partner wax and wane over the five, ten, or more years an alliance may be in existence, and interpreting which managerial variables determine just who gets what out of the collaborative process. In most successful alliances, value creation is the work of a decade or more. Simplistic typologies and grand metaphors about "eco-systems" and "co-evolution" are of little value to executives charged with extracting profit and competitive advantage from complex partnerships in tumultuous times.

Our concern with the process of value creation within strategic alliances led us to delve deeply into the "forerunners" of today's fluid and uncertain alliances, such as the alliance between computer makers ICL in the United Kingdom and Fujitsu in Japan, and AT&T in the United States and Olivetti in Italy; the relationship between Rover and Honda; the evolution of Airbus; the alliance between Alza and Ciba-Geigy to develop new drug delivery systems; and other alliances from which one can now draw informed judgments about what really drives value creation. In all, we carefully reconstructed the history of about twenty alliances and followed their evolution in real time over several years. We tested our emerging generalizations on much wider samples of alliances on which we collected more limited data. We also ensured that we had, indeed, picked up forerunners (and not dinosaurs) by testing the applicability of our findings with executives building and managing very current alliances, the ones that *are* making headlines in the business press today.

As is typical of alliances, our process of working together was slower, lengthier, and more difficult than anticipated. A lot of people provided useful insights to help us develop our findings and build our argument. First and foremost, C. K. Prahalad, our close friend and colleague, was an early stimulant to our interest in strategic alliances and a significant contributor to our thinking. Others at INSEAD, in particular

Philippe Haspeslagh, Ingemar Dierickx, Ben Bensaou, Mitchell Koza, and André Laurent, and in other institutions, in particular Ranjay Gulati, Peter Ring, Bala Chakravarthy, and Eleanor Westney, shared their insights with us.

Even more important, thousands of executives—both in the companies that opened their doors to help us carry out our research, and in the many seminars at INSEAD, the London Business School, and scores of companies—challenged our thinking, helped sharpen our ideas, and provided constantly renewed and demanding "testing grounds" for our findings. We owe much to their collective understanding and experience.

To Amy Shuen, who worked at INSEAD as a research associate in the late 1980s, Yves owes much of the process analysis of the early cases and a contribution to their conceptualization. Amy also worked with Gary on several cases. Several other assistants helped us with the field work, in particular Mark Bleakley at LBS and Robin Millington and Mark Cunningham at INSEAD. Gerda Rossell did very useful archival searches on a variety of alliances. Most critically, Alison James at INSEAD and Karen Moss at LBS protected our schedules so we could devote enough time to our research in otherwise overcommitted lives. Alison Connell and Stéphanie Pons played a critical role in seeing the manuscript through countless revisions with great patience and dedication.

The editors and staff of the Harvard Business School Press were extremely supportive and patient. Dick Luecke greatly helped us shape the manuscript; Carol Franco, Hollis Heimbouch, Nick Philipson, and Marjorie Williams provided valuable feedback on our work and our writing, and kept us moving.

Finally, we owe a great deal to our families, who endured weeks when we were away on field work, countless evenings and weekends when we had to "work on the book," and many days and weeks when we conducted seminars all over the world to test our thoughts and findings.

❖

INTRODUCTION

TEN YEARS AGO, when we asked participants in our executive seminars whether their firms needed alliances, the answer was most often "No." Corporate managers from Stuttgart, Armonk, Ludwigshafen, Midland (Michigan), Peoria (Illinois), Munich, and other business centers were content to go it alone, confident that they had the resources and know-how to compete and win. Today, our question is purely rhetorical.

An unprecedented number of strategic alliances between firms are being formed each year. These are not limited to a few industries but occur broadly in transportation, manufacturing, telecommunications, electronics, pharmaceuticals, finance, and even professional services. They bridge national borders and continents. Indeed, the strategic alliance has become a cornerstone of global competitiveness, one that all executives must now understand and manage with skill.[1]

Strategic alliances are a logical and timely response to intense and rapid changes in economic activity, technology, and globalization, all of which have cast many corporations into two competitive races: one for the world and the other for the future. Globalization opened the race for the world as firms entered once-closed markets and pursued untapped opportunities. The race for the future compels firms to discover new market opportunities, new solutions for customers, new answers to poorly met needs.

Together, technical and political upheavals have thrown many firms into both races at once. Consider telecommunications. Here, entirely new services and means of content delivery are now possible. As computers and communications converge, cable television, data networks, telephony, and traditional broadcasting become substitutes and merge. At the same time, deregulation, privatization, and the opening of national markets in Asia, Latin America, and Europe to global competitors pose a threat to local competitors, whose traditional protections are evaporating, and represent new opportunities for global firms.

Ten years ago the question was: "Who can still run these races alone?" The answer today is: "Nobody." Today a more relevant question is whether alliances should be a cornerstone of corporate strategy. Proud companies such as Ericsson, BMW, and Procter & Gamble, while acknowledging the importance of alliances, used to say "No." Those few companies which did make alliances a cornerstone of their development years ago—such as Corning in engineered silica materials and Robert Flemings in investment banking—were exceptions. Alliances were usually confined to peripheral businesses, marginal markets, and emerging countries where they could not be avoided. Not so today. Alliances now play a central and strategic role in a growing number of companies.

Ironically, a decade of reengineering and refocusing has made many corporations more needful than ever of strategic allies. Most management teams have addressed demands for greater shareholder value creation by a mix of refocusing around core competencies and core businesses—becoming more selective about what they do—and reengineering, downsizing, and delayering—becoming leaner and more productive in doing what they still do. The self-contained, vertically integrated companies of yesteryear are largely extinct.[2]

If few firms can now create and deliver products and services on their own, fewer still can control leading-edge technologies. Technologies are seldom controlled by single firms. Consider flat panel displays. The leader in this important area is the Toshiba-IBM alliance. The challengers are also alliances: small entrepreneurial companies such as France's Pixtech—itself allied with Motorola, Futaba, and Raytheon for new product technology development and with United

Microelectronics in Taiwan for manufacturing processes—and major groups, in particular Korean *chaebols* such as Samsung and LG, which are allied with Compaq, Acer, and others.

Whether they are racing for the world or for the future—or for both—more and more companies are deciding not to compete alone but in the company of allies. Unfortunately, few managers are prepared for a world in which the boundaries between collaboration and competition are unclear and in which the answer to the questions "Who are my friends? Who are my enemies?" is not easy and can change overnight. Nor has their experience with traditional joint ventures prepared them for the more complex world of alliances and alliance networks.

To date, most intercompany collaborations have involved the setting up and management of joint ventures in well-circumscribed areas. In most cases, these ventures are designed to contain and share known risks, not to create an expansive future. These risks are well understood, and the strategic foundations of the joint venture are clear to the partners, whose managers focus most of their attention on the economics and contractual design of the agreement. Once agreement is reached, one of the partners usually assumes operating responsibility and, for all practical purposes, runs the operation as if it were the sole owner. This arrangement lacks the dynamism, collaboration, and mutual learning characteristic of successful strategic alliances. The strategic alliance, in contrast, is characterized by the following:

- There is greater uncertainty and ambiguity.
- The manner in which value is created—and the way in which partners capture it—is not preordained.
- The partner relationship evolves in ways that are hard to predict.
- Today's ally may be tomorrow's rival—or may be a current rival in some other market.
- Managing the alliance relationship over time is usually more important than crafting the initial formal design.
- Initial agreements have less to do with success than does adaptability to change.

Unfortunately, few managers are prepared to handle these issues. Very little in their experience—including traditional joint ventures—

has provided suitable training. As a result, many alliance managers falter, procrastinate, or just burn out, and the collaborative linkages they are charged with nurturing come apart.

This book aims to help managers and their companies to be more successful in creating and guiding their strategic alliances. To that end it offers both conceptual and practical tools for analyzing the design and performance of alliances and presents a wide range of examples of both successful and unsuccessful collaborations. Although the traditional approach to this subject—and the attention of most executives—gravitates toward initial deal making, our focus extends more broadly to what strategic foundations make it possible for alliances to create value and what dynamic processes and partner interactions make it possible for allies to meet their strategic goals.

Chapter 1 explains how the race for the world and the race for the future compel companies to create alliances. It describes how these new alliances challenge the conventional wisdom inherited from earlier partnerships and joint ventures and call for a new mindset in their management.

Chapter 2 establishes the strategic foundations of sound and robust alliances: how alliances create value and what are the enabling conditions for value creation. Using the definitions and practical concepts developed in this chapter, readers will be able to assess the strategic soundness of their own alliances.

Chapter 3 argues that the expectations of partners with respect to alliance duration, scope, coordination of joint tasks, and so forth should be driven by how the partners want the alliance to create value. Put differently, consistency needs to be achieved between the value creation goals of the alliance and the way its design and processes are defined and implemented. This chapter offers guidelines for achieving this consistency.

Building on the understanding gained in Chapter 3, Chapter 4 examines how each partner's respective positions and ambitions affect the robustness or fragility of the alliance. It provides templates that will help managers to select potential partners and to assess the strategic compatibility of themselves and their partners, particularly in the more difficult circumstances of collaboration between industry competitors.

Managers can minimize conflicts by design—both through alliance configuration and coordination. Chapter 5 shows them how. Coordination is achieved through both the governance structure and the interface the partners put in place to perform joint and coordinated tasks.

Chapter 6 shows how the similarities and differences between partners' frames of reference, organizational cultures, decision-making processes, and "ways of working" can facilitate or hamper collaboration. Some allied companies find it fairly easy to work together, while others discover deep differences. This chapter helps managers to conduct a systematic review of the organizational compatibility between partners.

The initial design of the alliance and the similarities and differences between partners interact to make alliance processes more or less cooperative. Chapter 7 provides managers with guidance on how to build and manage constructive and collaborative processes between themselves and their partners.

Chapter 8 examines the cooperative processes that influence the costs and benefits of each partner, balance within the alliance, and, ultimately, the value of its outcomes for each partner. It also reviews sources of stability and instability over time and the way in which balance can be monitored and sources of instability addressed.

Chapter 9 turns from the analysis of single alliances to the issue of their embeddedness in a wider web of alliances. It discusses various types of alliance portfolios and networks and the various approaches to their management.

The final chapter, Chapter 10, considers "alliance readiness"—the cooperative capability of the organization and its managers. It will help readers answer the questions "Does my firm have the makings of a good alliance partner?" and "Can I manage an alliance effectively?"

Chances are that different readers of this book will have very different experiences with alliances. On one extreme, some will have no experience; on the other, they will have been involved in one or more alliances from inception to termination. Most readers, we suspect, will fall somewhere between these ends of the experience spectrum. Since these different readers are likely to find specific chapters of more immediate relevance than others, each chapter is designed to be relatively self-standing. Nevertheless, the text provides an integrated approach to helping managers avoid the most common and dangerous pitfalls we have observed.

The Appendix is designed to serve as a template to highlight the important questions to be addressed in planning, designing, starting,

and managing an alliance over time. It recasts key issues in our argument as questions to managers and provides a checklist to cover the
various facets of alliance management. Its outline parallels that of the
text, but it is not meant to be read sequentially. Instead, it is
intended to be used as a tool for helping the reader apply insights
gained in the main text to the specific alliance situation he or she
may be facing.

1

THE NEW ALLIANCE GAME

POWERFUL FORCES are driving the formation of strategic alliances between firms in the world economy. The movement toward globalization has opened many new opportunities to companies, triggering a desperate race for the world by major global suppliers of everything from credit cards to telecommunications. Once they are in the game, many find themselves eyeball-to-eyeball with ambitious global players as well as local competitors whose friendly home governments restrict market access to a chosen few. Countries like China, for example, select key investors and partners and give them privileged market access while excluding others. In this game, companies cannot play without partners both local and global.

As we saw in the 1970s, when Western car makers struggled to close the quality gap with their Japanese competitors, in global competition, gaps in skills between competitors have become both more painfully apparent and very much less tolerated. Who develops the best products fastest? Who achieves the highest quality at the lowest cost? Which company has the resources and know-how to install a world-class phone or cable system in a short time? In the intensely competitive global arena, companies must identify their skill and competency gaps and fill them rapidly. Very often they find that the fastest way to fill them is with the capabilities of strategic allies.

The globalization movement is paralleled by a new industrial revolution: an information and communication age driven by technological breakthroughs that have spawned entirely new industries, such as mobile communications and interactive multimedia. As this new age takes form, it is dramatically altering existing markets and reconfiguring established industries, triggering a race for the future among the world's fleetest competitors.

Three features of the race for the future make alliances essential. First, many of the great opportunities of the information age call for the melding of skills and resources that few individual companies now possess entirely. Second, this revolution isn't being built on vertically integrated structures of single corporations, as was the industrial revolution that preceded it. More and more, it is being built on "seamless" networks[1] that must be standardized across vast expanses and complementary applications. Digital cash and global payment systems are the archetypes of these new service networks. The value of a good or service to each customer depends on how many others use the same good or service. Whoever is first with a strong network solution enjoys lasting first-mover advantages, as there is room only for a very few successful competitors. Third, the uncertainty inherent to the information economy, with its myriad of new markets to create and emerging technologies to define, calls for alliances not only to serve the usual purpose of bringing together complementary strengths but also that of combining insight and understanding to reduce uncertainties and accelerate learning.

The races for the world and the future require the development of insight, capabilities, and infrastructure at an ever faster pace that few companies can master, and yet they must be swifter and swifter if strategic advantage is to be gained. If a company cannot position itself quickly, it misses important opportunities, whether they are in China or cyberspace. It may also find itself in a precarious competitive position. In most cases, in-house developments and new "green field" investments are simply too slow and problematic for rapid positioning. By contrast, well-chosen alliances make it possible to bypass slow and costly efforts to build one's capabilities and to access new opportunities.

In principle, acquisitions are an alternative to strategic alliances. But an acquisition is a blunt tool, often leading one to acquire more, for a higher price, than one needs. And some of the very resources one hopes to gain through acquisition—such as the close government relationship that in many countries confers insider status or the commitment of key scientists to do their best—may not survive the transaction. Further, as companies refocus around core competencies, it makes less and less sense to acquire only part of a business; disconnected from its supporting competencies, the part loses some of its value; yet acquiring the whole company might not be feasible nor desirable. The value of an acquisition, in any case, is often difficult to establish in advance, particularly in the context of underdeveloped markets and uncertain technologies. Alliances have therefore emerged as the vehicle of choice for many companies in both the race for the world and the race for the future.

Iridium

Consider the case of Iridium, a broad alliance initiated by Motorola in the early 1990s to develop and build a global satellite-based mobile communications network.[2] By ringing the earth with sixty-six low-orbit satellites, Motorola planned to overcome the limitations of ground-based cellular phone networks and leapfrog its competitors. Unlike current cellular systems, Iridium's would use its satellites to beam signals directly to and from small phone handsets. Iridium was Motorola's bet both on the complete globalization of wireless telecommunications and on its concentration in a few global networks.

To implement its ambitious project, Motorola needed funds, traffic rights, and complementary capabilities (particularly for space technologies). To secure these, it brought together an exceptional coalition of seventeen equity-holding partners, including local national telecommunications companies, whose concerns over the bypassing of their infrastructures (and their traffic fee collection process) had to be placated, and an array of industrial partners, including Raytheon, Lockheed Martin, Krunichev Enterprise (the Russian launch rocket supplier), China Great Wall, and Nippon Iridium (itself an alliance of eighteen Japanese partners). The inclusion of these industrial partners had a clear purpose: to provide the technologies that Motorola needed but could not (or did not wish to) master, from ground communication to the whole range of very demanding technologies inherent to space-based communications. And it needed them fast. Other consortia, notably Globalstar, led by Loral, a specialist in space communications and defense technologies, were racing for the same opportunity.

The first Iridium satellite launches took place in 1997, with wireless global telecommunication services slated to begin in late 1998. The $3.4 billion investment is intended to capture most of the demand from "high-end" travelers around the world and to bolster Motorola's leadership in cellular communications. For Motorola and its partners, Iridium was (and remains) a formidable bet.

Primary Purposes of an Alliance

Like Motorola, many leading companies find themselves racing for both the world and the future. And since few have everything they need to succeed on their own, alliances play a key role. In this, alliances have at least three distinct purposes:

1. *Co-option.* Co-option turns potential competitors into allies and providers of the complementary goods and services that allow new businesses to develop. Here we use the term *co-option* in the sense that (a) potential rivals are effectively neutralized as threats by bringing them into the alliance and (b) firms with complementary goods to contribute are wooed, creating network economies in favor of the coalition.[3] As princes and warriors have observed through the centuries, often the most painless way to neutralize potential foes is to bring them into one's own camp. Both competitors and "complementers" need to be co-opted into coalitions.

   Motorola, for instance, needed the national telecommunication service operators in its coalition on both counts: to provide Iridium with traffic rights (complementer co-option) and to make them supportive of Iridium's deployment and also unavailable to rival coalitions (competitor co-option).

2. *Cospecialization.* Cospecialization is the synergistic value creation that results from the combining of previously separate resources, positions, skills, and knowledge sources. Partners contribute unique and differentiated resources—skills, brands, relationships, positions, and tangible assets—to the success of their alliances, and alliances create value when those resources are cospecialized, that is, they become substantially more valuable when bundled together in a joint effort than when kept separate. For example, Motorola needed the cospecialized resources of its aerospace industry partners to develop and build a complete space-based communications network.

   Cospecialization becomes increasingly important, and more likely to be at the heart of an alliance, as companies refocus on a narrower range of core skills and activities and as opportunities become systems and solutions rather than discrete products (Iridium, for instance, is a complex, tightly integrated system). This makes the individual company less likely to be the sole source of the skills and capabilities needed for exploiting new opportunities.

3. *Learning and internalization.* Alliances may also be an avenue for learning and internalizing new skills, in particular those which are tacit, collective, and embedded (and thus hard to obtain and internalize by other means). Core competencies are not for sale on an open market. When these skills can be learned from a partner, internalized, and exploited beyond the boundaries of the alliance itself, they become all the more valuable. Thus, the learning one gains from an alliance partner can often be leveraged broadly into other activities and businesses beyond those covered by the alliance.

These three purposes of an alliance are discussed in detail in Chapter 2. In combination with the fluidity and uncertainty of competition, they create fundamental challenges for many firms. The strategic significance of these purposes makes alliances much more central to corporate strategy. Alliances are becoming unavoidable. They are taking firms into new and uncertain territory, at the edge of their current domains and skill sets, and they are testing the ability of these firms to manage complex relationships. Much of the critical resource base that will determine the success of a company now lies outside its boundaries and escapes its direct control. In a word, alliances are becoming both strategically critical and harder to manage.

New Alliances versus Old Joint Ventures

On the surface, one might not see a great deal of difference between an alliance and the more familiar joint venture. Both, after all, seek to accomplish what the individual firm cannot, or chooses not, to attempt on its own. Nevertheless, the two differ in at least five ways.

First, strategic alliances are often more central to firm strategy than traditional joint ventures. In the past, very few companies created joint ventures close to the core of their businesses; fewer still made them a cornerstone of corporate strategy. Those which did were clear exceptions. Typically, joint ventures were formed to exploit specific opportunities that were somewhat peripheral to the strategic priorities of the firm. In the 1970s, for example, Peugeot, Renault, and Volvo, three midsize European car makers, created a joint venture to make six-cylinder engines for the top of their product range, but all three were more focused on mass markets and midsize cars, for which four-cylinder engines were quite sufficient. Also, joint ventures were rarely used by leading companies in the pursuit of fundamentally new markets and technologies. Their main purpose was most often to obtain economies of scale and scope in marginal but well-known market segments that were too small for each firm to serve separately, such as that for large powerful cars in Europe.[4]

Second, traditional joint ventures combined known resources and most often shared known risks, such as in the oil industry. What each partner brought and what it gained was clear. New alliances, in contrast, face much greater uncertainty, both in the resources they bring together and in the external turbulence they confront. They push the leading edge of technologies and bring together emerging and rapidly evolving skills, often for the first time. The ultimate value of each partner's contributions as well as the value of the benefits each will draw from the alliance are unclear at the outset. New alliances are used to reduce uncertainty rather than simply combine known resources.[5]

Third, new alliances increasingly involve multiple partners, whereas old joint ventures were often bilateral. Iridium encompasses no fewer than seventeen main partners, and this is not that unusual. Fewer and fewer of the alliances intended to exploit new opportunities comprise only two partners. The more partners, the greater the risk of divergence and the development of subcoalitions between them.

Fourth, alliances are now forged seldom to coproduce single products but increasingly to develop complex systems and solutions that call for the resources of many partners.

Fifth, being less certain, less stable, and at the competitive edge, alliances are inherently more difficult to manage. What resources are going to be needed and how best to combine them are not known for sure at the outset. How best to manage the interface between partners and to govern their relationship is something to be discovered rather than determined at inception. Partner relationships are highly ambiguous, and today's partner may be tomorrow's competitor. So where should the boundaries between areas of competition and collaboration be fixed? And as alliances proliferate, it becomes impossible to manage even simple bilateral alliances without taking into account the web of other relationships in which the partners engage. Any alliance may trigger unforeseen operational or strategic interdependencies with any other alliance in which one or both partners are engaged.

Given the strategic role that alliances now play in business competition, it is disappointing to find how few managers pay attention to their fluidity and evolution and how many academics and consultants offer simpleminded analyses and prescriptions for their management. To a great extent, both management literature and practice are influenced more by the experience of traditional joint ventures than by the less certain, more fluid, and more ambiguous environments of alliances.

To see the challenges facing alliance managers more clearly, let's revisit the Iridium example.

As of this writing, Iridium was at the leading edge of new technologies. Its sixty-six Lockheed-developed satellites were designed to be affordable, each costing about one-tenth the price of current satellites. The low unit cost of these satellites would not be simply a function of production scale; cost-saving technologies and innovations would be needed. But their development would require careful integration with the work of allies who would be responsible for developing the ground-based stations, system software, and the like that would make the entire system work. Getting all of the parts to fit together seamlessly would be a complex exercise in technology integration.

Iridium faced several further challenges. First, how would it compete against rivals such as Globalstar? The answer was not clear. Globalstar's reliance on the ground infrastructures of conventional telecommunications networks would give it an obvious advantage over Iridium: traditional service providers would more naturally ally themselves with Globalstar. Second, the future shape of worldwide long distance mobile communications was unclear; as a result, Iridium's place in that future industry was equally unclear. Pricing, too, was problematic. Third, the relationships between Iridium partners could potentially unravel. Some partners already found themselves in conflicted situations. Lockheed, for instance, after its acquisition of a 20 percent equity position in Loral Space & Communication, found itself with a significant stake in both Iridium and Globalstar. Would it be able to maintain a "Chinese wall" between the two projects and not let its interests and activities in one influence its behavior in the other? Finally, the many alliances in which Iridium aerospace partners took part on their own accounts had created a tangled web of relationships that Motorola executives had to understand and deal with intelligently. A change anywhere in the web of alliances would have repercussions for either good or ill within Iridium.

The challenges just described are not uncommon in other alliances, and they raise four fundamental questions for partners:

1. *Will the alliance create value, and for whom?* Put differently, what can the partners realistically expect from the alliance? How will it create value, and where? Will the benefits be commensurate with the efforts of partners? How should the alliance be structured and managed to maximize the odds of creating value?

2. *Will the alliance stand the test of time?* Although longevity per se should not be a goal, the fact remains that most alliances only create value over time. Hence, the ability of the alliance to survive external turbulence and internal dissension is an important concern. Will the alliance last long enough to create value? What elements of design and management will increase the odds for survival?

3. *Will the partners reconcile conflicting priorities and concerns?* Conflicts between partners are common and usually unavoidable. These can undermine the commitment of individual partners; in the worst cases, they can torpedo the entire alliance. The question is, how can conflicts be contained or resolved? How can the commitment of the alliance partners be maintained or strengthened?

4. *How will each partner manage its growing web of alliances?* During the Cold War period, the United States was a member of many mutual defense alliances in North America, Europe, and Asia. Whatever happened in one part of the world inevitably affected its relationship and credibility with allies elsewhere. Large global corporations are little different; they are parties to several alliances, and what occurs in one has implications for the others. How should a company respond in one alliance to developments in another?

These are the key questions we will address in this book. In doing so, we will first explore each question in greater depth, identifying the managerial challenge involved in each and indicating how each defies the conventional wisdom and usual assumptions about joint ventures and alliances.

Table 1-1 presents the perspective we will take. The left-hand column highlights what we have observed conventional wisdom to be, and the right-hand column outlines a new perspective, one that is more useful in managing today's alliances. The table suggests the deep differences between the conventional wisdom we inherit from our experience with joint ventures and the new perspective that successful strategic alliances require.

Before we embark on the analysis of how to design and manage alliances to beat the odds, we need to explore these changes in perspective and mindset that firms and their executives must make as a precondition to successful alliance management.

Value Creation

In new strategic alliances, managers need to take a broader view of performance than they did in traditional partnerships, focusing on a wide range of economic and strategic outcomes. Some of these outcomes are the *options* that accrue to partners; their values cannot be

TABLE 1-1 *Conventional versus Current Thinking on Alliances*

CONVENTIONAL WISDOM		A NEW PERSPECTIVE
WILL THE ALLIANCE CREATE VALUE? AND FOR WHOM?		
• Cost-benefit analysis	→	• Complex strategic assessment
• Value-creation priority	→	• Value-capture emphasis
• Simple complementation	→	• Complex cospecialization
• Initial structure	→	• Evolving process
WILL VALUE CREATION STAND THE TEST OF TIME?		
• Managing a set of objectives	→	• Tracking moving targets
• Implementing a single bargain	→	• Striking multiple bargains
• Making a commitment	→	• Creating and maintaining options
• Achieving longevity	→	• Contributing to competitiveness
WILL THE PARTNERS RECONCILE CONFLICTING PRIORITIES AND CONCERNS?		
• Collaboration	→	• Collaboration and competition
• Interdependence	→	• Risk of unbalanced dependence
• Trust	→	• Enlightened mutual interest
HOW WILL EACH PARTNER FIRM MANAGE ITS GROWING WEB OF ALLIANCES?		
• Marriage	→	• Realpolitik, diplomacy
• Single relationship	→	• Alliance networks

measured easily. If more strategic choices become available or, on the contrary, if strategic opportunities are foreclosed, it is difficult to place a value on the alliances that produced these outcomes. Here a shift from simple cost-benefit analysis—of inputs versus outputs—to a probabilistic assessment of strategic value is required.

Traditional partnerships are not the best training ground for managers who must make strategic alliances create value. This is particularly true in new environments where the melding of complex and heterogeneous skills and the interaction between dissimilar organizations are the bases for value creation. Value creation is heavily dependent on successful cospecialization between the skills of different partner organizations, and the payoff of this cospecialization is hard to predict. So, too, are opportunity costs, which are much harder to assess than are the costs and benefits of highly circumscribed joint ventures operating in known markets with proven technologies. Assessing value creation is much easier in traditional joint ventures, where the economics are simpler and better understood.

Conventional wisdom encourages managers to look for value creation potential in the initial design of the alliance and in terms of governance. It supports a natural tendency to focus on contractual terms. In answering the question "What's in it for us?" traditional joint ventures rely heavily on initial structure and governance. In a strategic alliance, however, initial structure and governance need to be complemented with attention to management process over time.

Cost-Benefit Analysis versus Strategic Assessment

Value creation in traditional joint ventures, and in customer-supplier partnerships, is usually easy to measure. In mature, well-established industries with known markets, known technologies, well-identified skills, and reference prices, measures of both inputs and outputs are generally workable. In upstream collaborations, such as joint R&D projects, it is easier to assess the respective contributions (inputs) of the partners than the relative benefits (outputs). In downstream ventures, such as joint distribution, the opposite is often the case: market results (outputs) may be easier to measure than relative efforts (inputs).

The new alliances we have observed pose tough valuation challenges, and they do so for the following reasons:

- They are more strategic than traditional joint ventures.
- They create value in many different ways.
- Their ultimate consequences cannot be anticipated with precision.

As a result, simple attempts at economic valuation break down.

The measurement of costs and benefits—in particular value capture benefits that accrue outside the alliance and that are strategic rather than financial—calls for a broad understanding of value creation and a keen sense for value capture. This is especially true when the alliance is used to learn about a new environment and thereby reduce the uncertainties present in a new territory. The strategic benefits of this activity are difficult to quantify. Here, allied firms that have long experience with traditional joint ventures must be cautious. Applying measurement methods used successfully with simple or strategically peripheral joint ventures to strategic alliances with greater ambiguity and strategic importance is inappropriate and will likely produce a misleading assessment.

Costs and benefits are also unclear because they accrue both in what the partners do *jointly* and in what they do *separately*. For example, when JVC, the Japanese consumer electronics firm associated with Matsushita, supplies components to a joint venture it runs in Europe with Thomson, also a consumer electronics firm, it creates and draws value both from the joint venture's own activities in Europe (visible to Thomson) and from incremental economies of scale derived from making components in Japan for the joint venture (at a cost not known by Thomson).

If value creation is difficult to measure, value *capture* is even harder to calculate. This is because so many alliance benefits are indirect. What matters most may not be the balance of direct alliance inputs and outputs but the impact of the alliance on the competitive standing of each partner and the strategic options made available or foreclosed. Thus, some alliance value can be measured directly, but other benefits enter the ledgers of partner companies "surreptitiously." These may be intangible and difficult to link with the activities of the alliance, but they are real nevertheless.

Consider the General Motors–Toyota NUMMI joint venture to produce automobiles in California. In learning how to apply "lean" manufacturing to a restive unionized work force in North America, the two firms created value together. That value manifested itself in at least two ways: high-quality, efficiently produced cars, and the learning that accrued to the partners. The efficiency with which the cars were jointly produced was a tangible measure of value creation, but what about the learning? Did it have value to GM? Did it do anything to enhance GM's competitiveness? We would argue that the learning had value only to the extent that it was *captured* by GM—that is, to the extent that GM succeeded in applying what it learned to GM-owned plants in North America and elsewhere. This is a measure of value capture from GM's point of view, not of overall value creation in the alliance.[6]

While simple in principle, differentiating value capture from value creation is difficult in practice. For example, GM's yardsticks for measuring value creation and value capture, respectively, might have entailed measurements of manufacturing productivity, on the one hand, and, on the other, the number of managers it rotated through the joint venture. Yet unless the costs of producers (the minimum staff needed to operate the plant) and learners (those managers and specialists there to learn but not essential to lean plant operations) among the GM staff sent to the joint venture were clearly differentiated, measures of value creation and value capture would quickly become blurred, leading to conflicting imperatives. Value creation, after all, would lead GM to understaff managerial ranks by design in order to stretch productivity, while value capture would lead the auto maker to overstaff the venture's management team and thus provide more of its managers and staff with the opportunity to maximize learning.

Unless value capture opportunities are explicitly identified and attended to, value capture is unlikely to take place. In other words, what should really matter to GM is not the financial performance of the NUMMI joint venture or even what it learned in working with Toyota. What is important is how effectively GM appropriated and transferred the lessons from that learning throughout its manufacturing network and the degree to which those lessons produced productivity gains and quality improvement throughout GM.

In sum, the key is to keep an eye on both value creation and value capture, to separate the two clearly in developing yardsticks for measuring alliance performance, and to manage both.

The Challenge of Effective Cospecialization

Value creation for many alliances is a function of cospecialization between partner contributions; in other words, the value of each partner's contributions is enhanced when combined with the contributions of other partners. We are not referring here to the sharing of capacity by two chemical companies or to the agreement through which Peugeot, Renault, and Volvo jointly make engines but to arrangements that bring together very different kinds of partners, with strongly differentiated but highly cospecialized contributions.

Today's alliances often involve melding differentiated skill sets from vastly different and often very distant partners. In many instances, each partner's skill set is not only foreign to the other partners but may also be relatively new. The success of this skill melding determines the value partners can realistically expect from the alliance.

Skill melding cannot be taken for granted. For instance, when Alza and Ciba-Geigy began development of advanced drug delivery systems (ADDS), which regulate the slow release of a treatment substance into the patient's bloodstream through the skin or the intestinal tract, the partners had to meld very different capabilities and skills.[7] Alza operated with multidisciplinary teams that responded in unplanned and creative ways to technical difficulties as they arose. Ciba-Geigy, in contrast, had a highly disciplined and structured process for drug development in which specialists intervened sequentially, one after the other. Both skill sets were needed, but bringing them together proved to be a marriage of oil and water.

The challenge of skill cospecialization is not simply one of geographic distance but is bound up with strategic, organizational, and cultural differences between partners. The Alza–Ciba-Geigy alliance, for example, reflected differences in company origins, histories, and core skills. Alza was a small, entrepreneurial new venture launched in Palo Alto, California, by a visionary physician, Alex Zaffaroni. Zaffaroni believed deeply in the value of an informal, egalitarian environment in which unique talents could bloom through self-structuring teams. Alza's teams worked quickly and informally to integrate the many technologies needed to develop advanced drug delivery systems. Ciba-Geigy, on the other hand, was a two-hundred-year-old company and one of the major Swiss pharmaceutical groups. It was the epitome of a traditional, disciplined, dedicated European company. And as a large multinational company, Ciba-Geigy was formally structured and bureaucratic.

Deep historical, cultural, and organizational differences between the two companies made the melding of their cospecialized skills and resources particularly difficult. This difficulty was compounded by the genuine challenge of the task they faced together. Market, technology, and competitive instability added to the burden. Nevertheless, each of the allies saw the benefits of working together as greater than the accompanying difficulties. One of the very reasons for entering an alliance, as opposed to obtaining technology licensing deals or product supply agreements, concerns the need to adapt and commingle tacit skills to achieve an objective.

New alliances increasingly seek to meld together cospecialized but widely different skills, contributed by deeply dissimilar partner organizations of different sizes, histories, and management styles. If cooperation is difficult between Aérospatiale, British Aerospace, and Daimler-Benz Aerospace, all three large European companies in the same industry, consider Hewlett-Packard and Microsoft, or Toshiba, IBM, and Motorola.

INITIAL STRUCTURE AND EVOLVING PROCESS

As described earlier, the static view of alliances inherited from traditional joint ventures encourages managers to pay too much attention to the initial crafting of alliance design and too little attention to the likely impact of that design on the subsequent process of collaboration between partners. The initial architecture of the alliance (contracts and/or legal and organizational entities, governance mechanisms, interface formats, etc.) can become a straitjacket as the alliance evolves. It should be reassessed and even revised as the partners learn more about the structures and relationships needed for value creation and capture.

For example, the alliance between AT&T and Olivetti in the mid-1980s was initially designed as a series of arms-length cross-supply contracts inspired by traditional original equipment manufacturer (OEM) relationships. The two companies merely exchanged existing products. While this design got the alliance off to a quick start, it locked the partners into a series of periodic price and supply negotiations that infected the relationship with adversarial spirit. This made it extremely difficult for the two companies to move toward the level of cooperation and mutual trust required by the next step in their strategic alliance: the joint development of completely new products.

The AT&T–Olivetti alliance began to stall, particularly as the dollar fell against the lira in the late 1980s, making Olivetti products less attractive to AT&T. Although other problems plagued the alliance, the initial design was a major contributor to its eventual failure. The initial design not only bred conflicts, it also short-circuited learning between the partners. Restricting the partner interface to product trading failed to provide a broad enough "window" through which the partners could interact, share expertise, and learn to work together.

We have observed many other cases in which alliance designs adopted for the sake of efficiency and a "quick win" hampered subsequent evolution. Unfortunately, the most efficient early forms of complementation, such as the mere arm's length exchange of products, are seldom conducive to the depth of collaboration required when complex, intangible assets must be brought to bear on difficult tasks in the face of high uncertainty. This dilemma is seldom an issue in traditional joint ventures, but it is a major stumbling block for many strategic alliances as they move from simple "quick wins" to more ambitious and complex tasks. In these alliances, the initial design of the relationship needs to encompass both the achievement of "quick wins" and the beginning of a joint learning process that will foster further collaboration over time.

The Test of Time

Instability is endemic to alliances that aim to create the future. It is more natural for them to come apart than to stay together. Whether an alliance will stand the test of time hinges on its ability to learn and be flexible in the face of change. Perhaps more than any other organizational form, the alliance faces a trade-off between too much rigidity—where design becomes a straitjacket—and too much flexibility—which may cause loss of direction or balance. Managers of enduring alliances master this difficult trade-off by doing the following:

- developing a process for tracking moving targets
- periodically renegotiating the "bargain" between partners
- reassessing the value of the options created by the alliance

Alliance managers cannot simply "set it and forget it." They must continually sense and respond to what is happening within the alliance and within its larger environment. This requires a managerial mindset very different from the one that negotiates and implements one-time contracts with fixed objectives. Alliance managers must understand the sources of instability and anticipate and react to the events and forces that undermine cohesion and purpose.

Let's review briefly the main sources of instability and see how they affect alliances.

1. *Emerging markets.* Instability is intrinsic to emerging markets. The cast of customers and competitors is constantly churning, and

market size and evolution are often unpredictable. In the 1980s, for example, all the companies involved in the cellular phone industry underestimated the pace of growth of that market—and by a wide margin. Conversely, it is now clear that Apple and other companies considerably *over*estimated the market for personal "pocketbook" computers and communicators (also called personal digital assistants), at least given what the available technologies could deliver.

History indicates that even the innovators who launch new industries are usually wide of the mark in foreseeing how their inventions will be used, altered, and adapted. Engineer Guglielmo Marconi, inventor of the wireless telegraph, imagined the only application of his device to be ship-to-shore communications; he had no idea that it would prove to be the basis of radio broadcasting. Nor did the early titans of the digital age—IBM, Digital Equipment, NCR, and the like—foresee how the development of micro- and workstation computers would shake the foundations of their industry.

2. *Emerging technologies.* Even when customer needs are clearly understood, the technologies and applications that emerge to meet them may not be. The search for a vaccine and cure for AIDS—an obvious need—provides a useful example. Beginning in the early 1990s, pharmaceutical giant Merck assembled a complex network of research institutes, universities, biotech entrepreneurial companies, and other organizations to develop AIDS vaccines and cures. Given the still serendipitous nature of pharmaceutical innovations, and the nature of AIDS and its evolving virus, there was no way of knowing which—if any—part of this web of R&D alliances would be productive and which would not.

3. *Competitors.* The actions of competitors are another source of alliance instability. Intel's actions, for example, created instability in the PowerPC alliance of Apple, Motorola, and IBM. Each of these firms had been a loser in the battle of personal computer standards—a battle won decisively by Intel, which captured 90 percent of the market. The PowerPC alliance was formed to develop a new microprocessor and computer architecture capable of challenging Intel's dominance, which had left Apple as the only significant user of Motorola's microprocessor products.

Paradoxically, the threat of the PowerPC alliance spurred Intel to accelerate its own program of innovation and product development, which in turn undermined the assumptions on which the PowerPC alliance was built. The appearance of more advanced Intel processors made aggressive pursuit of the PowerPC product less attractive for IBM, one of the key alliance partners. What for Apple was a "do or die" project was simply an option for IBM. IBM was a partner *and* a competitor of Intel, a fact that may have further dampened IBM's commitment to the PowerPC, whereas Apple and Motorola had only to gain with its success.

4. *Partners.* In some cases, alliance partners are themselves a source of instability. Each partner may want to keep its options open, so that any given partner's commitment is never quite secure. Better options may develop, or strategic constraints may be imposed by shifting corporate priorities and decisions in other businesses. This is particularly true in the case of specific product lines or geographic alliances; although these alliances may be important for the subunits involved, they may become victims of changing corporate strategies or resource constraints.

5. *Regulatory changes.* Some alliances are predicated on the expectation that the partners can obtain a favorable change in the regulatory environment. These alliances may, however, trigger an unexpected regulatory response. Perhaps the most striking example of this kind of instability is provided by the Bell Atlantic–TCI non-alliance of 1994. After announcing their plan to provide interactive home video services, the two firms received regulatory approval only on terms that made the venture less financially attractive than they had anticipated. As a result, Bell Atlantic and TCI scrapped their collaboration before it had even begun. Meanwhile, their initial announcement had triggered a wave of investments by competitors in a "digital superhighway" to serve the home video market, making the potential Bell Atlantic–TCI alliance even less attractive.

Given the sources of instability just described, the management of strategic alliances must be seen over the longer term. An alliance must be an evolving relationship capable of tracking and hitting a moving target—even as its own foundations are shifting beneath it. This need for self-correction stands in stark contrast to the traditional joint venture's contractual partnership arrangements aimed at static objectives. Instability demands that partnerships evolve from a single initial "bargain" to a series of bargains struck over time as conditions change. They must follow the commonsense approach of John Maynard Keynes: "When the facts change, I change." Partners must be prepared to reassess their relationships, adjust, and even renegotiate as the facts change, as intended objectives shift or disappear altogether, as partners lose interest or find better options. And partners should be prepared to disband alliances altogether. Uncertainty almost unavoidably makes some alliances short-lived.

Set Objectives versus Moving Targets

Conventional partnerships serve set objectives and face well-circumscribed risks; their economics are usually clearly understood from the start, and their strategic scope is usually limited and clearly bounded. Thus, a relatively static perspective on their implementation may be sufficient to ensure success. Not so in the strategic alliance, in which the partners must be flexible and must see theirs as a relationship whose objectives are bound to evolve in ways that cannot be fully planned at inception. Doing otherwise would be highly dysfunctional.

The process of partner collaboration may itself lead to the discovery of unforeseen value creation opportunities and to windfall benefits. For example, while ICI and Enichem, two large European chemical firms, entered their joint venture in the plastics business (Eurovynil Corporation) largely to rationalize manufacturing, they quickly discovered they had much to learn from each other—Enichem bringing technical expertise and ICI marketing know-how. Myopic attention to fixed objectives would likely get in the way of such discovery. Partners must keep a sharp eye on their own interests and have a sound yardstick for measuring value, but they must not establish objectives once and for all. As of this writing, Iridium, for instance, has already gone through at least one major redefinition of its market objectives—to give priority to business executives as customers—and of its technology base—to connect to and use existing telecommunications networks. Changes in the market and technology mean that the stated objectives of many new alliances must accommodate revisions.

The concept of alliance objectives as moving targets is easy to accept intellectually, but it is difficult to reflect organizationally, where plans, budgets, and resource allocations are often rigid. Managers closest to the alliance may see the need to change objectives, but they may be reluctant to depart from the basis on which they initially "sold" the alliance to their own management. Shifting the goalpost is also difficult for senior executives. This rigidity may impose a deterministic approach on partnerships.

Single versus Multiple Bargains

The evolutionary nature of alliances calls for an iterative approach to deal making. In this, orthodox thinking may be counterproductive. The strategy literature, for example, advises managers to "formulate, then select, then implement." The traditional prescription for mergers and acquisitions—to "search, negotiate, acquire, and integrate"—may also be misleading.[8] In partnerships, all processes are ongoing. The search for partners does not stop when the alliance agreement is signed: other options will continue to exist, and existing partners might not deliver. Nor should negotiation stop when the deal is signed; external conditions keep shifting, and the contributions and benefits of the various partners change.

Integration of activities between partners is rarely effected in a single stroke, as the level of trust shared and each partner's understanding of the joint task may be too low to permit it at the outset. On the contrary, integration must take place over time. Cospecialization, too, is often built over time as a function of perceived benefits and as trust and commitment develop. Partners in successful alliances increase their commitments in a series of steps over time, as they perceive a balance between their commitments and the related benefits.

Therefore, an alliance is perhaps best conceived as an evolving relationship punctuated by a series of commitments, steps, and "bargains" explicitly negotiated or implicitly accepted over time. In the course of that step-by-step evolution, many possible changes in the relationship are reviewed and considered by the partners, who reinforce or limit their commitments accordingly. This evolutionary approach is different from that observed in the traditional partnership, where partners usually merely implement the initial agreement. This does not mean that joint venture relationships do not evolve;

likely shifts in the economics of the relationship are usually understood well enough at the outset and are often incorporated into contingent contracts.

Evolution in the newer alliances, however, is less predictable. Rivalry between partners makes multiple bargains over time almost unavoidable, particularly when one partner begins in a weak position but gains strength, as did DASA, the aerospace arm of Daimler-Benz, in the Airbus alliance. Shifting relative strength between partners must be recognized in the structure of the alliance. The relationship between Fuji-Xerox and Xerox Corporation, for instance, went through a series of periodic adjustments to reflect the unanticipated but growing role of Fuji-Xerox in restoring the competitiveness of the Xerox group against Japanese competitors.

COMMITMENTS VERSUS OPTIONS

Alliances must balance the need for commitment with the desire of partners to keep their options open. Obviously, commitment facilitates cooperation. But in a fast-changing world, companies must be free to pursue better opportunities when they appear.

In traditional joint ventures, commitment often stems from an absence of compelling alternatives. ICI and Enichem did not have obvious alternatives. When market access is the goal, for example, the partners may not be uniquely good choices for each other, but they may have no choice but to work together. When the German air force needs some new weapon systems, DASA, as Germany's leading aerospace system integrator, is almost necessarily involved. There simply is no credible local alternative as a partner.

The cost of abandoning the alliance or of switching from one partner to another may be a further source of commitment. Alliances seeking economies of scale have very high exit costs. Once Peugeot, Renault, and Volvo started making engines together, it became absurd for any one of the three to exit the venture. The same is generally true of upstream material and component supply and capacity optimization ventures. In many contemporary alliances, on the other hand, the volatility of technologies and markets, the complex nature of the tasks undertaken, and the shifts in rivalry and competitive position among the partners all contribute to making commitments more tentative. Indeed, many alliances are simply options, not strong commitments.

For Merck to pretend to be fully committed to its AIDS network partners would be useless; everyone involved recognizes the technological and market uncertainties faced by Merck's alliances. Commitment may grow as these uncertainties are resolved, or it may dissolve if new developments reduce their potential for value creation.

Just as all of life's options are never exercised, some planned alliances are never activated. Some may not even be meant to succeed. Their purpose is simply to forestall rival alliance negotiations or, in some cases, to catalyze the formation of other alliances or competitive developments. We have seen a number of these short-lived "virtual alliances" in multimedia information technology, for instance, between Canal Plus (the French television broadcaster) and various companies in Germany. Their value lies more in what their announcement prevents or triggers—in a complex, multistage coalition-building game—than in what they might actually accomplish.

Despite the lack of fixed objectives in the newer alliances, and the wish to keep some of their options open, we have observed partners in successful alliances make increasingly significant and irreversible commitments, building value-creating cospecialization into their alliance over time as their level of mutual understanding and trust increases and as they become more comfortable with the uncertainties confronting their alliance. Expecting such cospecialization commitments up front would, in many cases, prevent an alliance from getting started. Partners balk at binding commitments when uncertainty is high and trust and mutual understanding have not yet been established. Yet the limited level of mutual commitment that makes alliance entry feasible is seldom sufficient to carry it through to success. As long as alliances are viewed as relationships to be constantly and patiently improved on, the level of commitment they enjoy from their partners can be gradually increased.

Calls for "commitment" make good rhetoric but are a poor basis for action. Commitment increases only over time, and an uncritical belief in commitment is naive and misleading. Nor can one ignore the fact that alliances, like other courses of action in business life, are always challenged by the existence of options and have value only in comparison with alternative choices. People, being largely risk averse, will always be tempted to hedge commitments and keep their options open in the face of uncertainty.

Longevity versus Competitiveness

Some observers equate alliance longevity with alliance success. They view an alliance as a marriage and the duration of the marriage as a yardstick of success. But are the couples married the longest always the happiest? In jurisdictions where divorce is illegal or highly restricted, the average marriage is long lasting. But this may be less a function of satisfaction than of a lack of alternatives. Not all alliances need to stand the test of time to create value, and, conversely, a long-standing alliance does not always create value for its partners.

Our observations of alliances indicate two things about longevity. First, longevity is driven by different factors in different types of alliances. It is only a revealing yardstick if one clearly understands the strategic logic of the alliance being measured. Indeed, what the alliance contributes over time to the competitiveness of each of its partners is a more important measure of success than longevity of the alliance proper. For example, some companies, such as Siemens in microelectronics, have used a succession of learning alliances to gain ground in an industry or regain competitive advantage. Given this strategic logic, using the longevity of each alliance as a proxy for success is like measuring a climber's progress on a ladder by how long he stays on each rung.

Second, uncertainty is bound to tax the longevity of alliances. Uncertainty itself can be taxing as it leaves room for divergent expectations between partners. Further, uncertainty may be resolved by unexpected changes, calling for changes in the alliance. Either the partners to an alliance adapt their relationship over the course of time or the relationship is unlikely to last. Hence to equate success with longevity, once the conditions have changed, would be misleading in the absence of other criteria.

With respect to longevity and success, the experience of traditional joint ventures may be misleading to the managers of strategic alliances. In many of the former, the partners combine assets in a common entity. The joint venture is thus a stand-alone, self-contained business, like any other; it just happens to be owned by two or more parents. For such a venture, longevity is indeed a measure of success, but no more, really, than the longevity of any business firm, particularly when the parents have relatively similar strategic and financial priorities. Consider the Dow Corning venture, which has endured for more than fifty years. It is not clear what lesson of its longevity can be applied to the newer types of alliances, except perhaps that the alignment of performance demands between the parent companies is a prerequisite for long-term survival. If Dow and Corning, as coinvestors, are satisfied with the performance of Dow Corning, they will remain committed to it. But their commitment does not necessarily make them strategic partners.

Reconciling Priorities

Conventional joint ventures sometimes occur between actual or potential competitors. Nevertheless, they usually separate areas of competition and cooperation. The economics of the venture are sufficiently well understood by the partners for joint activities and their consequences to be clearly delineated. In current alliances, we find that separation between where partners compete and where they collaborate is much harder to achieve, partly because of the more strategic role of alliances and of their relatedness to other activities, partly because of the intrinsic uncertainty confronting many alliances, and partly because of the greater fluidity of partners' respective positions.

Rather than being separated, cooperation and competition must often be handled jointly, an exercise in ambiguity and duality for which few managers are prepared and that makes them acutely uncomfortable. They are naturally concerned about the acceptability of cospecialization and the risks of dependence it creates, about the trade-offs between value creation and appropriation, and even about the wisdom of trusting their partners.[9]

COLLABORATION VERSUS COMPETITION

Competition between partners was seldom an issue in traditional joint ventures. In market entry arrangements, global and local partners often collaborated, but the local partners rarely had global ambitions. This is no longer true. Following the example set by Japanese companies as early as the 1960s, many local partners now see their joint ventures with global firms as stepping stones to new technologies and world markets. For example, a South Korean consortium entered an alliance with GEC-Alsthom, the European electrical equipment firm, to sell and build a state-of-the-art, high-speed train system in South Korea. The agreement, however, did not end there; it also called for extensive technology transfers and a licensing agreement that would allow the Koreans to compete directly with GEC-Alsthom.

In traditional arrangements of the type just described, the global partner controlled markets and avoided rivalry with local partners. Local partners received a share of profits or revenues but seldom turned into global competitors. Moreover, when several global companies joined forces, as in oil exploration and production projects, the economics of their ventures were usually transparent, and the interests of the partners sufficiently well aligned to leave little room for competition within the alliance, even though the partners remained competitors in the marketplace. In many of today's alliances, however, neither the economics nor the interests of the partners are clear. Furthermore, the shape of future competition is so ill defined that attempts at containing rivalry within the alliance are usually futile. Rivalry between partners in today's alliances can occur in the marketplace, within the alliance itself, or in both arenas at the same time.

Marketplace rivalry between alliance partners is a frequent source of tension. This was the case in the PowerPC alliance described earlier, which, in addition to semiconductor supplier Motorola, brought together Apple and IBM, both supplying personal computers. These firms had contrasting approaches to introducing the PowerPC. Apple rushed in, while IBM moved more gingerly. The differences may reflect not simply disparities in organizational agility but also divergences of strategic interest: Apple was driven to develop and roll out a more powerful microprocessor to compete with producers of Intel-based machines (of which IBM was one), whereas IBM may have been concerned about the risk of obsoleting its existing Intel-based products too quickly. It may also have expected to benefit more from using PowerPC to drive down Intel's prices and accelerate Intel's innovations than from sharing in the success of the new processor.

In the Airbus alliance, DASA, Aérospatiale, and British Aerospace aligned their strategic market interests as they competed as a group against Boeing. DASA wanted to increase its say in the alliance, and presumably its share of returns, and the company used Boeing's attempts to woo it as leverage in getting what it wanted. This made the Airbus alliance, for DASA, a form of competitive collaboration with its partners.

Other partners find that rivalry calls for a totally new arrangement. ICL and Fujitsu, which formed an alliance in the 1980s, worked together closely on product development and manufacturing even as they competed in the market. Their competition for retail applications in the United States was a factor in their decision to shift from an alliance to a full merger.

Any form of rivalry between alliance partners complicates alliance management. The balance of power within the alliance (either between the partners or between the joint venture and one or more partner companies) can shift widely over time, particularly as the relative importance of the skills and experiences contributed by each partner varies. For example, when Xerox and Fuji created Fuji-Xerox in 1962, both the joint venture and Fuji itself were totally dependent on Xerox for product and process expertise, technology, brand credibility, and the business system of Fuji-Xerox, which emulated Xerox's North American leasing business. Over the ensuing decades, the relationship incrementally reversed itself. Fuji contributed major process skills,[10] then developed products that made Xerox and Rank Xerox (the European organization) increasingly dependent on it. Fuji-Xerox pioneered new sales and service approaches, such as indirect sales, within the Xerox group. By the 1990s, the balance of relative influence had shifted in Fuji-Xerox's favor. So too had the balance of financial return, with Fuji-Xerox charging up to a 20 percent R&D royalty on the price of its shipments to the rest of the Xerox group, whereas Xerox charged only 5 percent royalties on its sales to Fuji-Xerox.[11]

For many companies, collaboration through alliances has become competition by other means. IBM's participation in the PowerPC alliance was partly competitive and partly cooperative; it both collaborated and competed with Apple, gaining indirect leverage on Intel through the alliance. Analyses that do not acknowledge or understand that allied firms can be both partners and competitors miss the point of many contemporary alliances. Rivalry can emerge even in cases in which the partners do not compete in the marketplace, as occurred in the Iridium case.

INTERDEPENDENCE VERSUS UNBALANCED DEPENDENCE

Interdependence, stemming from cospecialization between partners, is the foundation on which successful alliances are built. Yet to stop here without asking whether cospecialization is balanced or one-sided is downright dangerous. One-sided specialization makes the specialized partner dependent, for example, by giving up key competencies and taking the risk of being subsequently dumped by partners who have found better alternatives or lost interest. Despite such obvious risks and well-publicized examples, we have often seen managers taking a simplistic view of dependency, again inherited from traditional joint ventures. For example, managers sometimes gain a sense of safety from formal measures of balance, such as equity shares in a joint venture, and fail to notice that their alliances, no matter how carefully balanced from a formal point of view, broaden the range of strategic options for their partners while foreclosing options for their own firms or that their partners come to control the tasks and competencies most critical to the success of the alliance, providing the basis for one-sided renegotiations of alliance gains.

Here again, as we already signaled in our discussion of outcomes being more important than mere inputs and outputs, complex strategic alliances require a wider, more strategic perspective on benefits and risks than do simple joint ventures. In the latter it was usually possible to separate areas of competition from areas of cooperation and to manage each area quite differently. Not always so in today's alliances, where both competition and cooperation coexist in the same areas. Alliance managers must have the capacity to handle duality and ambiguity and to take an attitude of self-interested cooperation—something that does not come naturally to managers steeped in the Manichaean dichotomy of "good guys" and "bad guys" (and in John Wayne movies).

TRUST VERSUS ENLIGHTENED SELF-INTEREST AND MUTUAL INTEREST

Trust, like interdependency and commitment, figures prominently in the lexicon of the alliance. Who could possibly say anything against trust between partners? Trust is obviously a good thing. Either we

trust or we distrust. But trust cannot be guaranteed before a relationship is established. Unless one collaborates repeatedly with the
same partners, or unless a partner's reputation is very strong,[12] trust
must be earned. Managers cannot be ordered to trust their partners,
particularly when those partners are potential rivals. Instead, they
can be encouraged to build trust over time through a collaborative
process. In this process they should neither trust blindly nor act
with such caution that cooperation is made impossible.

"Trust" means different things to different people. To some, it
means putting one's interests in the hands of a partner, confident that
that partner will act as a good steward. In business alliances, trust may
take the form of giving another company the use of one's best
resources, trusting it to use them in the best interests of the alliance.[13]
To others, trust is a function of dependence: the other party can be
trusted because it is so dependent that it cannot afford to do anything
"foolish." Another form of trust rests on confidence in one's ability to
predict the behavior of another party. This confidence, in turn, is
based on a superior understanding of the other party's situation and
self-interest.[14] To still others, trust is a matter of ethical standards.

Trust is a simple, powerful, and emotionally laden word. As such
it can be a source of confusion if used prescriptively for alliances. To
avoid possible confusion, we suggest that partners replace trust with
"enlightened self- and mutual interest," a concept that drove British
diplomacy and foreign policy in the nineteenth century. As a basis
for alliances, this is more appropriate than the idealistic but perhaps
hollow concept of trust.

Managing in a Web of Alliances

A fourth distinguishing feature of many contemporary alliances is
that they cannot be understood except as part of a web of relationships, a "web" being an interdependent set of alliances.

Traditional joint ventures were self-contained to the point of
being manageable without considering other relationships. For
instance, Dow Corning, created in 1943, mostly makes silicon-based
lubricants and has been an outstanding success. One does not need
to understand the entire range of Corning's or Dow's other alliances

to understand Dow Corning's strategic development. As we will note in a later chapter, Corning followed a policy of keeping each alliance and each partner strategically separate. Most recent alliances, on the other hand, belong to an interdependent web. Thus, we cannot understand the strategic linkages between Motorola and Toshiba without also understanding each company's other alliances. Similarly, positions taken by Aérospatiale and DASA in one or another alliance may have been motivated by linkages between them in other fields and by their alliances with other companies. One cannot understand alliances in satellites without being aware of alliances in missiles, helicopters, or aircraft.

Bilateral alliances still account for the bulk of all alliances, but fewer and fewer can be understood outside of a broader context of multilateral collaboration. The level of ambiguity created by these cross-linkages can be confusing and can defy logical structuring. Some companies, confronted with a proliferation of alliances in their various businesses, have given up trying to maintain order in the myriad alliances in which their operating units participate.

If one does not give up to chaos, though, it may useful to distinguish various ways in which the multilateral nature of today's alliances makes their management difficult. Multilaterality creates difficulties at the following three levels:

1. *Between partners who comprise a single alliance.* Within a single alliance, a multiplicity of partners, each with its own stakes, constraints, and ambitions, can create problems. CASA of Spain has a small stake in Airbus's work share (4.2 percent) but a full partnership role, including veto power over joint decisions. This veto power complicates Airbus management. Its members acknowledge that differences between the major and minor partners delayed the launch of Airbus's first narrow-body, single-aisle jetliner, the A320, by more than a year. That delay gave rival Boeing a strategic opportunity to establish its second-generation B-737 in the early 1980s.

2. *Between multiple alliances involving the same partners.* DASA and Aérospatiale are allied in many businesses: space launchers and satellites, missile systems, helicopters, jetliners, military transport, and others. Yet the two companies competed actively in the commuter plane market. There, Aérospatiale was allied with Alenia of Italy, and DASA had acquired Fokker, a manufacturer

of commuter planes in the Netherlands. That acquisition was viewed with concern by some at Aérospatiale, who feared that DASA would cut prices in the already crowded commuter plane business, making it quite unprofitable for Aérospatiale. Weakened profits, in turn, would deprive Aérospatiale of the cash flows it needed to match DASA's investments in other businesses and thus to hold its own, financially, in the many alliances and joint ventures between the two companies. While this fear was exaggerated, the concern was sufficiently plausible to threaten relationships between the two companies.[15]

3. *Between different alliances in a network of coalitions.* Finally, a multiplicity of separate alliances may lead a company to lose focus and consistency as well as bring about a fragmenting of its resource commitments—the chaos alluded to earlier in the chapter. In 1992, for instance, Olivetti's chairman, Carlo de Benedetti, publicly praised his company's participation in 229 strategic alliances. Although Olivetti was run strategically and centrally, one can only wonder at how strategic consistency was maintained across these many alliances. The issue becomes even more problematic in companies such as DEC (or, for a while, IBM) that have decentralized themselves into small entrepreneurial units. For these companies, a web of alliances may look very impressive, but they may also be disjointed and lack cumulative logic. Contrast this with Fujitsu's approach: in mainframe computers it achieved half the R&D and manufacturing scale of IBM through a purposive web of alliances with ICL in the United Kingdom, Amdahl in the United States, Siemens in Germany, and other partners. Multilaterality was exploited by Fujitsu to build a strong nodal position at the center of the web linking its various partners.[16] More often than not, however, multilaterality seems to result in confusion, conflict, and loss of focus, if not worse, or in one company being "cherry picked" or held hostage by better strategically coordinated partner-competitors.

Marriage versus Realpolitik

Marriage is the most commonly used analogy in the popular literature of strategic alliances. This analogy is emotional and affective and speaks to a sense of unity and common purpose: in "sickness and in health until death do us part." Perhaps this is an apt analogy for mergers, which create a common entity, but not for alliances. Contemporary alliances maintain the separate identities and integrity of individual partners, and in so doing, protect their self-interests.

Better analogies for alliances are found in statecraft—in particular, the past few centuries of European diplomatic and military history. Here we observe the simultaneous management of viable coalitions built on a number of bilateral relationships, each with its own history. A notable example is found in World War II, when the United States allied itself with both Britain and the Soviet Union. The U.S. alliance with Britain was anchored in a deep-rooted "special relationship"; its relationship with the Soviets, in contrast, was opportunistic. The United States had little in common with the Soviets, and many Americans viewed it as a pariah state; yet both countries had a common enemy in Nazi Germany. The issues of trust, collaboration, cospecialization, ambiguity, and rivalry—all of which have been described in this chapter—were present in the U.S-British-Soviet alliance. Indeed, the parallels between geopolitical and business alliances are many, and managers should turn to history as a worthy source of inspiration and guidance.[17]

SINGLE RELATIONSHIPS VERSUS ALLIANCE NETWORKS

While analyzing individual alliances can be useful, they make little sense outside of the broader web, or network, of relationships in which companies and their partners are involved. We believe therefore that being sensitive both to the integrity of individual alliances and to the embeddedness of each alliance in a broader web is fundamental. This, of course, becomes more difficult as a company's alliance web expands. Only a simultaneous consideration of all the linkages in the web makes it possible to understand and manage effectively. Few companies, and fewer managers, are equipped to grapple with the complexities of this task.

Summary

We have found in our research that the most important starting point in a successful alliance is the adoption of a mindset and set of attitudes by managers that allows them to function in environments characterized by instability, few fixed objectives, ambiguity, and evolving partner relationships. Alliances cannot be crafted and set on "autopilot." They require ongoing management of the relationship within a clear strategic framework. Nor can they be treated as mere "projects." For most companies they have become too central to strategy to be relegated to project status.

Alliance management is a wonderful test of general management skills—here, purpose and flexibility, analytical powers, entrepreneurial instincts, and organizational and political skills must come together.

2

❖

DISCOVERING VALUE
IN ALLIANCES

WINNING THE RACES to the world and to the future requires speed and a strong sense of direction and purpose. Common sense would suggest this is best accomplished by a single organization, not by a motley alliance of partners. Yet few organizations, if any, have what it takes to run these races alone. The idea that many heads and many complementary sets of skills working together are better than one is intuitively appealing. Still, it is natural to expect that partners will not be of one mind. When the path suddenly branches into several different directions, it is too much to expect level-headed discussion, agreement, and a decision to follow one or another. Running as a loose coalition, allies must pause to debate which path to take among many and whether running the race is still worth the effort. Too many of these pauses will surely cost them the race. This suggests that a strong shared commitment to playing as a team is critical.

Racing as a team requires several preconditions. One needs to be able to keep one's bearings in unstable conditions and uncharted territory. A compelling but realistic motive for running a particular race is key. Partners must want to win the same race, even if each one has a different reason for running. Each partner must understand the value of running as a team, that is, what and how each member contributes to increase the odds of winning. The difficulty, obviously, is that an alliance race often lacks a clear goalpost, or at least one that can be identified at the start. Partners also need to share a common map of the terrain their alliance will lead them to cross.

Given the challenges most alliances face, partners must fully appreciate all the benefits they can expect from the alliance, so they do not lose their sense of purpose when confronted with unexpected setbacks. It's important to use a scorecard to measure the progress of both the alliance and each partner toward value creation and benefits. This scorecard should be sufficiently robust to capture the hard-to-measure values and benefits described in the previous chapter. The map can be used to direct efforts in the race toward those benefits, and the scorecard, both for the alliance and for each partner, can measure progress toward them.

Alliance partners who attempt to assess potential benefits often fall into one or both of two traps: (1) making excessive ambitions and overly optimistic assessments of benefits and (2) defining the range of potential benefits too narrowly. Excessive ambition over a narrow front is often a recipe for disaster. Ambitions are either too grand to be realized or so narrowly defined that other value creation opportunities are overlooked.

Some companies run into both difficulties within the same alliance. The partnership between AT&T and Olivetti mentioned in Chapter 1 is a case in point. Both AT&T and Olivetti had lofty but very broad ambitions: to position themselves strategically for the future convergence of communications and computing; to combine AT&T's technical strengths with Olivetti's marketing capabilities; and to complement their presence in Europe and the United States. Unfortunately, the two companies' minicomputer products were so far apart in architecture, standards, operating systems, applications software, and target markets that bridging the gap between them through a single new product line was unrealistic. Short of implementing the grand visions of their CEOs, which tended to dissolve on close inspection, the partners fell back on simply trading products.[1]

Even this limited initiative had little success. AT&T lacked the skills to distribute Olivetti's personal computers in North America, and Olivetti had little experience in marketing private telecommunications switching systems. Each partner thus found it very difficult to move from extremely ambitious, yet abstract, statements of potential benefits to actual value creation through real cospecialization. Disappointment quickly crept into their relationship.

Too exclusive a concern with immediate tangible benefits, such as measurable financial returns, prevents alliances from realizing their full potential. Less tangible, less easily predictable benefits, such as knowledge transfer between partners, benchmarking against partners, reducing market uncertainty, and so forth, are often ignored. When these benefits are not part of the initial alliance expectations, they may remain unsought, unnoticed, and unexploited. AT&T and Olivetti, for example, learned relatively little from each other about technologies and markets even though they recognized the benefits of doing so. They focused so much on tangible benefits that they failed to take the time and trouble required for learning.

Whether facing an excessively ambitious or overly narrow plan for the scope of the alliance, the essential point remains the same: discovering the full range of potential benefits is a prerequisite to building an alliance that creates value.

The Logic of Alliance Value Creation

Most strategic alliances serve one or several strategic imperatives. If a company is racing for the world—that is, attempting to make the most of global opportunities—it will form an alliance to do what it cannot do alone, which is usually one or more of the following:

1. build critical mass globally or in a specific new market

2. learn quickly about unfamiliar markets and become an insider

3. access skills concentrated in another geographic location (such as fashion design skills in Italy or software design skills in the United States)

These are the most common requisites for winning the race for the world. Each represents an opportunity to create value for the alliance and its partner firms.

The firm that is racing for the future may also find that alliances have their own means of creating value:

1. building nodal positions in coalitions aimed at creating new markets

2. creating new opportunities by combining skills and resources

3. building new competencies faster than would be possible through internal efforts

While the strategic use of alliances in the races to the world and to the future appears much different on the surface, we find that the use of alliances in both races shares a common set of underlying "logics." The benefits to be gained from each of these logics is what managers should look for as they design their alliances, set objectives and score-keeping procedures, and guide day-to-day activities. As shown in Figure 2-1, these common, underlying, value-creating logics are:

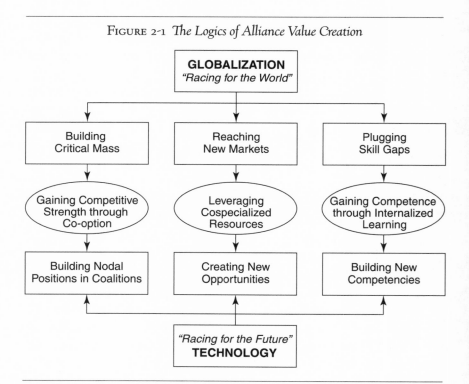

FIGURE 2-1 *The Logics of Alliance Value Creation*

1. gaining competitive capabilities through co-option
2. leveraging cospecialized resources
3. gaining competence through internalized learning

Not surprisingly, these are the fundamental imperatives that drive companies to form alliances: the need to position themselves strategically and gain competitive capabilities through the co-option of rivals and complementary firms, the need to combine their resources through cospecialization so as to access new markets and create or pursue new opportunities they could not consider on their own, and the need to learn through alliances, both to overcome skill deficits and to acquire new competencies.

Alliances make it possible to build the critical mass and global presence the race for the world requires. British Airways (BA) discovered this in its efforts to break into the larger U.S. and Latin American markets dominated by United Airlines and American Airlines. In its proposed partnership with American Airlines, BA is hoping to build critical mass in the American markets. Further, partly to make itself more attractive as a partner in global alliances, such as that with American Airlines, BA has co-opted, through alliances and acquisitions, weaker regional airlines in continental Europe and gained access to additional hubs, such as the Orly airport in France, which American Airlines uses as well. Similarly, Fujitsu sought ICL, Amdahl, and Siemens as partners, in part to acquire "virtual market share"—that is, to build critical mass and become competitive with IBM. In the 1980s, Fujitsu's visible market presence under its own brand was only about a tenth of IBM's, but including its partners, its actual market presence was roughly half the size of IBM's. Fujitsu was pursuing a clear co-option strategy, wherein the starting assumption was "My enemies' enemies are my friends."

The race for the future also calls for critical mass of a sort; the competitive momentum and the coalition skills needed to lead a race that leaves room for very few winners. This "winner-takes-all" contest can often be traced to technical standards and the network effects they trigger.[2] Building critical mass in one's industry to establish a "de facto" standard and making one's own coalition attractive to customers through accessing and tying "complementers" (providers of complementary goods and services that enhance the value of one's offerings to customers) from related adjacent industries are the two fundamental drivers of alliances in that situation.

The current wave of media alliances—from Kirch-Bertelsmann in Germany to Dreamworks-Microsoft or Hughes's direct TV in the United States—is an example. Leading firms in these new coalitions attempt to build nodal positions to control the high ground of future reconfigured industries.[3]

Alliances also allow firms to meld resources and capabilities that are "cospecialized" (that is, to create value by virtue of their very combination and melding) and that could not be easily combined by means other than alliances.[4] This is particularly true when the resources are very specific to each partner and hinge on their continued independence and integrity. For instance, as we discuss more fully later, the French state-owned jet engine maker, SNECMA, brought to its U.S. partner, General Electric, both its privileged relationship with the French government (and the Airbus consortium) and its expertise in military engines, which could be applied to civilian jet engines.[5] An acquisition of SNECMA by GE, assuming it was politically feasible, would not have preserved either, whereas a simple codevelopment contract might not have provided for a strong enough commitment on GE's part. With its politically savvy French partner, GE was able to short-circuit the long and tortuous process by which a foreign firm becomes an insider in a nationally sensitive industry. Of course, in essence, Iridium provides another example of a cospecialization alliance.

Alliances may also serve as privileged vehicles for learning and internalizing new skills, particularly when those skills are embedded, tacit, and collective and require extensive "copractice" to be learned. In this, conventional technology transfer and licensing agreements would not suffice, and independent development would be slow and difficult.

Thus, alliances create value in different ways depending on the motives they serve. Figure 2-1 offers a comprehensive view of the various imperatives of the races for the world and the future and of the alliance strategies through which companies respond to them.

These different paths to value creation naturally affect the ways in which alliances should be designed and managed. They also call for different expectations and performance measures. Thus, a first key step in developing a value-creating alliance is to understand how these different logics achieve alliance objectives, performance, and value creation.

Value Creation through Co-option

Co-option turns actual or potential competitors and "complementers" into partners. In the race for the globe, co-option is a means of reaching the critical mass needed for effective competition. In the technology-driven races to create new markets, co-option supports the building of powerful nodal positions in emerging coalitions, particularly where standards play a key role and network effects create strong first-mover advantages.

BUILDING CRITICAL MASS

As competition widens from national to regional and even global arenas, the rules of competitive engagement often change, and new rivals appear. When this happens, critical mass is extremely important. The case of European telecommunications provides an example. In 1997 Deutsche Telekom and France Telecom, two of Europe's most traditional national telecommunications service operators, faced the prospect of the complete liberalization of telecommunications services. Both worried about the strength and the entrepreneurship of major competitors, British Telecom in particular. British Telecom would challenge the two companies in their home markets (it had already stationed hundreds of marketing and sales people in France). It had also spun a web of alliances in other parts of Europe and was teaming up with MCI, a major U.S. long-distance provider. Deutsche Telekom and France Telecom were also threatened by AT&T, the kingpin of U.S. telecommunications, which was building its own network of alliances with national operators in smaller European countries.

Faced with these developments, Deutsche Telekom and France Telecom entered into an alliance designed to merge some specialized services, avoid rivalry between themselves, and counter British Telecom. This alliance gave the two firms a critical mass in continental Europe that improved both their competitive capabilities and their bargaining power in subsequent alliances. Together, they could gain a joint 20 percent stake in Sprint (the third largest long-distance service provider in the United States), giving them access to North America and to other markets where Sprint had expanded. These combined alliances, they hoped, would secure their home bases and give them global reach.

Building Nodal Positions

Besides building critical mass in a market, alliances can also help a company become a "node" in a network, a position from which it can lead the development of new industries and competitive arenas and command the lion's share of profits. This challenges companies to seek alliances with both complementers and competitors, their goals being to:

1. exploit new opportunities and meld a wider set of differentiated resources than any company would possess on its own

2. co-opt "unaligned" competitors and complementers into their own camp, sometimes because they can contribute valuable cospecialized and differentiating resources, sometimes to prevent them from falling in with a rival coalition[6]

3. build market leadership quickly; being first matters most when the advantages that accrue to first movers are substantial (most often because technical compatibility needs—what economists call network externalities—leave little room for incompatible new solutions once the first one is established on the market)

Co-option makes potentially attractive partners unavailable to competing alliances. This triggers a race for control of the critical differentiating resources that will confer competitive advantage externally and bargaining power internally, within the alliance.

Perhaps nowhere more than in the current development of the digital broadcasting industry have efforts to gain nodal positions by means of co-opting competitors and complementers been so visible. Consider digital television in Europe. In their race to establish their own digital system, broadcasters have allied with content providers, usually the owners of rights to existing material—movies and televised events, such as large audience sporting events. Such access allowed the broadcasters to differentiate themselves from their competitors. Members of coalitions that failed to gain exclusive access to unique popular content were often quick to shift allegiance. These coalitions collapsed, and their members took back seats on other coalitions. Broadcasters have also allied themselves with companies that control distribution channels, in particular with cable-TV companies and some major retailers, to gain mass market access quickly. Put differently, the broadcasters took the initiative to introduce digital television. Conscious of the high network externalities of broadcasting, each tried to make itself attractive to consumers quickly by entering into alliances (depicted by the vertical arrows in Figure 2-2) with content providers, to differentiate their program offering from that of their competitors, and, with existing distributors and service providers, to gain instant access to the consumers' homes (except for direct broadcast satellite services, which sometimes promoted their services and distributed their hardware—antennas and set-top decoders—directly). In doing so, the broadcasters jockeyed for position in a complex, Europe-wide chess game and staved off potential entry by other types of communication companies, such as traditional print publishers or content owners (although at least one British soccer club went into broadcasting). The "vertical" alliances across market segments (the "layers" of Figure 2-2) allowed some broadcasters, such as Canal+ and Newscorp, to take a leading position in digital television and keep new competitors out. While the exact configuration of alliance linkages differs from country to country and keeps evolving, the underlying patterns are similar. The logic of interactions between competitor co-option and complementer co-option is depicted in Figure 2-2.

The speed at which alliance webs such as the one sketched above are spun and coalitions are built varies with the nature of the opportunity. Speed is of greatest importance when network externalities leave room for a single or, at most, very few winners. This is the case in digital TV, where consumers are unlikely to enter several subscriptions and equip themselves with multiple decoders and other access devices. The race for subscribers is very intense, and the right partners can help. The proliferation of information and entertainment businesses based on one type of network or another explains why we see such a rush on the part of such innovative companies as Kirch, Murdoch, and Canal+ in Europe and Hughes, Microsoft, and Time Warner in America.

In these situations, first-mover advantages are strong, provided the first mover manages to capture the opportunity. A flashback to a "classic" competitive race between Sony and Matsushita for the VCR market in the late 1970s illustrates the point. Sony failed to take advantage of its first-mover position, making it possible for Matsushita to capture industry leadership. This case shows how alliances can be used to set the terms of competition in one's favor.

FIGURE 2-2 *Patterns of Co-option Alliances in Digital Television Broadcasting*

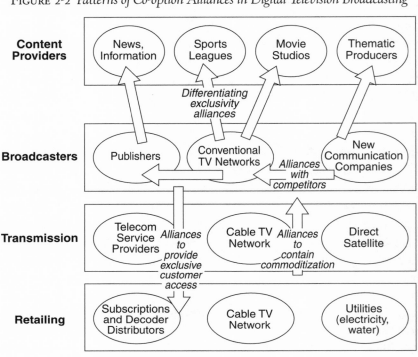

In the mid 1970s, when home-use VCRs first became available, the industry leader was Sony with its "Betamax" standard. In 1976, JVC, a partly owned affiliate of Matsushita, introduced the "VHS" standard in direct competition. In the space of only two years, JVC took industry leadership away from Sony and established VHS as the dominant standard. JVC became the nodal company in the VCR industry. At the same time, it thwarted entry by Philips and its standard and launched the VCR industry on a fast growth track that made it the biggest consumer electronics success of the 1980s. All of this was achieved with a product that was generally regarded as technologically inferior.

How did JVC do it? Its alliance strategy provides most of the answer.

The VCR is an example of a product that had significant network externalities. For consumers, a great deal of the value of a home VCR depended on how many other customers were using the same tape format. The more people who owned VHS machines, the greater the availability of retail VHS cassettes. And as VHS cassettes gained share in the video stores, fewer and fewer new VCR customers would buy anything other than a VHS machine. Soon many video stores stopped carrying Beta cassettes altogether, and VHS became the undisputed leader.

This outcome was heavily influenced by the alliance web JVC put together. Rather than adopt a restrictive and costly licensing practice—as Sony had done with Betamax—JVC made the VHS standard available to all for a modest licensing fee and actively promoted adoption of the standard. The establishment of VHS as a standard facilitated prerecorded videocassette distribution, especially in the video rental market. There the existence of a single, dominant standard made it possible for video stores to carry a much wider selection of movies and other recordings (and more copies of any given title) than would have been feasible with two or more incompatible standards. Video rentals, in turn, contributed to the rapid take-off of the home VCR market.

JVC, despite its somewhat inferior technology (at the time this crucial battle was won, Betamax's image quality was slightly better and its tapes allowed longer recordings), succeeded in co-opting companies such as Thomson in Europe and RCA in America and in occupying the nodal position in the coalition it built. These were companies that might otherwise have joined forces with JVC's rivals. This wide co-option and coalition strategy gave JVC parent company Matsushita three distinct advantages:

1. Matsushita was able to preempt distribution capacities. Companies such as Thomson and RCA brought their market shares and distribution channel strengths into the VHS camp. Matsushita could then feed that distribution pipeline with a fast ramp-up of manufacturing capacity.

2. Widespread acceptance of the VHS standard fostered faster market development.

3. Matsushita could play the game it is most effective at: rapid ramp-up toward mass manufacture of components and OEM products, cost reduction, a flooding of the market with high-quality, low-cost standardized products, and preemption of slow-moving competitors.

Where high network externalities exist, strategic co-option through the establishment of common standards generally brings several specific benefits to the members of winning alliances: strong first-mover advantages; the ability to define what will and will not become a basis for product differentiation; and the ability to collectively define technological trajectories, making the path of innovation more predictable and more favorable to alliance partners.

Co-option alliances, along with the building of strong coalitions and nodal positions, not only foster leadership of the nodal firm at one particular stage in the value-added chain. They may also enhance the profitability of that particular stage and enable firms active in it to collectively capture a bigger share of the total margins in the value chain, attracting partners at that stage and weakening companies that participate to total value creation at other stages in the chain. In the context of using alliances to redistribute margins between stages in the value chain, let's briefly consider the PowerPC alliance again.

When Apple, IBM, and Motorola teamed up to develop a new computer chip compatible with both Intel's and Motorola's, they clearly wanted to increase the rivalry in the microprocessor industry, to Intel's detriment and to their own advantage. They also wanted to increase rivalry in the software industry—to Microsoft's detriment—by broadening the market for Apple software (Apple uses the Motorola chip). For IBM, this rivalry in the microprocessor and software industries could create more competition upstream, where Intel and Microsoft exercised strong market power, and redistribute some of the PC industry's total margins toward the end-product business. IBM faced more intense competition there than either Intel or Microsoft, which were protected by their intellectual property rights on microprocessors and operating systems, respectively, and by strong network externalities for Microsoft.

Finally, co-option can channel rivalry: influencing which race will be run and who will be best positioned to win it. Standards, as described above, have a tremendous impact on competition and outcomes. Standard-setting alliances direct competition to specific areas or products and may throw some competitors off their preferred migration path. They lead markets toward the strengths of the alliance partners and away from those of competitors, making the latter's migration toward new competitive arenas and new markets less likely.

Some contests, such as that for high definition television (HDTV), are fought largely on this issue of migration paths. The opposition of European consumer electronics companies to Japan's "Hi-vision" MUSE standard for HDTV in 1987 stemmed from MUSE's incompatibility with existing TV broadcasting standards.[7] Adoption of MUSE would have encouraged the rapid replacement of existing sets with HDTV sets built to Japanese specifications and drawing on Japanese manufacturing strength. European firms, who were then busy trying to plug major skill, productivity, and quality gaps in TV manufacturing, would have been in a poor position to compete for this tidal wave of new business. European insistence on compatibility between installed broadcast standards and HDTV blunted the Japanese advantage by ensuring slow replacement of the existing base of TV receivers.

Compatibility also had the advantage, for Japan's competitors, of making access to software (mainly libraries of movies) less important, thus neutralizing the effects of Sony's and Matsushita's massive investments in the U.S. movie industry. This threw Japanese suppliers off their preferred migration path and onto the one favored by their Western rivals.

In sum, in activities characterized by high network externalities (a common feature in interactive information technologies), standard-setting alliances influence market development and direct its course. These alliances win the race for the future and, in "winner takes all" contests, are the only ones to cross the finish line. Companies that manage to build and sustain nodal positions in these alliances stand to reap huge benefits and to gain an influence that extends well beyond their size and resources. JVC for consumer electronics yesterday, and Microsoft for personal computers today are perhaps the most consummate masters of that approach.

Value Creation through Cospecialization

Cospecialization is the second compelling logic that drives value creation through alliance. Firms that race for the world often need local partners to gain market access and global partners to complement their skills. In the technologically driven race for the future, partners with specific skills likewise find value in combining forces to create and exploit new opportunities that call for a broader range of skills than either partner has on its own.

BECOMING AN INSIDER IN NEW MARKETS

New markets are eagerly pursued by global companies, particularly in oligopolistic industries like automobiles, whose home markets are often mature and slow growing. Alliances with local firms in emerging markets are a favorite mechanism in this pursuit. This is often a necessity when market entry is restricted by government and when companies must secure a local partner to become an insider. For auto makers, for example, the Chinese government has closed the window of opportunity to all but a few large ventures. Even in new segments, such as minivans and sports utility vehicles, Chinese authorities have restricted entry to a single supplier, Mercedes-Benz, which was chosen over Chrysler and others on the basis of past commitments to China and its stated willingness to transfer technologies and relinquish intellectual property rights. In the elevator industry, China originally left room for only a very few joint ventures. Although this number was later expanded, the early entrants, Schindler, Otis, and Mitsubishi, kept an advantage over later entrants.

Competition to access markets around the globe is even fiercer in telecommunications, where network economies remain enormous and leave room for only a few operators. Thus France Telecom and Deutsche Telekom, as noted earlier, have sought to gain access to new markets through an alliance with Sprint, while also shoring up their domestic positions. In Latin America, in the meantime, France Telecom has rushed to acquire a stake in potentially lucrative telephone system operators in Argentina and Mexico, while the Spanish firm Telefónica has invested in Chile and Argentina. The American regional Bell companies are partners to many telecommunications alliances in newly opening economies. Table 2-1 illustrates the extent of European and U.S. alliances in the telecommunications services of Argentina. The structure is similar in Chile, Mexico, and a growing number of other countries.

Why do competitive races for access to new markets lead to alliances? In the race for the world, companies find that their skills—no matter how sophisticated—are insufficient for rapid expansion into unfamiliar new markets. For example, in taking over part of

TABLE 2-1 *European and U.S. Telecommunications Alliances in Argentina (selected examples)*

SECTOR	KEY PARTNERS AND OWNERSHIP PERCENTAGES
Local Telco: Telecom (Northern)	NORTEL Consortium (60%) [consists of STET (32.5%), France Telecom (32.5%), Perez Companc (25%), and J. P. Morgan 10%)]; Public/Telecom employees (40%)
Local Telco: TASA (Southern)	COINTEL Consortium (60%) [consists of Telefónica de España (10%), Citicorp (20%), Banco Central (12%), Invorsora Catalinas (8%), Sociedad Comercial del Plata (5%), and other (45%)]; Public/TASA employees (40%)
Wireless: MOVICOM	BellSouth (31%), Motorola (25%), BGH (20%), SOCMA (16%), and Citicorp (8%)
Wireless: CTI*	GTE Mobile (23%), AT&T (10%), Telefone SA (20%), TCW Americas Development Association (5%), Compañia Austral de Inversiones (20%), and Intelcel SA (20%)

* Due to rounding, percentages do not total 100.

Argentina's telecommunications network in 1990, France Telecom had to rely on the contributions of others: Italy's STET (the diversified telecommunications services and equipment group) for complementary experience and competencies; J. P. Morgan, one of Argentina's most important international creditors, for financial engineering; and the Perez Companc Group (a diversified Argentinean business empire) for "insider" expertise and a means of maintaining a credible local face. Operating on its home turf, France Telecom did not have to worry about the fact that its lacked these capabilities. Once it stepped into Argentina, they mattered. Globalization requires access to new and complementary skills, and alliances make it possible to acquire them quickly.

The relationship between the big foreign partner and the more politically savvy local partner is often delicate. The balance of contributions between local and global partners generally follows this model: the local partner contributes the knowledge and insider skills needed to crack the local market; the foreign partner provides the specialized skills and other resources to serve it efficiently. Subsequent balance between the partners is conditioned by the nature of the products involved, by the characteristics of the market, and, to a degree, by the experience of the global company and the ambitions of the local partner(s). As the foreign global company accumulates experience and self-confidence in the local environment, its need for the local partner may diminish. Yet once it has made a commitment, and invested resources, the local partner and its local allies may hold it hostage. This evolution is most clear in alliances between global manufacturers and local distributors, where many distributors are ultimately taken over or replaced by the manufacturers. BMW, for instance, set up its own distribution in Japan, abandoning its former distributor. Japanese car makers do the same in Europe.

On the other hand, local partners have used alliances to propel themselves into global competitive arenas. In the 1960s, for example, many Japanese companies used alliances with American and European partners to learn technologies and skills and to gain an understanding of foreign markets. While their Western partners typically saw these alliances as traditional market entry joint ventures, the Japanese companies saw them as stepping stones in the race for the world. More recently, Taiwan's Acer used its alliance with Texas Instruments to propel itself into the world market for personal and, more recently, laptop computers.

CREATING NEW PRODUCT AND SERVICE OPPORTUNITIES

Many opportunities, such as the satellite-based telecommunications system pursued by Iridium or the Hughes satellite direct broadcast television system, are simply too complex for any single company to tackle alone. The range of required skills is too broad. Ironically, these opportunities are appearing at a time when many companies are more narrowly focused and prefer to "stick to their knitting." Companies have become more selective about what they do in-house, and they place greater focus on the maintenance and development of core competencies. Competence-based strategies, in turn, reinforce the need for alliance-based skill complementation when pursuing new opportunities. Even traditional industries such as auto makers call for a wider and wider range of skills as, for example, their electronic content increases.

In newer industries, product complexity calls for an even greater skill range. Take personal computers. In the early days, a PC was a black-and-white monitor, a crude printed circuit board, a basic microprocessor, and a simple keyboard. In contrast, today's laptops require high-resolution color displays with complex flat-screen technologies, a high-performance hard disk drive, a CD-ROM drive, high-energy batteries, and world-class packaging and miniaturization skills. No single company can produce all of these key components or provide all the requisite skills. Sharp and Toshiba are the leaders in flat-screen displays, Sony in miniature disk drives, while other companies provide CD-ROM technologies. This diversity of technologies and skills makes it necessary for companies to work together—often as partners. Apple's Powerbook laptop and its Newton personal digital assistant, for example, taxed Apple's capabilities for miniaturization, leading it to seek out Sony and Sharp as partners.

Alliances bring together partners whose capabilities are complementary for the exploitation of a particular opportunity (such as laptops) but rooted in a much broader range of activities—Apple's broad range of personal computers, Sony's tradition of miniaturizing consumer electronics, and Sharp's skill in densely packaged electronics. The various partners thus bring to the alliance competencies that have already been cultivated across a much wider range of opportunities than the ones they pursue together.

Many of the new opportunities in the race for the future are based on "hybrid" technologies that combine scientific disciplines, as have biotechnology, optoelectronics, and bionics for biological computers for instance. Here the underlying specialized know-how is likely to be spread across several firms, uncertainty is high, and the melding of necessary skills is extremely difficult. If combining disparate scientific disciplines into a single, usable technology is a first-order complexity, combining various technologies and integrating them into products is a second-order challenge.

Many other new market opportunities involve complex systemic solutions—a third level of complexity. These solutions hinge on integrated service and network-based systems that blend hardware, software, and services and that call for the coordinated development of complementary innovations and the successful integration of technical, political, regulatory, and financial requirements. Highway traffic management and travel guidance systems, such as those Siemens will supply in Europe, are examples. Siemens systems will rely on information collected by individual automobiles and automatically broadcast to traffic management computers, which will send recommendations back to motorists. These systems will require the cooperation of public road departments, town governments, telecommunications equipment suppliers (in this case, Siemens and Philips), software designers, radio frequency regulators, automobile manufacturers, and car audio systems suppliers.

Like many such solutions, these will be subject to high network externalities and first-mover advantages. Network externalities and first-mover advantages require the solution to be "right the first time," as there may be no chance to be a follower and catch up, while not getting it right may stifle market development and leave room for a "second-generation" solution. In these types of alliances, the coalition acts as a convergence arena and a forum for validating technology and architectural choices; it mobilizes the knowledge and insights of a constellation of players to reduce uncertainty, and it ensures that their interests and limitations are considered in the design of the solution. Such alliances thus simultaneously pursue the goals of strategic co-option (through a setting of the terms of competition in a given market, as in the case of the VCR) and resource/skills complementation (in the exploitation of the opportunity itself). As in the case of Iridium, these motives interact in the building of such alliances.

The developments we have described—hybrid technologies, products that bring together many technologies, and system solutions—explain why so many firms now race toward the future with alliance partners. Increases in the pace of technical change and in the complexity of available opportunities make alliances a natural response for individual firms. The current tendency of these same firms to focus on a narrower range of competencies and technologies only exacerbates the need for capable allies. Figure 2-3 sketches the nature of the challenge posed by the evolution and speed of technology.

Value Creation through Learning and Internalization

As companies compete in global markets, skill deficits are soon apparent and quickly debilitating: globalization makes local companies vulnerable to competitors that have developed and polished skills in distant and more demanding markets. U.S. auto makers, for example, hemorrhaged during the early 1980s when superior Japan-

FIGURE 2-3 *Shifting Opportunities in the Race for the Future*

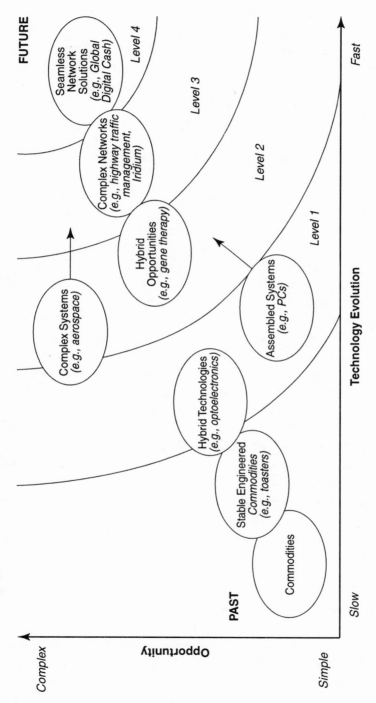

ese imports invaded their domestic markets. The Japanese had superior skills in design, manufacturing, quality control, and management, and the value of these skills was tangible and apparent in the products they sold. Had the American firms not plugged the skills gap, the U.S. auto industry might have withered away.

Unless plugged rapidly, skills gaps can kill or debilitate weaker competitors, particularly as their rivals continue to build new skills and use them for competitive advantage. Thus, competitive races are also races to learn and internalize new skills.

Companies often turn to alliances to win the learning race. These are often faster and more effective than alternative approaches to learning. Internal development, for instance, is often slow and uncertain. Even purchased technologies require time to learn and may be linked to other company-specific skills. Acquisitions, another approach to skill acquisition, are often filled with unpleasant surprises: competencies may not move to the acquirer easily; the skilled personnel employed by the acquired firm sometimes resign and join competitors.[8] Given these pitfalls, alliances are often the best way for companies to quickly acquire and deploy new skills.

The experiences of American and Japanese auto makers offer a good illustration of the relationship between the race for the world and the formation of learning and internalization alliances. Back in the late 1940s—long before anyone was talking about "globalization"—Toyota and its domestic rivals realized that if they hoped to build their industry and stave off foreign competition they would have to match the productivity of American auto makers on smaller volume, with less capital, and with fewer (but more permanent) workers. They also recognized the need to reverse the Japanese reputation for shoddy workmanship.

Japanese auto makers had no choice but to innovate, and over a period of time they discovered what is now called lean manufacturing. By the 1970s, continuous improvements in productivity and quality had made them formidable competitors to the American oligarchy headquartered in Detroit.

In response to Japan's rising share of the U.S. market and the obvious quality of its products, all three major American car makers entered alliances with Japanese competitors. Ford moved as early as 1976, taking a minority equity position in financially troubled Toyo Kogyo, the maker of Mazda (and now also Xedos) cars. This investment gave Ford access to Toyo Kogyo's process technology. Toyo Kogyo was on a steeper learning curve than its domestic rivals, decreasing unit costs faster on a smaller relative volume than its larger competitors. Its Hiroshima plant was, at the time, both the most flexible auto-making facility in Japan and the one with the most rapidly increasing productivity. Its Hama plant was Japan's most focused. Thus, the alliance gave Ford an opportunity to learn from the master of flexible and focused factories.

General Motors—whose long-standing involvement with Isuzu had already given it a window on the Japanese car industry—entered into a more targeted alliance with Toyota in 1984. The two companies agreed to comanufacture small cars in a former GM plant in California, using Toyota's methods and rehired laid-off GM workers. The project—called NUMMI—would be comanaged by a Toyota-GM team. NUMMI gave GM managers and technical personnel an opportunity to learn lean manufacturing methods from its proven master, while testing those same methods on a traditional U.S. workforce.

Chrysler entered an alliance with Mitsubishi Motors. Initially, this arrangement made it possible for Chrysler to plug product and component gaps and to weather a financial crisis in the late 1980s. The company subsequently learned a great deal about quality management and integrated product development. By the 1990s, many considered Chrysler the most competent product developer in the U.S. auto industry.[9]

Naturally, the Japanese companies that entered these alliances did so because they anticipated measurable benefits. And these were forthcoming. The first was a public relations benefit. The Japanese companies were seen as taking a cooperative stance toward U.S. industry at a time of mounting pressures for protectionism. The fact that American workers under Japanese management performed spectacularly, particularly at the joint GM-Toyota plant, shifted the blame for distress in the U.S. auto industry squarely onto the backs of management, further deflecting anti-Japanese sentiment. Besides these public image advantages, cooperating with U.S. rivals offered the Japanese partners insights into the competitive strategies of their partners cum competitors as well as perspective on how fast their capabilities were improving.

The Japanese partners also gained complementarity advantages in scale and skills. For instance, Mitsubishi increased its production of key components and systems—such as engines—which were sold in large volume to Chrysler. Toyo Kogyo contributed its technologies and engineering skills to Ford but also learned how to develop models and features better suited to Western markets. Ford also provided its Japanese partner with financial support after the failure of Toyo Kogyo's rotary engine got the company into trouble. Finally, the Japanese partners learned how to apply their principles of production and management in the United States. Toyota, in particular, used its alliance with GM to learn to deal with U.S. labor practices. This knowledge paid major dividends when it opened its own fully owned U.S. manufacturing plant, where it had to blend American labor management practices with the Japanese production system.

In sum, many skills were to an extent geographically isolated and grew in response to demanding local circumstances. Global competition exposes the world to the best available skills and threatens companies that do not adopt them. Alliances are a way to tap into the whole world's knowledge base.

The race for the future heightens the need to maintain or acquire key competencies. The new structure of competition it fosters—focused companies, broad opportunities—calls for collaboration. To hold their own in these collaborations, companies may still want to internalize enough of the critical underlying competencies—an issue for Motorola in Iridium, as we discussed. An alliance with a highly capable partner can offer a wonderful laboratory for a company eager to gain control over critical skills. Further, the speed with which this race is run means that companies may suddenly and unexpectedly find themselves behind the curve with respect to key technologies. Technologies that seem irrelevant or peripheral to an industry today may become critically important tomorrow. And once a company falls behind the technology curve, it is difficult to catch up. Alliances can be an effective means of complementing existing skills and acquiring new ones and for getting back into the race.

The experience of Germany's Siemens provides an example of how to use alliances to learn and internalize key competencies in the area of microelectronics. Siemens had fallen behind in microelectronic technology, but soon recognized its growing strategic importance. It also foresaw the danger of becoming dependent for this technology on suppliers who were also competitors. So in the early

1980s Siemens mounted an ambitious effort to catch up with the leaders in microelectronics.

Siemens used a series of alliances and joint projects (many under the sponsorship of ESPRIT and EUREKA, the European government-sponsored collaborative research programs) to catch up. Its first collaboration was with Toshiba on manufacturing technology. This was followed by work with Philips on the development of high-density computer memories. Next came a broader alliance with other European partners (the Joint European Silicon Structures Initiative). Other collaborations with IBM, Toshiba (again), and Motorola followed. Each successive alliance was used as a rung in a learning ladder, so that between its first and second alliances with Toshiba it had transformed itself from a humble apprentice to a near-equal partner. By 1995 Siemens could be counted among the world leaders in microelectronics.

The Siemens case underscores the fact that an alliance almost always has two dimensions: one is concerned with what the partners can achieve together, the second with what the partners can gain for themselves. Therefore, alliances create value by improving the competitive standing of their partners against others, and alliance partners attempt to extract value for themselves from within the alliance. The dual process of value creation and value extraction in alliances can be thought of in terms of baking and then sharing a pie, with each partner contributing different resources and skills (one furnishing the ingredients, another the recipe, and so on) and then having to agree with the others on how to divide the finished product. This means that, quite apart from any issues of rivalry in the marketplace between partners, relationships between alliance partners entail both cooperation and competition. Thus winning through alliances is, to a significant degree, also a matter of winning *within* one's alliances.

Being a good partner, of course, is a give-and-take proposition. Besides closing its own skills gaps, a partner must contribute unique competencies of it own if it aspires to maintain influence in an alliance. As we illustrated in the Iridium example, Motorola could hardly expect to maintain its leadership of the Iridium alliance if it were to relinquish responsibility for contributing all key technologies to Lockheed, Raytheon, or other strong partners.

Summary

Whether they are racing for the world or for the future, companies pursuing value creation by means of alliances can be found in any of three activities: the co-option of rival or complementary firms, the melding and leveraging of cospecialized resources, and the learning and internalization of critical skills.

Globalizing firms can use alliances to build the critical mass needed to stake out and hold market positions. They can also use alliances as vehicles to reach new markets and plug skills gaps.

Technology-driven firms find a parallel set of value-creating benefits. For them, alliances make it possible to build nodal positions in the coalitions that define the technology future. These same alliances also open new opportunities for products and applications, and they keep the partner firms on the cutting edge of knowledge and skills.

3

❖

CONCEIVING THE ALLIANCE
FOR VALUE CREATION

WHAT MAKES THE DISTINCTIONS between co-option, cospecialization, and learning/internalization, described in the previous chapter, so important? The short answer is that an alliance should be both conceived and managed according to its value creation logic. If this consistency is not maintained throughout the course of the alliance, disappointment is bound to follow. The logic of value creation should set the agenda.

This chapter explores the link between the different logics of value creation and the management agenda. We have observed that the expectations set by an alliance's value creation logic drive six key aspects of its management agenda.

1. *Assessment of each partner's contribution to the alliance.* Value creation expectations should drive the assessment of each partner's contribution: What does each partner bring to the alliance and why? How clearly can the assessment be made in advance or retrospectively?

2. *Agreement on the scope of the alliance.* Value creation expectations should also determine the scope of the alliance: what to include

in the tasks jointly performed by the partners, over what product markets, in what technological and operational domain to assess the economic and financial consequences of the alliance for each partner, and in the context of which strategic goals and intents.

3. *Agreement on tasks critical to the success of the alliance.* Value creation logic also defines the tasks critical to alliance success. In co-option alliances, the most critical tasks may be the initial negotiations and subsequent coordination of strategic actions between partners; beyond these, little joint work may be required. For cospecialization alliances, the most critical tasks are crafting the working interface between partners and subsequent effective and efficient skill combination. Copractice of new skills (for one partner at least) is usually the most critical task in learning alliances.

4. *Measurement of success.* Scorekeeping should also be defined against value creation expectations. Increased competitive strength, success in cospecialization tasks, and learning effectiveness must be measured in very different ways, and none can be measured solely in terms of the alliance's short-term financial performance.

5. *Progress and duration of the alliance.* Value creation logic is the strongest indicator of likely alliance duration. The timeline on which value creation occurs is likely to be quite different for co-option, cospecialization, and learning alliances.

6. *Points of tension.* Value creation expectations may also help anticipate areas of tension. Tension tends to accumulate around key areas of value creation.

Assessing Contributions

Perhaps the most critical determinant of value creation is the degree to which the partners' contributions are complementary. Thus, alliance architects need to determine which contribution to seek from each partner. While the ideal contribution is highly situational, the value-creating logic should guide the assessment of potential contribution.

CO-OPTION CONTRIBUTIONS

When co-option is the basis of value creation, the most critical contribution is the ability to tilt the competitive balance in favor of the coalition and to allow members to gain competitive strength. There are usually several contributors to an alliance's competitiveness. Here are a few examples.

In its battle against Sony for leadership of the emerging VCR market, JVC brought a new standard, new products, and the Japanese manufacturing advantage to its coalition. In Europe, the partners were sufficiently strong to provide market access, but sufficiently weak that they could not go it alone. Thus, JVC avoided Philips while co-opting that company's weaker, but not minuscule, European competitors: Thomson, Thorn, Nokia, and others. While each was relatively weak, they collectively provided large-scale access to European markets and the ability to lobby their respective governments and the European Community. Fujitsu followed a similar approach in its co-option of ICL, Nokia, Amdahl, and other mainframe computer makers against IBM.[1]

Riding the coattails of another firm's brand identity and reputation may help weak and unknown newcomers to establish strong positions. For example, PixTech, a new and relatively unknown French venture company developing field emission displays, a new unproved flat panel display technology, found an early R&D alliance with Texas Instruments essential to building credibility with investors and subsequent technology partners. While its alliance with Texas Instruments has since lapsed, it now has R&D alliances with Motorola, Raytheon, and Futaba and a manufacturing alliance with United Microelectronics in Taiwan.[2]

Interestingly, some twenty years after the JVC–Sony VCR battle, the Toshiba–Time Warner coalition won a similar contest for digital video disk standards. In doing so, it bested the same adversaries that lost in VCRs, Sony and Philips.[3] All competitors in the video disk contest faced strong pressures to adopt a single standard. When this happens, some are likely to gain more strength than others, depending on the standard ultimately adopted. What made the difference this time around? The Toshiba–Time Warner video disk technology offered advantages in terms of capacity and pricing over the Philips-Sony approach, which was derivative of the audio and CD-ROM technology at which the two companies excelled. But technology alone did not make Toshiba–Time Warner the winner. The enterprise built common ground across a wide range of coalition participants.

Cognizant of Hollywood's desire to influence standards for home delivery of digital pictures, Time Warner organized an ad-hoc committee of seven major studios to examine potential technologies and articulate its own wishes, which, perhaps not so surprisingly, came to match rather well the capabilities of the Toshiba product. Philips and Sony, in the meantime, worked in relative isolation, obtaining inputs only from the studios they owned, Columbia and Polygram, but built no broader industry support. Their product achieved higher compatibility with existing CD-ROM manufacturing technology, a characteristic prized by the CD-ROM makers, and by Philips and Sony in particular, but of little value to others. Toshiba–Time Warner also co-opted potential competitors when incorporating the technologies of some of these competitors, such as Matsushita, into their own solution.[4] Computer makers were also brought on board the coalition, and they put strong pressure on suppliers for the adoption of a single standard. In fact, the computer makers strongly encouraged the two emerging coalitions to negotiate a common approach in 1995. Sony was ultimately won over by pressure from the entertainment and computer industry coalitions, by Toshiba's willingness to incorporate Sony and Philips's signal processing and error correction technologies into the standard, and by its backward compatibility with audio and video CDs where Sony and Philips were the leaders.

Although Toshiba and Time Warner clearly won by building common ground and a powerful support base across many groups, they were also wise enough to co-opt members of the rival coalition.

Whether the main goal is to co-opt competitors, customers, or complementers, the contributions that initiators of co-option seek are the same:

1. To co-opt competitors who are collectively strong enough to build a valuable and successful coalition but individually too weak to seriously challenge the leadership of the nodal firm.

2. To use the coalition to surround major competitors that either will not join the coalition or would extract too many concessions or advantages as a price of joining.[5]

3. To co-opt the most desirable complementers in "system building" alliances to increase one's competitive strength and bargaining power over competitors. These partners may provide complementary goods (such as components), strength in complementary steps in the value creation process (such as distribution), or control over critical system complements (such as sporting events and movie rights for the broadcasters of digital television). Alliances at one step in the value chain give valued exclusivity to specific competitors, or partners, at other stages still exposed to competition. In the battle for the German digital television market, for instance, the Kirch group emerged as the winner largely on the strength of its preemption of broadcasting rights to movies and other programs, placing it in a leading position relative to other broadcasters.

4. To erode the competitive strength of the dominant industry player(s), as we see today in the myriad anti-IBM, anti-Intel, and anti-Microsoft alliances.

COSPECIALIZATION CONTRIBUTIONS

Cospecialization alliances create value by bringing together skills and, more generally, ownership-specific resources. When contributions to this type of alliance are analyzed, each partner must ask: "What does my potential partner bring that is unique?" Uniqueness has three aspects:

1. *Unique contributions cannot be traded easily across companies.* They lose their value if transferred or sold. Government relationships, for instance, are ownership-specific contributions that cannot be sold to another company, particularly to a foreign one, and may not survive the sale of a business to a foreign investor. Hence the importance of alliances with local partners when local government relationships play a key role.

2. *Unique contributions cannot be easily substituted.* To continue the government relationships example, a local partner is an absolute necessity when selling in some government-controlled markets, such as defense systems. In some cases, there is only one suitable partner. Partnering with that company is unavoidable; its support and goodwill cannot be substituted.

3. *Unique contributions cannot be independently developed or replicated within any reasonable time frame.* Again, the kind of relationships and understanding that confers insider status in closed markets provides obvious examples.[6]

The beginning of the GE–SNECMA alliance in the 1970s is an example of a partnership in which value was created through the cospecialization of a number of owner-specific, unique contributions. GE had entered the civilian jet engine market in the late 1960s—before the SNECMA alliance—with a large engine (the CF6) used on both the Douglas DC10 and the Boeing 747, two American civilian jetliners. Pratt & Whitney, however, remained the undisputed American leader in civilian aircraft engines, while financially troubled Rolls-Royce remained a strong global contender.

Why did GE turn to SNECMA? GE had identified an opportunity to build close links with European airframe makers as a way of first circumventing and later challenging Pratt & Whitney's dominance in North America and of preventing the development of a European alliance centered on Rolls-Royce. SNECMA's strong French identity, and its close links with Airbus and Airbus's French and German partners, seemed an opportunity to develop a leading position in Europe. GE's CF6 engine would be suitable for the Airbus A300 then under development, and various European airlines were also customers for the DC10 and the B747, which could be equipped with engines made by GE or its major rivals. SNECMA could also count on French government funding to develop its products.

Both partners thus brought unique "relational" assets to the alliance—assets that were rooted in their respective nationalities and in privileged positions with their home country governments.[7] But complementation extended beyond government support. GE brought SNECMA infrastructure and expertise in selling, supporting, and servicing civilian engines worldwide—a critical element of the business that its partners could develop only at great cost. Each company, moreover, brought specific technical skills to the alliance: engine core development on the part of GE, fan development on the part of SNECMA.

Finally, the high launch cost of the CF6 engine would have made it difficult for GE to fund the development of a new midsized engine on its own. Yet GE believed that being first with such an engine might deter other competitors from developing one, offering GE a limited strategic window.

In summary, GE had no other suitable potential partner in Europe and was co-opting the only viable complementary European engine maker other than Rolls-Royce, its global rival. Although SNECMA viewed Pratt & Whitney as a potential alternative to GE, it understood that Pratt & Whitney's leading position would make a true alliance difficult. Thus, the GE–SNECMA alliance seemed promising. Partner substitutability was low on both sides, and each company would bring unique complementary assets to the other. The relationship each partner enjoyed with it own domestic government further reinforced the "unsubstitutability" of their contributions. Put differently, cospecialization existed here not exclusively and not even so much between skills as between relationships and positions.

Inability to imitate was clear as well. As an American company, GE could not independently develop the close relationships it needed to operate in Europe. Any effort on SNECMA's part to enter civilian markets alone and try to earn the credibility GE already enjoyed with Boeing and McDonnell Douglas would have been a long, difficult, costly, and perhaps futile effort.

Finally, the partners' assets were not tradable. GE could not *buy* SNECMA's government relations, and SNECMA could not *buy* GE's technology or experience in dealing with airlines and American plane makers.

The GE–SNECMA alliance—which enjoyed great success—underscores several key points. Cospecialization between the two partners was very high on many dimensions and met our three conditions for uniqueness. Equally important, the partners' contributions, if kept separate, would not assure success in a demanding race; if combined, the chance of success was high. Every successful cospecialization alliance must meet these same tests of contributing uniqueness and of enabling new opportunities for its partners.

Cospecialization does have costs, however—commitment costs. Cospecialization entails irreversible commitments, making each partner a hostage of the other as each concentrates on delivering its unique contributions and comes to rely more and more on its partner for the partner's unique contributions.[8] The effects of this condition are difficult to assess in advance. This is why many alliances start with the exchange of information as a way to reduce uncertainty and build trust before committing to cospecialization.

LEARNING AND INTERNALIZATION CONTRIBUTIONS

When learning and internalization are the goals of the alliance, the criteria for assessing contributions are most obvious: partners need to provide valuable tacit or embedded skills—skills that are difficult to acquire, transfer, and learn except in a master-apprentice relationship. The alliance relationship may be balanced in that all partners learn from each other in roughly equal proportion, each partner being an apprentice of the others in one or another skill area.

To understand how to value each other's contributions in a mutual learning alliance, it is useful to come back to the motives underlying each partner's learning and internalization efforts. We have observed that efforts to learn the partner's skills are driven by a few key motives. One is the opportunity to leverage learning across an entire organization, not just in the alliance proper, as in the NUMMI situation described in Chapter 2. Another is fear of dependence on the partner(s) for key skills. This could leave one partner vulnerable to a loss of key skills should the partner(s) decide to leave the alliance, to diminishing returns from the value created by the alliance should the partner(s) decide to take advantage of the firm's dependence, or to a divergence of interests that would make continued cooperation impossible but leave one unable to pick up from the alliance and continue alone. Another significant motive to learn a partner's skills stems from one party's desire to rebalance the alliance in its own favor by becoming less dependent on the partner's contributions.

Analyzing the ways these various motives may affect a partner's value creation calculation helps one understand how the partner is likely to value the other's contribution and, in particular, the learning opportunities offered by the alliance.

Rather than balanced, the learning relationship may be one-sided, with one partner paying "tuition" to the other for the privilege of being its apprentice. We observe this to be a feature of many alliances, though it is rarely formalized. Here the value of the partner's contribution is a function of the "exchange rate" between learning and economic benefits (tuition). In cases where the exchange is clearly formalized—via technology transfer and royalty agreements between partners, for instance—formalization seldom covers the full range of learning opportunities. Strategically, if a company is only partly aware of its partner's learning aspiration, or is perhaps even entirely unaware, it will not extract an appropriate price for the learning opportunities it offers. Certainly many Western companies now feel they offered tuition to their Japanese or Korean partners at bargain-basement prices.

The relationship may also aim at extending each partner's skill base through jointly building new skills rather than trading preexisting ones. This has been the explicit logic of many R&D consortia in Europe, Japan, and the United States in microelectronics, new energy forms, and health care. Partners in bilateral alliances, such as EDS and Xerox in their attempt to develop "The Document Company" (a business concept integrating information management in print and on networks), also often believe an alliance will accelerate their joint learning. In other cases, networks of individual companies outsource and share some of their competencies to accelerate the development of these competencies, as in the case of local banks in the United States entrusting their information technology development to a common third party, such as EDS or Andersen Consulting.

The availability of the relevant skills in the partner organization or in the alliance and a mutually acceptable resolution of the valuation issue are necessary but insufficient conditions for learning and internalizing knowledge. Paradoxically, a long-time master of relevant skills may not be the best teacher. Its learning tracks may be so deeply buried in the past, and its skills so embedded in tacit understandings, that its partners would find it a poor teacher. A company that has acquired its skills more recently, or that is still at an earlier stage of competence development, may be easier to learn from and imitate.

A partner's learning *speed* is another element of the contribution assessment. Learning is not simply about capturing a partner's current skills but about riding on its learning coattails. Companies that seek the fast track to the future should latch onto a fast-learning partner. Ford accomplished this when it allied itself with Toyo Kogyo. This was not the most efficient Japanese car maker, but its rate of productivity improvement was faster than that of its Japanese competitors. Interestingly, though, despite its productivity gains, Toyo Kogyo was simply not quite large enough to compete on its own. Over the years of its alliance with Ford, while Ford was learning from Toyo Kogyo, Toyo Kogyo (now Mazda) became dependent on its American partner for financing and for global market access. Ultimately, a good student surpasses the teacher, and Mazda today is essentially run and operated by Ford as a subsidiary.[9]

Beyond availability, recentness, and rate of improvement, skill *accessibility* is another key factor. The alliance must make learning possible and easy. In its alliance with JVC in Europe, for instance, Thomson used JVC's need to increase local content to access JVC's expertise in micromechanics. Thomson also offered its European distribution channels as a bargaining chip, committing to large orders from the joint venture only in exchange for the transfer of knowledge to manufacture "mechadecks" (the mechanical parts of a VCR) to Thomson.

Acquisition may be another path to learning if an alliance partner proves unreliable. When a partner lacks a stable commitment to the business, or cannot maintain its commitments, an acquisition may be preferable to an alliance. Samsung, for instance, in its efforts to acquire new capabilities, acquired plants and complete companies and operated them locally. Ultimately, some of these facilities were dismantled and reassembled in Korea as pilot plants. But Samsung acquired companies that either would not partner with Samsung or would lack staying power in the alliance.

VALUATION CONUNDRA

Although valuing the contributions of partners for co-option, cospecialization, and learning and internalization may be simple in principle, it is difficult in practice. Most valuation difficulties stem from five specific characteristics of partner contributions. We call these the five valuation conundra:

1. The alliance brings together nontraded assets that are hard to value.
2. The relative contribution of each partner to alliance success is hard to assess, even retrospectively.
3. Much of the value, and the costs, of an alliance accrue *outside* the relationship, making it difficult for partners to monitor each other's balance of costs and benefits.
4. The relative value of each partner's contribution may shift over time in ways that are difficult to anticipate and recognize.

5. Partners may be less than totally forthcoming in declaring the value they seek from the alliance.

Each conundrum creates a distinct challenge to alliance design and management. Let's explore each in detail.

Hard-to-value assets. Hard-to-value assets, such as relationships and competencies, are combined through alliances precisely because other forms of combination and exchange would not work. Further, it is difficult to value contributions when external benchmarks and markets don't exist and when partners' skill and experience bases differ.

Interestingly enough, GE and SNECMA agreed rather easily that their work shares were roughly equal. They transferred a few small tasks from one partner to the other until they were satisfied that equality was reached. But GE's trust in SNECMA to "deliver" Airbus was an act of faith, as was SNECMA's trust in GE to secure access to leading U.S. airlines. Put differently, the partners could agree relatively easily on the value of their respective tasks but not on the value of their relationships.

Western companies going to China or Russia today face a similar difficulty: it's relatively easy for them to assess the tasks their partners can perform, but it's extremely difficult to assess the value of the relationships their partners bring to the table. Yet it is these relationships that make their alliances valuable.

Partners' relative contributions to success. It is often difficult to separate value created by the partnership from value created by individual partners acting alone. How to sort this problem out is far from clear. The problem is most acute in the development of new opportunities, where both the alliance and the specific efforts of the partners matter.

Consider the Alza–Ciba-Geigy alliance to develop advanced drug delivery systems. "TTS-nitro" (an Alza-designed transdermal "patch" used to treat angina pectoris) was one of the most successful products to result from the alliance. But which firm should have gotten credit for its success? And how much? Alza had the outstanding technology. Ciba-Geigy contributed its considerable worldwide marketing capability and bankrolled Alza R&D for years. Given these contributions, what benefits should each partner draw? Royalties from Ciba-Geigy to Alza would be a typical solution, but what should be the level of royalties? Should the royalty rate decline over time to reflect Ciba-Geigy's role in the product's ongoing success? Should decline in the royalty rate be a function of sales volume? Should royalties cease a preestablished number of years after commercialization? Or, on the contrary, should the royalty rate increase once Ciba-Geigy's investment has been paid back?

The questions just cited are familiar to all those involved in sharing and trading technologies. If partners were perfectly cospecialized—that is, the contribution of one is worth nothing at all unless combined with that of the other, and no contribution can be substituted, even in part—the difficulty would almost disappear and the partners could presumably agree on parity in benefits. Very few alliances conform to this ideal pattern. Complex contractual formulas can provide sophisticated solutions to the valuation problem, but they do not make the problem go away. There is no simple analytical answer to the problem.

Deferring valuation to a retrospective assessment through contingent contracts does not necessarily solve the valuation problem, particularly in the face of remaining causal uncertainty, or even ambiguity, about the reasons for success.

One "solution" is to create a joint venture with boundaries sufficiently broad to minimize transfer pricing issues. Philips and DuPont, for example, found it difficult to agree on transfer pricing. DuPont was the maker of magnetic tape products that Philips sold under its brand names. To avoid transfer pricing problems, they created a joint venture that bought raw materials at market prices and sold end products using competitors' trade prices as a point of reference.

The joint venture approach raises two major issues with respect to valuation. First, the valuation question has to be tackled at the outset, before the process of cooperation allows the partners to better gauge the value of their respective contributions. Second, the joint venture formula works best when the partners create a stand-alone entity that does little "trade" with its parents. Ideally, one would like to minimize interdependencies between the activities put into the operating scope of the alliance and those left with the parent organizations. While this is possible for stand-alone joint ventures, it makes no sense for the many alliances in which value creation is based largely on exploiting interdependencies between the alliance and its parents (often by pooling volumes and combining core competencies). Short of setting boundaries that separate the partnered activities from the parents', provisions for periodic reassessment and revaluation of benefits and contributions, past and future, may help solve this conundrum, albeit imperfectly.

Value accrued outside of the alliance. When interdependencies between shared and independently performed operations are strong, trade issues between the partners and their joint venture are likely to be thorny. JVC-Thomson provides a useful example. If J2T, the companies' European joint venture, enabled JVC to move from producing, or purchasing, 4 million sets of components per year to 4.8 million, and if there were significant economies of scale in component manufacture or procurement, how should the transfer price between JVC and J2T be set? We present the issue graphically in Figure 3-1. By entering the alliance with JVC, Thomson saves the difference between P_t (what it would pay per unit on a volume of 800,000 units) and P_p (the price the partnership can get by pooling JVC's and Thomson's purchasing volumes) multiplied by the volume it would have achieved on its own (the area shaded as "A" in the figure).

FIGURE 3-1 *Setting Transfer Price in the JVC–Thomson Alliance*

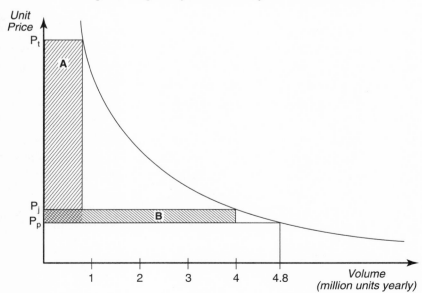

By a similar logic, JVC saves a lesser amount (Pj–Pp) but on a much higher volume (4 million, with the reduction of price times volume represented by the area shaded as "B"). Does this mean that the transfer price should be set to equate "A" and "B," so that each partner gets an equal share of the value created by the pooling of purchases? Or should JVC charge J2T price P_t, on the grounds that JVC's previously independent manufacture of 4 million VCRs a year ought not to give the alliance a "windfall" that it has done nothing to earn? Or should the total savings be apportioned to respective volumes (that is, 83.33 percent for JVC and 16.67 percent for the joint venture)? Obviously, although this last suggestion is in principle a fair choice, there is room for negotiation and conflict in setting a "fair" transfer price.

In fact, JVC first charged the joint venture a price close to P_t. It was induced to gradually reduce this transfer price after Thomson obtained much lower quotes from other suppliers for similar components (some of which were made by JVC's own subcontractors). In this particular case, new sources of cheaper components would naturally become available over time as more companies began building VCRs, thus decreasing the uniqueness of JVC's contribution, a shift legitimately reflected in falling transfer prices.

Shifts in partners' relative value over time. The fourth conundrum in valuation is the shift in the relative value of each partner's contribution over time. This shift occurs in ways that are difficult to anticipate or recognize. As these shifts take place, the pricing of any contribution will, in principle, raise problems similar to those faced in the transfer of components and perhaps lead partners to suggest unworkable solutions, for example, to include components. While this was a solution for Thomson, which did not have an established VCR manufacturing volume base of its own, it was not a feasible option for JVC. The Japanese firm saw no advantage in separating J2T's component volume from its own, or in letting Thomson share in JVC's total economies of scale, or in manufacturing components in Europe. The tension-ridden reduction of transfer prices in this alliance, which took place as Thomson gained better information and developed alternate supply options, was probably unavoidable, even with some expansion of the alliance boundaries. JVC saw cost reductions in Japan and high margins on the exports of components to France as essential parts of its "trade" with Thomson.

Actual value sought by partners. Partners may not always see it as in their interest to share their full value creation expectations, partly because they believe they can underrepresent the benefits they get to their partner, particularly when these benefits accrue outside the scope of the alliance. Yet there are obvious advantages to being very transparent and building trust between partners.

Handling Valuation Conundra

While it may not be easy to resolve these valuation conundra, a few steps can be taken to limit their impact:

1. *Clearly define alliance scope and trade terms between partners.* Valuation conflicts can be minimized by bringing into the alliance activities of mutual interest and by creating a joint receptacle, such as a joint venture, to hold them. This also limits the disruptive impact of hidden agendas by making the partners' respective costs and benefits mutually visible.

2. *Create a separate economic entity.* The decision to create a joint venture rather than rely on contractual trade moves the need to solve some key valuation conflicts to the outset of collaboration. When the economics of the situation are well understood, this is easy. When the economics are very uncertain, early resolution of conflicts requires an act of faith on the part of the partners.

3. *Seek external benchmarks.* As in many other cases in which exchange is sought, external reference points provide independent calibration of each partner's assessment of value-creating contribution (as Thomson found out by seeking quotes on VCR components).

4. *Plan for recurring bargains.* By not making decisions a priori, companies avoid initial difficulties, but they must prepare themselves to deal with conflicts on an ongoing basis. The issue of recurring bargaining obviously is more difficult when the relative values of partner contributions shift over time in ways that are hard to measure or even recognize. In other words, the valuation conundra discussed above also have a dynamic dimension and often cannot be solved once and for all. Such shifts can become disruptive, locking partners into periodic renegotiations of transfer prices. This was the case in the AT&T–Olivetti alliance. Once an

adversarial climate has settled in, it may become difficult or even impossible to move on to a more constructive relationship. Conversely, Xerox has shown great ability to adapt to reflect the growing role of Fuji-Xerox, its joint venture with Fuji, in its global operations.

The managerial challenge raised by all five valuation conundra is the need to define the economic "trade" between partners early, when information and mutual understanding are poor. The issue of valuation often boils down to a choice between which conflicts to solve up front by design and which to accept and manage later when better information is available. This choice will, of necessity, be based on partial information and an incomplete understanding of each partner's contributions and the benefits of the alliance. Either of these—contributions or benefits—may change as the partners work together. Accepting the notion that better information yields better judgment, partners should recognize that initial agreements may need renegotiating.

This recognition may be the most critical shift in mindset between traditional collaboration and the new types of alliances. Partners should not cling to an obsolete bargain, or pretend that it remains valid, or make unilateral choices to reduce or increase their own commitments. Instead, they should accept the need to renegotiate based on a new and more accurate assessment of relative contributions. Thus, a healthy alliance is a series of microbargains made over time, something we will discuss more fully in Chapter 7.

Agreeing on the Scope of the Alliance

The *scope* of an alliance has three dimensions: areas of interest, net benefits, and joint operations. Interests determine an alliance's strategic scope and usually encompass its widest territory. Benefits underpin its economic scope; some benefits accrue within the alliance proper (for example, the profits of a joint venture), while others accrue separately to each partner. Joint activities provide operational scope, which is typically the narrowest definition of the alliance territory.

The GE–SNECMA alliance helps us to see the tangible aspects of these three dimensions. The *strategic scope* of this alliance encompasses the entire jet engine business of the two companies, both civilian and military. Civilian and military engines are developed in the same labs and made in the same plants; product policy and product engineering choices, as well as investment decisions, cannot be made for one market independently of the other. Both civilian and military business depend on the same competencies.

The *economic scope* of the alliance is seen in the activities that GE and SNECMA carried out for the alliance and in the impact of those activities on each company's performance. Development, manufacturing, sales, and field support and maintenance were performed by each partner on behalf of their alliance, and each made or lost money on its share of these activities. Ultimately, in any alliance, it is only the performance of the partners that matters. In the absence of a joint venture, there is no legal accounting entity other than the partners.

The *operational scope* of GE–SNECMA is the sum of the activities performed within the venture and the activities performed by people whose jobs are at the interfaces between the venture and the two partner companies.

Let's consider the details of each of these important dimensions of the strategic alliance.

STRATEGIC SCOPE

Let's stay with GE and SNECMA to consider the impact of strategic scope. Although the two companies began collaborating on a narrow front—a single product—they quickly found it necessary to expand collaboration to their entire range of civilian engines. This expanded scope was needed to prevent conflicts between them.[10] Across-the-board cooperation also reassured customers, who saw the common interest of the partners extending to the entire range of their engines.

Partners whose strategic scope contains unresolved conflicts may experience a less favorable outcome. Two American suppliers of industrial systems (which, unfortunately, must remain anonymous) formed what appeared to be a promising alliance. Let's call them X and Y. Prior to their alliance, X had formed a partnership covering Europe with a European competitor of Y. Y competed in Europe on its own. The X&Y alliance was confined to North America. Ultimately, the fact that they were now partners on one continent but competitors on another bred suspicion and made their alliance ineffective. For instance, being on its own in Europe, Y was reluctant to share technical information for fear of X leaking it to X's European partner to Y's detriment. Widening the strategic scope of the alliance to include the partners' European interests, a rather obvious solution to this conflict, was not possible because of X's preexisting alliance with its European partner. Predictably, the alliance between the two U.S. suppliers was short-lived.

An important task for managers in cospecialization alliances is to minimize conflicts between what is included in the strategic scope of the alliance and what is not. For the partners just cited, X's separate European alliance was the Achilles heel of their relationship—a source of inherent conflict. GE and SNECMA were free from this type of conflict, in part because of the nature of the business in which they operated independently. The military jet engine market was smaller and more protected, and competition there was indirect; nor was the GE–SNECMA alliance seriously threatened by the two companies remaining independent in the military field.

Decisions on strategic scope are most critical when companies in the same business form a cospecialization alliance. Here mismatched or misunderstood strategic scopes can lead to insuperable conflicts. Conversely, companies that learn new skills together or from each other find less difficulty with strategic scope, in particular, if they serve different markets or segments. Each will have its separate strategic ambitions for its own markets and will learn from the other. Strategic scope is also less likely to be a source of conflict in co-option alliances. Because strategic scope drives the alliance, strategic scope conflicts would likely prevent the alliance from being initiated.

Economic Scope

Economic scope is defined by the range of activities that takes place within the partner firms on behalf of the alliance. For example, both of the U.S. industrial systems companies referred to above were supplying products and subsystems to their marketing and distribution alliance. The plants from which they supplied these were obviously part of the economic scope of the alliance; the actual performance of each partner's plants was only partly influenced by the fortunes of the alliance. This bred suspicion of overcharging, as plant performance information was not usually shared. A similar arrangement existed between GE and SNECMA, but trade across similarly positioned boundaries was managed quite differently. Whereas the systems companies haggled regularly over transfer prices, GE and SNECMA had agreed to a "once-and-for-all" work share arrangement, whereby each would contribute equally, with no money exchanged or transfer prices set. The two engine makers estimated each other's share of the work—and of the costs—to be equal; this entitled each to 50 percent of alliance revenue (minus the costs incurred in the joint venture) no matter what their actual costs were. As a result, each was indifferent to the actual economic performance of the other and had a strong incentive to reduce its own costs. This work- and revenue-sharing arrangement was less conducive to conflicts than a profit-sharing one, as it minimized ongoing areas of discussion on costs and benefits.

The interests and attitudes of alliance partners cannot be fully understood if the full economic scope of an alliance is not considered. The benefits of the alliance to the partners may accrue largely outside of its operational scope—for instance, through the supply of components, leading to the valuation conflicts discussed above. These tensions are harder to avoid when the alliance is a stand-alone joint venture investment for one partner but is deeply embedded in another's related activities. The former will focus on shared performance in the alliance proper, the latter on benefits outside the visible shared operational scope of the alliance.

Consider the example of Ciba-Corning. In this medical diagnostics alliance, Corning was supplying part of the equipment (components of test machines, glass test tubes and plates, and the like), and Ciba was supplying reagents and other chemical and biological substances. The joint venture's activities were much more central to Ciba's strategy and learning priorities than they were to Corning's. They also generated a larger, steadier, and more profitable revenue stream for Ciba. After a few years, the partners realized that their economic scopes differed too much to support sustained cooperation, and Corning sold its stake in the venture to Ciba-Geigy.[11]

Short of minimizing interdependencies between each partner and the alliance—a difficult job in any case—ensuring that the value, or potentially the cost, of these interdependencies is recognized by all partners is essential. In other words, partners must recognize that the economic scope of the alliance is wider than its operational scope and develop a comprehensive view of each partner's benefits and contributions, including economic and strategic risks.

OPERATIONAL SCOPE

The operational scope of an alliance is what is actually done jointly by the partners. For instance, GE and SNECMA limited the operational scope of their alliance to program management. Partners may decide to minimize or maximize this operational scope. Minimizing has several advantages. First, coordination and integration needs are reduced. This translates into practical savings on the cost of collocation, travel, integrated teams, and the like. GE and SNECMA were able to develop their respective "parts" of the CFM engine separately, at least initially, limiting operational scope to a minimum. Second, because fewer activities are shared, minimizing the operational scope reduces the risk of unintended leakage of technology or skills from partner to partner. Alza, too, minimized the operational scope of its alliance with Ciba-Geigy, its intent being to limit Ciba-Geigy's ability to learn through joint work. Third, limiting operational scope may circumvent the problem of cultural distance by reducing requirements for two very dissimilar companies to work together closely. This was a concern on Ciba-Geigy's part.[12]

Minimizing the operational scope of an alliance can be costly, especially if later developments call for expansion. For example, when AT&T and Olivetti attempted to jointly develop a new minicomputer product line, they were hampered by the pattern of distance and mistrust that their previously contractual, conflict-ridden relationships had set. Their sudden shift to a cooperative relationship of broader scope failed.

A broader operational scope normally provides a larger "exchange surface" on which members of the partner firms can interact, communicate, and learn from each other. Therefore, another concern when setting operational scope is the creation of sufficient interface to facilitate joint learning.

WHAT SCOPE MEANS FOR MANAGERS

All three kinds of scope—strategic, economic, and operational—can create conflicts that may erupt in very different places. Operational scope conflicts emerge at the interface where partners work together. One partner may, for instance, want to work more closely with its partners, while the others may want to keep allies at arm's length. Economic scope difficulties typically manifest themselves at the boundary between those activities which are jointly performed and those which are not. The idea of giving price breaks to allied firms, for instance, can easily trigger a debate about whether the ally is "one of us" or a "third party." Strategic scope difficulties manifest themselves most strongly around market competition and situations in which each partner may push its own products rather than the "alliance" products.

Thus far, we have described scope-related conflicts in isolation. In reality, conflicts that center around one type of scope usually lead to tensions in another. For instance, in the case of the two U.S. industrial systems companies described earlier, the unresolved geographical conflict of collaboration in America and competition in Europe, a strategic scope issue, made the development of the appropriate operational scope impossible. Neither partner was willing to share know-how or to achieve enough cospecialization to make the alliance create value. Their alliance failed after about two years. This interconnectedness between strategic, economic, and operational scopes in an alliance, and between various—sometimes conflicting—alliances, means that issues of scope need to be considered in light of the alliance's value creation objectives. How the alliance is connected, strategically, economically, and operationally with other activities the partners leave outside the alliance, or even perform through other alliances, needs to be very carefully considered up front when conceiving a new alliance.

In sum, all three scopes are important to all three types of value creation logic, but not equally so. Market and competitor-driven considerations of strategic scope are key to co-option alliances, as their benefits are often more strategic and accrue outside the alliance proper. Conversely, in co-option alliances, the operational scope is often unimportant, as alliance success does not imply closely integrated joint tasks. In cospecialization alliances the economic scope often matters the most, as benefits and costs often accrue in activities that are closely related to that of the alliance but not part of its operational scope. In learning alliances all three scopes are important, but the operational one conditions what learning, and how much learn-

FIGURE 3-2 *The Relationship of Scope to Value Creation Logic*

	Co-option	Cospecialization	Learning and Internalization
Strategic Scope	Strategic interests must be similar (Success: Toshiba–Time Warner) (Failure: IBM–Apple)	Strategic materials must be compatible and result in comparable performance expectations	Differences in strategic market scope and similarities in skill sets and required capabilities facilitate cooperation (Success: Philips and Siemens in semiconductor memories)
Economic Scope	Each partner must find enough benefits in the alliance to remain committed to its continuation	Minimize interpartner trade by making the alliance a stand-alone joint venture (as in Dow Corning), or manage trade in as neutral a fashion as possible (Success: GE–SNECMA) (Failure: AT&T–Olivetti)	There must be careful separation of value creation performance from value appropriation costs (as in GM in NUMMI)
Operational Scope	Usually unimportant	Depends on the demands of the joint task (process integration or output coordination), and on concerns for skill leakage to partner	Must provide enough of a window for learning from the partner or from a joint learning ground (Success: NUMMI) (Failure: Ciba-Geigy–Alza)

ing, can take place. The relationship between alliance scope and value creation logic is depicted in Figure 3-2.

Understanding Joint Task Demands

Different value creation logics call for very different approaches to the tasks performed by partners. Co-option alliances entail the fewest demands from an organizational and managerial standpoint. Success is more a function of strategic foresight and negotiating skills than of the ability of partners to work together closely. The Microsoft–IBM alliance is instructive. When Microsoft, unknown to IBM's executives, simultaneously developed OS-2 for IBM and its own Windows operating system, the Microsoft organization needed little adjusting. Microsoft's interface with IBM was confined to a few people: CEO Bill Gates, several senior executives, and a handful of lawyers and intellectual property rights experts. How Microsoft worked, as an organization, was not material to the success of its interaction with IBM except insofar as it needed to deliver on its commitments. The key managerial tasks for Microsoft concerned Gates's strategic foresight, ambition, and cunning. The requisite skills were largely political and intellectual: conceiving a winning coalition, imagining migration paths to a favorable industry future, and negotiating in a self-interested but cooperative way to build common ground and obtain the key commitments for co-opting partners.

Co-option alliances also typically need to be maintained over time, even when they result in early and irreversible commitments, such as the adoption of a standard. The difficulties experienced by Sony and Philips in the digital video disk (DVD) contest in 1995 stemmed from their lack of ongoing attention to the entertainment industry once the adoption of CD standards had been achieved, a precedent that created ill will among media producers.

While co-option alliances generally require little organizational adjustment or management, alliances that involve many joint tasks—whether skill cospecialization, learning/internalization, or both—are much more demanding. For example, GM's alliance with Toyota required careful design and ongoing management. GM would have learned little from Toyota had it not designed a number of major joint tasks into the alliance: a common plant, mixed teams working together, and a dedicated effort to diffuse learning from Toyota into its own organization. Each of these activities had to be managed over time. Likewise, had they not worked diligently to make their respective organizations similar, GE and SNECMA would have found working together more difficult. Conversely, Ciba-Geigy enjoyed limited success in learning from its relationship with Alza largely because the two companies failed to learn how to perform interdependent tasks together. Successful products were developed, but Ciba did not internalize a new capability.

When collaborative R&D efforts succeed it is generally for two reasons: (1) the learning ambitions of the partners are well matched, and (2) the partners create an interface that makes learning possible. The Japanese very large-scale integration (VLSI) project provides a useful model. Designed to gain leadership in microchip design and manufacture in the late 1970s, the VLSI project was successful largely because of sponsors' efforts to learn how to work together closely without compromising self-interest.

The actual design of individual alliances is discussed in detail in Chapter 5; our purpose here is simply to state that the key tasks in an alliance depend on the value the alliance is expected to create. In most alliances, value creation is a function of the successful performance of joint or coordinated tasks. Thus, value creation should be the yardstick of alliance design.

Defining and Measuring Progress

Design based on value creation is only a partial prescription for alliance success. The value creation expectations reflected in the alliance design should define how success will be measured.

CO-OPTION ALLIANCES

The progress of co-option alliances ought to be measured against their specific aims. For example, an alliance to establish standards can be measured by:

1. the reduction in the number of competing standards and/or system architecture approaches

2. the acceleration in market development attributed to the standards being set

3. the growth and profitability of coalition members compared with that of counterparts outside the coalition

4. the coalition's market share and members' margins

Alternatively, the progress of a co-option alliance intended to restructure a mature industry can be measured on the basis of:

1. adherence to price discipline by its members and by other industry players in downturns

2. improvements in the balance between supply and demand

3. overall improvement of margins in the industry

Although the specific measurements vary in each case, the benchmark for the performance of co-option alliances can be summarized in terms of *the improvement of the structural attractiveness of the industry for the alliance participants and the strengthening of their competitive capabilities.*

COSPECIALIZATION ALLIANCES

Cospecialization alliances that rely on skills or other ownership-specific contributions have other relevant measures. These ought to be measured by *the value of the new opportunities they create compared with what partners could have achieved on their own.*

Increased revenues and cash flow streams are likely to be the most frequently used benchmarks for cospecialization alliances, but there are others. A defensive alliance may have limited positive effects, but these may still be improvements over the effect of having no alliance at all; hence the importance of using alternatives to the actual alliance as reference points, not just actual starting positions. Obviously, the comparison will always be clouded by the difficulty of answering the "what if?" question, but the strength of cospecialization should be able to swing the balance decisively in favor of an alliance as opposed to no alliance.

It is therefore both important and difficult to separate alliance performance from the performance of the underlying business. Eurocopter, the alliance between Aérospatiale and DASA, was established just before the helicopter market collapsed and has consequently performed poorly against expectations. Does this mark Eurocopter as a failure? Not if the separate performance of its partners would have been even worse.

LEARNING ALLIANCES

The success of learning alliances can be measured in terms of the intensity of skill improvement and the scope of learning application. The real test for GM's learning from Toyota was not the performance of NUMMI but the extent to which GM could reduce costs and improve quality at GM plants around the world. Learning alliances need to be assessed on the basis of the individual partner's appropriation of that learning. In this value creation logic, the real value of the alliance must be measured largely outside the agreement.

A more ambitious but perhaps less precise scorecard would include measures of "learning to learn." In other words, did working with Toyota give GM an advantage in practicing disciplines such as TQM and Kaizen on its own, so as to accelerate its own learning, or did GM merely transfer and diffuse internally what it picked up from Toyota via NUMMI?

A full scorecard would also assess time-to-learn versus the decay rate in the value of what is learned in the alliance, again against alternatives. Let's consider the Ford Motor Company's experience to make this point more concrete. Ford's alliance with Toyo Kogyo gave it a window on Japanese lean manufacturing as early as 1976. Based on what it began to learn, Ford launched an "After Japan" program of productivity and quality improvement. By its own admission, Ford only began to amass major benefits from that program in the mid-1980s. Could Ford have learned faster or differently? Could it have obtained the same benefits more cheaply? By the mid-1980s, lean manufacturing was well understood. In view of this, could Ford have bypassed its alliance altogether? These questions are obviously difficult ones to answer today. They were even more difficult to answer when Ford was deciding whether or not to create the alliance.

Relative dependence within a competence-building alliance is another criterion against which to measure success. Whether the coalition contributes to skills parity or maintains a disparity between the partners is perhaps the acid test of any learning alliance. Is GM now able to compete with Toyota in the small car market? Had Rover, by the time it was taken over by BMW in early 1994, learned everything it needed to learn from Honda in terms of productivity, quality, and development cycle times and costs?[13] Was it therefore dependent on Honda only for specific components and models but not for key competencies?

Not a Case of All or Nothing

Whatever the value creation logic followed, it's a mistake to evaluate the success of an alliance only on the basis of what might have resulted in its absence. This all or nothing perspective can blind firms in an alliance to opportunities for greater value creation and value capture. The reason is complacency about alliance benefits. In some cases, alliance benefits so exceed those of go-it-alone strategies that partners fail to make their alliances "efficient." For example, the cost of developing new weapons systems is so high for firms acting alone that European defense contractors have taken a lax attitude toward achieving efficiency in their alliances. The right benchmark is not alliance versus no alliance but the existing alliance versus the optimally efficient alliance. But what is the benchmark for the optimally efficient alliance? In competitive environments, alliance efficiency is policed by external market competitors. Airbus's benchmark is Boeing, not Airbus partners taken separately.

Different Goals, Different Measures

Beyond the problem of finding an appropriate benchmark, a second complication of performance measurement is the overall framing of the assessment. Some alliances should be measured as *options*. R&D alliances, for instance, may be assessed in terms of the range of available options they present to their partners.

Not all options are exercised, nor do all alliances lead to active business development efforts. Merck in particular maintains a network of relationships in its effort to find a preventive or curative treatment for AIDS. Given the scientific and technological uncertainties involved, these alliances should, for now, be measured as options. The value of the learning that takes place in alliances should be assessed in terms of strategic options as well. Ford, through its alliance with Toyo Kogyo, may have become a stronger, more competitive company than it could have been on its own.

Conversely, accepting permanent cospecialization in a complementation alliance reduces the options available to each partner separately. The cost of the loss of these options has to be factored into the assessment. Over the longer term, these costs can be substantial. Aérospatiale, for example, may have gained through its membership in Airbus, but it may have lost the capability of building a major aircraft on its own. There are opportunity costs associated with this lost capability.

The Danger of Measuring the Wrong Things

In all the alliances we have observed, it is all too easy for the management of one or more of the partners to lose sight of the value creation logic of the alliance and to fall back on purely financial measures of performance. This practice is both misleading and dangerous. Measuring NUMMI's success on the basis of its financial performance only might have cost GM the opportunity to learn from it by encouraging GM's management to cut the numbers and the quality of the managers and technical specialists it rotated through the joint venture.

Focusing exclusively on the financial performance of competitive coalitions is also misleading and dangerous. If Boeing were to successfully woo an Airbus partner to its own camp, the weakening of Airbus might be the greater benefit to Boeing, not the financial value actually created through collaboration with the new partner. Measuring only the latter benefit would miss the point. Indeed, a company such as Boeing might see its interest in giving a very sweet deal to an Airbus partner just to break the rival coalition.

The Balanced Scorecard

Ultimately, financial performance is still a yardstick in all alliances. Yet how, and over what scope of activities and time frame, financial benefits are to be generated varies greatly according to the alliance's value creation logic. Managers therefore need to develop a balanced and comprehensive scorecard to assess the performance of a strategic alliance, one that is consistent with the value creation logic that it pursues. Understanding that robust alliances create benefits according to all three logics is key. A comprehensive scorecard reduces the danger of missing value creation opportunities by focusing too narrowly on a few benefits and ignoring, or forgetting, others.

Keeping Time

The same value creation logic that sets the agenda for an alliance also influences its time horizon and the "critical moments" at which managerial action is required. For example, the critical moments for alliances bent on setting industry standards are at their inception. Once the partners have agreed on a standard, or it has won the battle for the marketplace, these alliances are usually stable. They require active managerial intervention only insofar as other companies may try to woo away partners and as changes in technology lead to new alliances. We observed this in the Sony-DVDs case. New standards are usually called for only under one or the other of the following conditions: (1) the appearance of a strong technological discontinuity or (2) open revolt by junior coalition members who feel "locked in" and economically exploited by the coalition leader and its standard. Thus, managers must monitor both external and internal destabilizing factors. Obviously, the lead partner in a standards coalition must be sensitive to the balance between maximizing its own gains and provoking partners to defect.

When the lead partner does not abuse its position, the incentive for alliance continuity remains strong for all partners. Sony's difficulty in challenging the VHS standard with its 8mm format is explainable, in part, by the behavior of JVC and Matsushita in their alliance. Most VCR makers remained loyal to VHS, partly because JVC and Matsushita did not use their control of the standard's proprietary elements to demand excessive licensing fees. Their introduction of VHS-C (for "compact") and of Super VHS also helped, until more recently, to blunt some of Sony's advantages for hand-held video cameras. It is only in the mid-1990s that the new standard made serious inroads.

The stability of the co-option alliance is a function of the benefits the various parties find in it. Each partner must be given a unique and well-defined role, and a role it can gladly accept.

Alliances that combine cospecialized ownership-specific assets likewise tend to be relatively stable and long lasting (as are many traditional joint ventures), particularly since their value usually accrues over time as a function of the performance of the joint work. Similarly, new businesses based on cospecialized assets tend to be stable, if only because their cospecialization makes the partners increasingly reluctant to dissolve the alliance. Airbus is a prime example; it was reinforced by a lack of potential substitutes to the current partners, strengthening perceptions of mutual uniqueness between the Airbus partners.

Only a substantial evolution of technologies and markets—one that challenges the value creation potential of the alliance, or the complementarity and cospecialization of the partners' respective assets—will put an early end to such alliances. The case of Oris and Syncor provides an example.

In 1985, Oris, a French supplier of immuno-diagnostic kits employing radioactive materials, entered an alliance with Syncor, a U.S. network of radiopharmacies. Syncor supplied hospitals and diagnostic centers with radiation-based diagnostic technologies, utilizing fleets of specially equipped vans driven by registered radiopharmacists for the delivery of radioactive materials and collection of wastes. Under the terms of their agreement, Syncor was to distribute Oris products in the United States. Oris bought a 15 percent participation in Syncor to facilitate its partner's development and foster mutual interest in Syncor's performance.

Within a few years, however, new nonradioactive technologies became more important for medical diagnostic tests, even as Syncor extended its network of radiopharmacies. With the shift to nonradioactive technologies, the benefits of cospecialization between the two companies disappeared: Oris could use ordinary drug distributors or even courier companies to distribute its products, while Syncor had to look for other opportunities to leverage its distribution investment and the skills of its pharmacists. Home care services provided an opportunity for Syncor, but one in which Oris had no interest. The alliance was dissolved in 1989.

In very turbulent, rapidly changing environments, the value of firm-specific assets to a cospecialization alliance is likely to be transient. Alliances in these environments are useful as hedging options, even though they may never be exercised—longevity is not a measure of success.

Learning alliances also have a unique time frame. Their duration is typically conditioned by the learning cycles on which they are based. When a learning-motivated firm feels that it has learned all that's worth learning from its partner—or all that the partner will reveal—the basis for the alliance evaporates. If and when GM believes that it has learned all that NUMMI can teach it, or all that Toyota is willing to impart, the value of NUMMI to GM may decline. Similarly, once Toyota has mastered U.S. labor relations and demonstrated that a unionized American workforce can be productive and disciplined, Toyota may also lose interest in the venture.

To summarize, partners must keep tabs on the benefits that remain to be gained as their alliances proceed through their life cycles. As those benefits are exhausted, partners are likely to opt out.

A sense of time is critical to planners and managers. Early expectations about the life of the alliance are useful for planning milestones and possible renegotiation points. It is also important to keep a long-term perspective, to avoid being swayed by the many crises and conflicts that are likely to punctuate the evolution of the alliance. The need for a long-term perspective notwithstanding, alliance longevity alone is not an indicator of success. Longevity is, among other factors, a function of the value creation logic that justifies the alliance.

Anticipating Points of Tension

When we look at the conflicts and tensions that afflict alliances, we notice that they accumulate around the key areas of value creation and capture. Managers who understand the different logics of value creation, then, are better prepared to predict where conflicts are likely to erupt and be most intense.

In co-option alliances, conflicts typically develop around the sharing of economic rent between the nodal firm (typically the innovator on whose technology the coalition's standard is based, or the initiator of an industry restructuring attempt) and the other coalition members. The lesser partners chaff at the risk of becoming hostages to the nodal firm's strategy. The turmoil within the UNIX alliance is a representative case. Here many different approaches were advanced to guarantee that AT&T would not exercise excessive influence over

UNIX users. The contrast between Intel's and Sun's strategies concerning proprietary microprocessor technology—control in one case, openness in the other—exemplifies how different focal firms in the same industry have handled these tensions. As a newcomer, Sun was originally willing to share benefits more widely to set a new standard than was Intel, a more established company. A similar example is found in the cases of Matsushita (in VCRs) and of Toshiba–Time Warner (in DVDs); unlike Sony, these companies adopted an inclusive approach to dealing with proprietary standards.

In cospecialization alliances, the value of partner contributions and the benefits each draws are a major source of tension at the inception of the alliance. Here, asymmetry of interests or expectations can be a problem. For instance, if Partner A looks to the alliance itself as a major source of benefits, while Partner B looks *outside* the alliance for its benefits, the potential for conflict is high. Asymmetric cospecialization, leading to unequal mutual dependence, is an obvious next order source of tensions. If one partner becomes strategically dependent on the other, the other will be tempted to take advantage of the situation to tilt the alliance in its favor.

In learning alliances, the most contentious issue is usually one of symmetry and balance in learning, assuming that both partners are interested in learning. Tensions may also arise from the difficulty of measuring learning when the following kinds of questions arise: How much will one partner make available to the other(s) to learn? How much is a partner actually learning? How much is a partner benefiting from its learning? Obviously, one partner will measure its contribution to the other based on what it has put on the table, while the other partner will attempt to measure how much of that contribution it has actually absorbed, digested, and applied. It is not unusual for each side to arrive at a different assessment of the situation. In other words, if GM did not benefit much from what Toyota made available, Toyota would see this as GM's problem, while GM might not see it that way.

Summary

We have argued that alliances create value in many different ways, but that the options can be clustered within:

1. the logic of strategic co-option, which makes a situation more attractive to alliance members and increases their competitive capabilities
2. the logic of cospecialization, which creates opportunities through the complementation of cospecialized skills and other firm-specific, nontradable assets
3. the logic of learning and internalization, which provides opportunities for learning and appropriating new competencies

Understanding these mechanisms for creating value is important in that they strongly influence key features of the alliance: the assessment of contributions; the scopes of the alliance; the priorities, tasks, and capabilities on which effort is to be focused; the criteria for measuring the alliance's success; and the expectations that a partner can harbor about the alliance's time horizon and prospects for stability. The key points of our argument on each of these themes as they relate to co-option, cospecialization, and learning are summarized in Table 3-1.

Our argument has so far concentrated on what kind of "game" is played in an alliance. It is equally important, however, to know how to assemble the alliance team, and then how to lead and coach it—the subjects of subsequent chapters.

TABLE 3-1 *Value Creation Logics and Alliance Management*

	CO-OPTION	COSPECIALIZATION	LEARNING/INTERNALIZATION
ASSESSING CONTRIBUTIONS	• Medium competitive strength for alliances with competitors (usually at same stage in the value chain) • Uniqueness and differentiating power of contribution for alliances with complementers (usually at different stages in the value chain)	• Uniqueness of contribution rooted in: nontradability nonsubstitutability nonimitatability	• Recent skill leadership • Pace of skill improvement • Access to copractice of key skills
AGREEING ON ALLIANCE SCOPE	• Consideration of overall strategic scope of each partner	• Focus on economic scope of each partner	• Focus on operational scope as learning ground
UNDERSTANDING JOINT TASK DEMANDS	• Strategic foresight—imagining winning coalitions and migration paths • Negotiating successfully for mutual gains • Maintaining and leading the coalition over time	• Effectively melding the skills of the partners • Jointly adjusting to the evolution of the opportunity to maintain a dynamic fit	• Ability to copractice: "apprentice to master" relationship • Codiscovery and development of new skills
DEFINING AND MEASURING PROGRESS	• Improved margins, increased market share for coalition members	• Revenue and profit stream or/and cost savings versus what is available to each partner separately	• New or enhanced skills • Leveraging opportunities of using the skills

TABLE 3-1 *(continued)*

	CO-OPTION	COSPECIALIZATION	LEARNING/INTERNALIZATION
KEEPING TIME	• Life cycle of the industry structure (e.g., of the standards or production processes, barriers to entry, or markets underlying an industry structure), unless alliance leaders use their position against their partners and encourage defection from the alliance	• Life cycle of the product/industry/technologies, provided cospecialization and complementation retain their value over time—or short-lived options in hedging strategies	• Learning cycle of the "apprentice partner(s)" with regard to the skills contributed by other partners, and renewal rate of the skills contributed to the alliance by each partner
ANTICIPATING POINTS OF TENSION	• Balance of costs and benefits among members of the coalition: rents of the coalition's focal or leading firm versus benefits to the other members of the coalition	• Relative valuation of contributions; sharing of the value created in the alliance, in particular when the alliance is partly embedded in the partners' own operations	• Symmetry and balance in learning • Potential versus actual learning • Competence replenishment versus competence transfer

4

❖

SECURING STRATEGIC
COMPATIBILITY

EVERY ALLIANCE PARTNER makes self-interested commitments in pursuit of its own objectives. This fact makes many of the alliances we have researched hydra-headed: while different partners agree on the logic of value creation, they operate with incompatible goals and yardsticks, making their priorities diverge over time. Sustained agreement on how to run the alliance and share the benefits becomes impossible.

Rivalry between partners may be the greatest deterrent to alignment of strategic interests. It aggravates strategic incompatibility, undermining the basis for cooperation and fueling distrust, especially when hidden agendas become visible. This problem is most acute in alliances involving companies in the same industry. These partners are rivals in both the alliance and the marketplace.

How the problems of rivalry and strategic incompatibility can be overcome are the central issues of this chapter. Partners may agree on how they will create value, but this is insufficient for success. They must answer other questions:

- How compatible are we?
- How will we agree on value creation priorities?
- How will each of us contribute to the success of the alliance?
- How can we overcome our natural rivalries?

These are critical questions that each partner must answer.

Value creation potential is a necessary but insufficient condition for entering an alliance. Strategic compatibility between the partners' interests is a second, often more demanding, condition. The assessment of strategic compatibility is complicated by the difficulty partners have in grasping each other's strategic intentions for an alliance. Organizational and cultural differences between partners can significantly complicate a reading of their strategic intentions and mask divergence. Partners who find it difficult to communicate and to understand each other are likely to misunderstand each other's strategic logic. Finally, partners who are otherwise like-minded may disagree on the best vehicle for reaching their objectives: where one sees an alliance, the other may see an acquisition, or a mere contract. We will focus on those organizational, cognitive, and cultural differences in Chapter 6, concentrating here on the first test of compatibility: the strategic interests of the partners.

We have found a number of useful predictors of strategic compatibility. First, among firms in the same industry, the relative competitive positions of the partners greatly influence both the strategic interest and the value creation logics that they individually pursue—that is, where one stands depends on where one sits! Although it is not always possible to clearly assess the competitive positions or strategic ambitions of potential partners, it is possible to understand *why* variously positioned firms in an industry typically cooperate, or do not, with each other. Second, a partnership's stability—or "robustness"—can often be determined by assessing the interaction between the partners' strategic positions and the value creation profile of the alliance itself. Finally, it is possible to anticipate how the relative positions of the partners may change over time and thus anticipate the evolution of the dynamics of their relationship. Let's consider each of these in turn.

Competitive Position

The relative competitive position of a company in an industry is a good predictor of the benefits, or value creation goals, that the company will seek in an alliance. There are many ways to determine industry position. Some involve quantitative measures such as relative return on assets and relative market position. Others involve more of a gestalt; these are broader in scope but lack precise measures. For example, when asked to name the leading firms in their industries, knowledgeable managers and other experts often arrive at the same selection even though they use slightly different criteria for industry "leadership." We have not found a single, simple index of industry position that is really useful for the analysis of partnerships. However, we use a method of categorizing that, while imprecise, yields useful insights for evaluating companies as potential partners. Our categories are:

1. *Leaders.* These companies have established and sustained strong (usually number one) positions in a business, a technology, or a market. Examples include Boeing in civilian aircraft, IBM in mainframe computers, Intel in microprocessors, Nintendo in video games, and Bristol Myers in anticancer drugs. It is often necessary, however, to define leadership more narrowly. Take the German aerospace company DASA as an example. Broadly speaking, one would not call DASA a leader in its industry. In terms of aerospace system integration in Germany, however, it exercises near-monopoly power, making it an "unavoidable" partner for any firm that wants to access the German military aerospace market. In this narrow sense, DASA is a market leader.[1]

2. *Followers.* Followers belong to the second tier of companies; they are major players in their industries but not leaders. Some followers may never improve their position but nevertheless remain strong "number two" (or three) challengers: for example, Motorola in relation to Intel in microprocessors. The relative position of other followers, however, changes over time, and we have found it useful to distinguish between two types of such companies: followers that succeed in improving their positions

to the point of being potent challengers to the leaders, and followers that must struggle simply to maintain their industry positions. Airbus vis-à-vis Boeing, and Fujitsu vis-à-vis IBM represent, over the past two decades, the group of improving challengers. Prior to its merger with Boeing, McDonnell Douglas represented the category of lagging followers. Most of IBM's U.S. mainframe competitors and Intel's Japanese microprocessor competitors now fall into this category of lagging firms.

3. *Newcomers* and *latecomers*. These firms are relatively new entrants to a business or to a market or technology domain. In the 1970s, Honda was a newcomer in the Western auto industry. Typically, the ambitions of newcomers vastly exceed their existing resources and capabilities. They see the industry as a major development opportunity.

As they look to alliances, leaders, followers, and newcomers usually see different benefits. We use a simple map to explore these different perceptions of alliance benefits. As depicted in Figure 4-1, the two dimensions of our map are (1) relative industry position and (2) the alliance's value creation profile.

FIGURE 4-1 *Relative Industry Position versus Alliance Value Creation Profile*

Primary Value Creation Logics

	Co-option	Complementation	Internalization
Leader			
Challenger			
Follower			
Laggard			
Newcomer			

Partners' Relative Competitive Positions

We now turn to analyzing how to position alliances on this map, starting with leader-driven alliances.

Leader-driven alliances. One of the most surprising aspects of alliances is the frequency with which leaders in the same industry, who would seem to be the least likely collaborators, enter into alliances. Economies of scale and scope are often the cause. Boeing, for example, engages in collaborative agreements with U.S. and international partners, the JADC among others, as a way of both sharing the costs and risks of individual aircraft programs and making the production of a full range of airliners more affordable. Not surprisingly, Boeing has collaborated most intensively when it has been the most financially strapped.[2]

This was the case in the 1980s as Boeing launched a sequence of new development programs to counter growing competition from Airbus. Its cash flows from existing programs were insufficient to fully fund new ones. It looked to its partners to fill the gap. The B767, for example, was developed in collaboration with a variety of partners, whereas earlier and later models involved less work sharing and codevelopment between Boeing and its partners. In other words, Boeing practices a form of asymmetric cospecialization: others depend on Boeing for critical competencies and relational assets (with airlines in particular), but Boeing depends on them only for undifferentiated contributions such as structural manufacturing or fungible inputs such as money. In that sense, Boeing has demonstrated that it is possible to collaborate successfully without relinquishing its industry "sovereignty."

Leaders are often pushed into extensive cooperation by coalitions built by challengers. Boeing probably cooperates more and more readily because it has Airbus on its heels. By building a web of relationships with its partners, Boeing preempts and co-opts companies that might otherwise ally themselves with Airbus or other rivals; it also preempts their ambitions to develop into potential rivals. This is evident in Boeing's approach to its Japanese partners; some agreements with these partners explicitly forbid their taking part in other coalitions.

To protect its leadership of the microprocessor business, Intel may find it necessary to cooperate more in the future, and on more equal terms. Intel's 1994 agreement with Hewlett-Packard on the

RISC microprocessor may be a first step in that direction. Similarly, Pratt & Whitney, historically the leader in the U.S. aircraft engine industry, may have recently grown more accommodating to MTU (the aircraft engine subsidiary of Daimler-Benz) and to other partners because of the success of the GE–SNECMA coalition. Toshiba cooperates eagerly with IBM to develop flat screens partly because of the challenge from Sharp. In these alliances, the leader's purpose is usually co-option, with strategic defense in mind.

For smaller firms, if a choice between coalitions exists, the important issue is which leader-driven coalition to join. The choice is largely determined by the benefits that coalition leaders are willing to extend to them and by the likely success of the coalition. These dual considerations sometimes create difficult trade-offs for smaller partners. Benefits have to be sufficient for the smaller partners to relinquish autonomy and to commit to the alliance.[3] Bigger, but weaker partners—laggards—may more easily commit to sharing benefits than will industry leaders, but they may have less to offer, as their coalitions are less likely to succeed.

Benefits to the smaller members may take various forms: sharing in the economies of scale and scope and in the profits these create, sharing market power with a leader, gaining access to leading-edge technology, and taking shelter from the direct winds of competition.

In leader-driven alliances, it is quite clear which party is in control: Boeing's partners, for example, are seldom more than glorified risk-sharing subcontractors. The same was true of Pratt & Whitney's "partners" in jet engines. As long as it was the industry leader, Pratt & Whitney saw no need for equal, or quasi-equal partners. Other companies needed Pratt & Whitney to be in the game, albeit marginally, but Pratt hardly needed them, except to share the costs of new product development. Cospecialization was very asymmetrical and in Pratt's favor. Indeed, it is only with very significant degrees of cospecialization that the relevance of leadership within such alliances decreases. When GE accepted cospecialization with SNECMA, it was the ambitious challenger to Pratt & Whitney; a stronger GE might have avoided binding cospecialization.

In completely cospecialized situations, where each partner brings unique contributions, the partners are de facto coleaders and equally codependent. When, on the other hand, cospecialization is limited or the contribution of one partner can be easily substituted for that of the other(s), this equality does not develop. This was clearly a difficulty in the relationship between GE and MTU that preceded MTU's agreement with Pratt & Whitney. GE did not need MTU, given its alliance with SNECMA; MTU, on the other hand, badly needed GE or an equivalent partner. After a few years, in 1990, MTU switched its allegiance to Pratt & Whitney. One of the reasons it did so (in addition to the fact that Pratt & Whitney was by then a more pliable partner) was that GE had already chosen SNECMA as its lead European partner, leaving little room for a second European company. In this type of situation, shared strategic ambitions and interests, focusing on a common enemy, are seen by managers as keys to overcoming rivalry between partners and maintaining a working alliance.

It takes more than shared strategic interests and ambitions, however, to make a successful alliance: zeal for strategically compatible partners can lead to alliances between similar firms when there is room for only one firm of each type in each alliance. Companies that share aligned strategic interests but lack genuine complementarity in strategic position or in potential for cospecialization rarely build robust alliances among themselves. What these alliances gain in strategic alignment, they lose in value creation. An alliance among similar companies is seldom successful. This may well have been the key factor in the failure of Unidata, a tentative alliance of European computer makers in the 1970s. It was certainly an important consideration in ICL's decision to join forces with Fujitsu rather than go for a "European solution." When skills are not differentiated, cospecialized, or world class, the alliance is doomed, particularly in technology-intensive industries where mastery of world-class skills is imperative. Put differently, compatibility does not usually stem from similarity in strategic position and/or other contributions but from complementarity, implying differentiated rather than similar positions and contributions.

Leaders often do, however, try to assemble differentiated coalitions in which each member plays a given role and contributes a cospecialized complementary skill. There is a trade-off in this between the likelihood of alliance success versus the risk of diminished bargaining power; this applies equally to leaders and to weaker companies. Leaders are sometimes persuaded to accept true cospecialization at the cost of diluting their own power in the alliance, an approach GE started to follow with SNECMA in the 1970s, and one Pratt & Whitney adopted with MTU in the 1990s.

In the absence of valuable cospecialization opportunities, leaders seldom collaborate with strong followers. They have too much to lose: today's allies might well be tomorrow's challengers. It is only when their leadership is fragile or poorly established that leaders seek the company of strong challengers, or when they fear these challengers might in turn be co-opted into an alliance by even stronger challengers. Instructed by the misadventures of Western companies whose Japanese partners used their alliances as stepping stones to global competitiveness, many managers are now cautious and systematically shun alliances with strong followers.

Leader firms are even less eager to cooperate with other leaders in the same industry, partly because of antitrust concerns and partly because of intense rivalry. In general, they cooperate only at the instigation of governments, and then in carefully structured and monitored schemes and in specialized "precompetitive" areas. For example, GM, Ford, and Chrysler agreed to cooperate in the development of electric car technologies at the behest of the U.S. government. This was not a strategic priority for any of the participating companies. In fact, without the compulsion of regulations, and in the absence of government funding, it is doubtful the Big Three would have conducted much research on electric vehicles. Government-instigated coalitions usually dissolve after the precompetitive work has been done. Some, such as SEMATECH, a research cooperative that develops semiconductor manufacturing equipment, endure because the partners have no shared commercial interests but do share interests in new core technologies, such as "submicron" manufacturing processes.[4]

Government-sponsored cooperations may also be good opportunities to practice the art of partnering. For example, through their involvement in a series of government-initiated collaborative R&D programs, Japanese electronics companies became very skillful at cooperating with strong rivals, while at the same time protecting their own proprietary interests. This experience made them potentially dangerous partners for less alliance-savvy Western companies.

Another pressure that brings leading firms together is the presence of strong network externalities. Particularly in strategically important areas, leaders recognize the risk of being excluded from the winning coalition. Visa International, the credit card coordination group, is an example of such a collaboration between banks; the common payment system in Europe is another. IBM's recent alliance with Gemplus, the fledgling French maker of smart cards, is clearly driven by their desire to take advantage of network externalities.

Excepting the motivations just described, alliances between leaders in the same industry are rare, and those which do occur are not always what they seem. The NUMMI alliance between Toyota and GM, for example, would appear to have been a compact between two industry leaders. In fact, when NUMMI was formed, Toyota was the clear leader in small car design and manufacturing, and GM was a laggard.

Obviously, there is always the possibility of tacit or secret collaboration, or even collusion, among leader firms to diminish or eliminate industry rivalry. Possible instances of collusion have been periodically investigated by the courts in both the United States and Europe, and some have been subjected to sanctions. In some instances, as in the European synthetic fibers and steel industries, collaboration between industry leaders is sanctioned by government to solve problems of overcapacity and "destructive" competition.

While collaboration between leaders of the *same* industry is rare, collaboration between cross-industry leaders, or leaders in very different segments, is common. These alliances are often of a kind in which each partner supplies the others with important technologies or products. This was the case in Siecor, Corning's joint venture with Siemens in optical fibers. In such interindustry alliances, leaders seek leaders as partners, as they can benefit from one another's respective strengths.[5] In the absence of direct competition, and without strong interpartner rivalry in end-product markets, alliances among leaders make obvious sense.

Follower-driven alliances. Alliances among followers in the same industry are usually based on an even simpler logic than those involving leaders. Most are driven by complementation and cospecialization: separately the followers would be relegated to laggard positions, together they can turn into challengers. This point was made painfully clear to the European aerospace industry in the 1960s, when the forerunners of both the British Aerospace and Aérospatiale consolidations attempted separately, and unsuccessfully, to compete against McDonnell Douglas, Lockheed, and Boeing. The French developed the "Caravelle" and the British developed an entire range of airliners, but very few of these were produced in economical volumes.

Most alliances of follower firms are initially driven by a broad desire to maximize partner specialization and benefit from the resulting scale economies. Like Airbus, most evolve toward greater cospecialization to obtain economies of scale and, through this, to achieve industry competitiveness. Other alliances between followers are prompted in part by the presence of some corporate "super-power" and the concerns of both follower firms and customers about the power imbalance it creates. Boeing was such a super-power. In Airbus, British Aerospace, DASA, and Aérospatiale built a credible challenger to Boeing. They were supported in this by cus-tomers—the airline companies—who saw their own interests threat-ened by Boeing's market power. The eventual strength of Airbus made it possible for the airline companies to pit the two suppliers against each other, as United Airlines did in 1992.

Despite their simple and robust logic, cospecialization alliances among followers do not always work. When followers share the same weaknesses and have few differentiated strengths, their problems are not solved by forming alliances. Two drunks seldom make a stable person! This is why national consolidation alliances such as Rover, which brought together many British car companies, or DASA, which federated the aerospace industry in Germany, have seldom been any-thing but the preamble to transnational alliances with more distant but also more complementary partners. Moreover, an alliance does not usually turn two or more laggards into market powers.

When alliances of followers do succeed, the reason can usually be traced to a long-term view, good timing, and lack of competitive reaction from leader firms. Airbus's initial offering, the A300 wide-body twin jet, succeeded to a great extent because none of its U.S. competitors had a comparable offering, and none had the resources to develop one in the short run. Similarly, GE–SNECMA succeeded in part because Pratt & Whitney stuck for too long to derivative ver-sions of an earlier-generation engine and was not in a position to quickly match the performance of the alliance's products. Airbus and GE–SNECMA, however, are more the exception than the rule.

The more successful alliances have also predictably widened the range of benefits they bring to their partners over time. For instance, the GE–SNECMA alliance transformed itself into a competitive coalition as the two partners cooperated across their whole range of civilian engines. Shared learning became more important as they complemented their alliance with manufacturing joint ventures for composite materials and advanced metallurgy.

Without a willingness to invest for the long haul, and without the benefit of passive competitors, success in follower-driven alliances is unlikely. An example is provided by GEC-Plessey, the combination of these companies' telecom equipment activities. The alliance started in the 1970s with a joint program to develop "System X," the British digital switching system. This led, in the 1980s, to a joint venture. But both companies suffered from the same capability deficits, found it difficult to overcome decades of rivalry, and failed to commit sufficient resources to the business. Moreover, their competitors did not sit idly by but left the alliance little room for development. Other difficulties surfaced, as the new partners had very different performance expectations. Eventually, GEC joined forces with Siemens. Again, *weak players with similar rather than complementary positions and skills do not build a successful alliance.* Airbus's success, conversely, stems largely from how quickly it pushed the partners into cospecialization, making them less and less similar and increasingly complementary and leading them to reap the benefits of cospecialization.

Alliances among followers are also unstable when the partners are asymmetrical in their intentions. Laggards may bring an installed base, market access, and technical resources but may not be in a position to share future development efforts equally with more aggressive followers intent on capturing industry leadership. This seems to have been the case of Honeywell and Bull in the computer business. Initially, in the 1970s and early 1980s, Bull was aggressively expanding and assuming alliance leadership while Honeywell viewed the alliance as a way out of the business. A decade later, faced with a fast-changing industry, loss of government funding, and its own competitive weakness, Bull found itself in an untenable position. Bull may now be playing with NEC and other partners the same exit game that Honeywell played with it a decade earlier.

In sum, followers tend to collaborate with other followers across the range of value creation logics: building coalitions to challenge leaders, combining cospecialized resources, and learning from one another. Ambitious followers seldom collaborate with leaders: followers fear their ambitions will be thwarted by the leaders, and the leaders feel they have too much to lose, making agreement difficult. Alliances among followers can work, but only when the partner firms see them as opportunities to make significant investments in the businesses in which they are allies in order to challenge and displace existing leaders. Follower-driven alliances tend to work best when the main benefits stem from cospecialization. Conversely, when the leader's positions are a function of highly proprietary technologies, and when technical standards yield strong network economies, alliances among followers are unlikely to succeed. An alliance against Boeing or Pratt & Whitney is more likely to succeed, competitively, than an alliance against Intel and Microsoft.

Newcomer-driven alliances. Alliances among newcomers usually follow a logic similar to follower alliances. Newcomers cannot stand alone, but together they can become credible challengers, if not future leaders, provided they are strongly complementary and willing to invest.

Newcomer alliances are often the most stable. The partners typically share a common strategic ambition; they either contribute already complementary and cospecialized assets (GE–SNECMA) or are driven by competitive pressures toward greater efficiency and cospecialization (as in Airbus). Newcomers are also likely to bring the greatest motivation for value creation. For them the alliance is likely to represent a major development opportunity and a way to accelerate their race for the future. While the motivation of followers in an alliance is often suspect—their top management may be tempted to use the alliance as an exit strategy at the first difficulty—no such ambivalence is found in newcomers. In this context, newcomers may use alliances with relatively vulnerable laggards as a way to gain quick access to the laggard's skills and markets.[6]

Typically the laggard is not falling behind in all areas and continues to have some skills and strategic assets (such as brands, channels, and customer relationships) that can be exploited by the newcomer. Yet because the laggard is on a broad downward trajectory it is unlikely to thwart the ambitions of the newcomer. This was probably part of Honda's strategy in entering into its European alliance with Rover in the late 1970s.

Rover gave Honda a shortcut to the European market and to the development of the large, fast sedans suited to that market. Honda had not yet developed the expertise needed for the engineering of fast sedans with European road-holding characteristics, and Rover brought just such expertise. Yet Rover's small size and poor manu-facturing skills made it critically dependent on Honda for its sur-vival, at least initially. Over time, Rover's learning reduced such dependence, although Rover continued to suffer scale and scope deficits relative to Honda; for this reason many Rover models were variants of Honda's products. Given the enduring dependence of Rover on Honda, one could have expected Honda to ultimately absorb or drop Rover, at least until BMW came along. BMW's motives in acquiring Rover were manifold, but denying Honda a sec-ond brand in the European market probably featured in the thinking of BMW's management.

This suggests that not all forms of strategic complementarity bring stable alliances. There is some objective complementarity between the waning ambitions and capabilities of the laggard and the growing ones of the newcomer, but the very nature of such complementarity makes for an unstable alliance.

Collaboration between newcomers and leader firms creates a dif-ferent dynamic. Newcomers see many advantages but worry that their own development will be thwarted, if not killed, by the larger partner. Indeed, the risks of this are real and have led some innova-tors to exercise extreme caution in their alliance strategies—and to miss out on opportunities. For example, Raynet, a subsidiary of the Raychem Corporation, created an important innovation in local tele-phone switching technologies, one that threatened to make the tech-nologies of the major telecom equipment suppliers obsolete. This put Raynet in a quandary. Should it go it alone or seek a major ally to help develop and market its innovation? Potential customers pushed it to enter partnerships with established equipment suppliers, such as Siemens or Alcatel in Germany, but Raynet's management did not trust the motives of its prospective partners. This reticence certainly contributed to Raynet's slow start in marketing its innovation.

For its part, an industry leader may wish to enter a series of alliances, if only to "hedge" its uncertainties. This leader knows that it can either thwart or back a technology as the layers of technologi-cal uncertainty are peeled back and possible paths of development become clearer. This is not a favorable situation for the newcomer firm, which explains why newcomers seldom cooperate with lead-ers, except when the newcomer accepts a position of permanent or long-term dependence, as the Japanese aerospace companies now appear to do vis-à-vis Boeing.

Newcomers may occasionally collaborate with leaders—and possibly score a role reversal over their larger partners—if they find a powerful home government to support them. The French company Framatome did this in the 1970s when it allied with Westinghouse in producing pressurized water nuclear reactors. In that case, the French government protected Framatome, mandated cooperation, provided a large domestic market (via the French national utility Electricité de France's massive nuclear reactor investment program), and subsidized Framatome's learning (via the national nuclear energy research program). Framatome's learning outpaced Westinghouse's to the point that the French could free themselves from their dependence on Westinghouse's technologies, become the leader, and exit the alliance.

Westinghouse is not the only established competitor to have been upstaged by an ambitious newcomer partner, particularly when the established partner has become a laggard. In these situations, the newcomer may appear as both a "white knight" and a threat. Today, Xerox executives acknowledge that their company was saved in the 1970s by its joint venture with Fuji. Xerox was unable to face Japanese competition on its own and became dependent for key competencies and products on Fuji-Xerox and, indirectly, on Fuji. The fact that Fuji was not a competitor made this situation palatable to Xerox.[7] This is perhaps an extreme case, as few companies face such strong and abrupt competitive threats as did Xerox when its patents expired, and few fall from leader to laggard in so few years. More usually, newcomers attach themselves to a leader, as the Japanese aerospace companies did with Boeing, or target a lagging company as a willing or unsuspecting Trojan horse (if they consider absorbing or dropping the partner as a possible outcome).

While leading firms may offer them some alliance benefits, newcomers may find more suitable partners in the ranks of aspiring leaders. Aspiring leaders need the newcomers to help break into the front ranks of their industries. For instance, GEC-Alsthom aspired to enter a non-European market for its high-speed trains. Korea provided that opportunity. To achieve this, GEC-Alsthom was willing to engage in far-reaching technology transfer with a Korean collaborator, even though it seemed almost certain that the Korean collaborator would become a competitor.[8]

Partners' Strategic Positions and the Value Creation Profile of the Alliance

The interaction between relative company position and value creation logics is captured in the map introduced in Figure 4-1. The relative status and positions of competitors in an industry are a good predictor of what kind of alliances they will seek and how robust they will be. It can also be helpful to anticipate the kind of tensions that may arise between partners. Figure 4-2 revisits that map and sketches the more robust alliance patterns we have observed; Figure 4-3 does the same for the more problematic ones.

The Usefulness of Mapping

Let's just suggest the usefulness of such mapping by interpreting briefly the less than fully successful alliances positioned on Figure 4-3. Value creation, value capture, or both were issues in each. As we've seen, alliances between unstable leaders and ambitious followers are fraught with dangers for the leader. In the alliance positioned at the top left position in the figure, Framatome learned all it could from

FIGURE 4-2 *Robust Alliance Patterns*

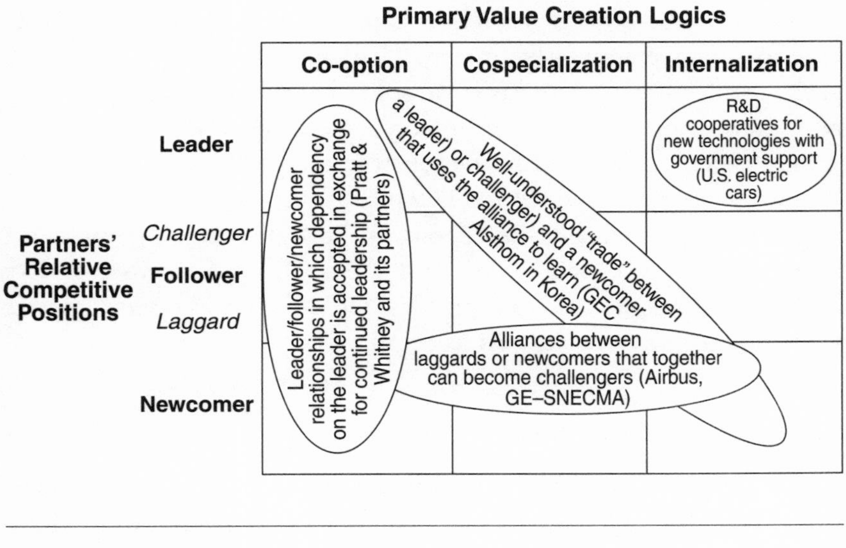

FIGURE 4-3 *Problematic Alliance Patterns*

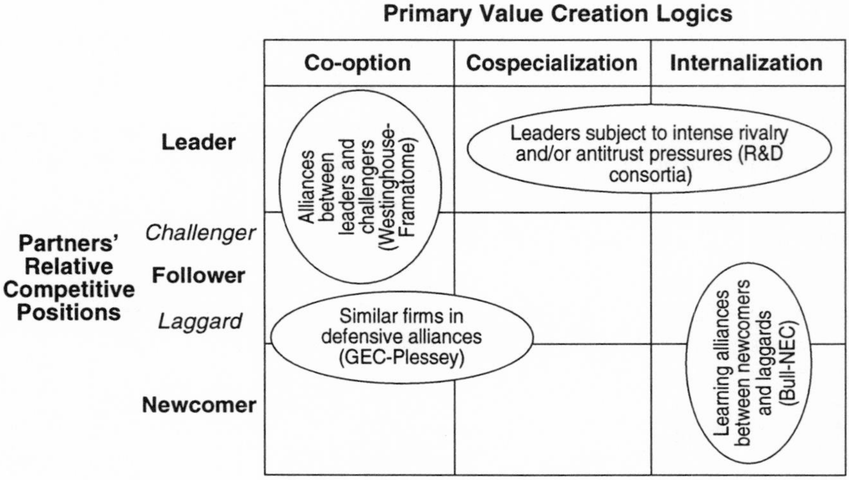

Primary Value Creation Logics

		Co-option	Cospecialization	Internalization
	Leader	Alliances between leaders and challengers (Westinghouse-Framatome)	Leaders subject to intense rivalry and/or antitrust pressures (R&D consortia)	
Partners' Relative Competitive Positions	*Challenger*			
	Follower			Learning alliances between newcomers and laggards (Bull-NEC)
	Laggard	Similar firms in defensive alliances (GEC-Plessey)		
	Newcomer			

Westinghouse and then set loose. Where Westinghouse saw a co-option alliance, Framatome saw a skill internalization opportunity. Accepting cospecialization and the risk of interpartner learning makes for difficult alliances between leaders.

Even when blessed with government support—such as SEMA-TECH, the U.S. semiconductor manufacturing technology research cooperative—rivalry among leaders may extend to the alliance and jeopardize both value creation and capture. SEMATECH's partners came to an agreement only after they had agreed to focus their effort on the semiconductor's industry supplier base, something more neutral than sharing their own technologies with one another. Alliances among leaders, positioned in the top row on the Figure 4-3, are usually less successful than SEMATECH.

In the two other alliances depicted, Bull, over time, grew more dependent on NEC, and GEC and Plessey found themselves too similar in strengths and weaknesses for effective cospecialization. Both alliances were rather unsuccessful.

THE LIMITS OF MAPPING

The mapping of alliance configurations can be a useful tool as long as one is mindful of its limitations, which stem from four complicating factors:

1. Many successful alliances create value in multiple ways and thus do not fit neatly into any box; they are multibenefit alliances.

2. Partners may view their positions within the alliance differently and therefore have very different perceptions of its costs and benefits.

3. Positions may shift over time.

4. Positions in emerging industries may be so unclear that a clear mapping is impossible.

Multibenefit alliances. When mapping alliances, there is a natural temptation to assign each alliance to a "box." This is not always possible. In robust alliances, the partners' positions complement one another in varied, complex, and balanced ways. For example, one partner is a leader in some areas and a laggard in others, while the other partner has opposite and complementary positions. This complementarity was clear between, for example, ICL (industry application know-how) and Fujitsu (hardware), leading to more complex positioning. Balance in an alliance is usually achieved only when such complementarity exists, providing a basis for robust cospecialization, and/or for reciprocal and balanced learning where partners can learn from each other. Successful alliances cover a "space," as shown in Figure 4-2, not a box.

Differing positions. Each partner may have a different reading of its alliance and either assign the alliance to a different box or draw the alliance space differently. To illustrate, consider an alliance in which the partners seek different values and also see value in different aspects of the alliance. This would make assessing their compatibility more difficult. The case of Boeing and JADC makes the point.

In the 1980s, Boeing enlisted the support of the Japanese Aerospace Development Corporation (JADC), a consortium of Kawasaki, Mitsubishi, Fuji, and Nissan, to develop a new smaller jet, the 7J7, as a potential replacement for its 737. Boeing believed that Japanese support would be useful for a number of purposes: for financing development expenditures and leasing planes; for facilitating access to the Japanese market; for providing manufacturing and quality management expertise; and for ensuring that the Japanese industry would be part of a coalition built around Boeing rather than around Airbus. Boeing would not make its most advanced engineering and design technologies available to JADC personnel. JADC's management

FIGURE 4-4 *Different Perspectives on the Same Alliance*

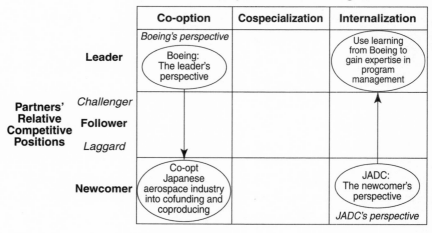

acknowledged Boeing's interests and the fact that Boeing intended to control technology transfers carefully. To Boeing, this was mostly a complementation alliance of a not very sophisticated nature, where cooperation brought market access, as sketched in Figure 4-4. Co-option and learning were secondary priorities.

JADC viewed the alliance differently. Its members saw the early phases of the new airliner program as a unique learning opportunity, given both Boeing's outstanding program management and "preengineering" skills. To them, the only other sources of such competencies, Airbus and McDonnell Douglas, appeared less advanced.

The Boeing–JADC partnership was discontinued before the different perspectives just described were fully understood by all partners, and before potential conflicts could erupt. In the meantime, JADC learned the "soft" program management skills it sought—a benefit that Boeing had not recognized, partly because it took program management capabilities for granted; it failed to see how valuable these might be to an inexperienced partner. In sum, the two partners positioned the alliance quite differently, as sketched in Figure 4-4.

In principle, position differences between partners should facilitate cooperation. Thus, if one partner is interested in economic gains, and the other in new competencies, agreement should be easy. One partner pays "tuition" to the other for the opportunity to learn. Indeed, the broader and wider the range of potential benefits discovered by each partner, the easier and more satisfactory the cooperation should be, as each partner will find in it a full range of benefits.

Does this mean that Boeing should have rejoiced? Perhaps not, particularly if interpartner rivalry was potentially high. A second assessment of this situation would argue that the partners' interests may be too weakly aligned. In the Boeing–JADC case one partner needed resources, the other needed help in learning, but no long-term mutual interest bound the two together, and they were likely to compete in the future. In this and similar circumstances, conflict can arise when the stronger firm believes that it is nurturing its own rival.

Boeing thus faced a complex set of considerations when it joined forces with JADC: the giant American firm could argue that there was much more to entering the civilian airliner business than anything JADC could learn from the 7J7 project. Working with the master of civilian aviation would no doubt strengthen the competencies of JADC companies, but not to the point of making them serious competitors. While Boeing understood its partners' technical learning agenda and closed off their access to its own hard technologies, it may have underestimated the value of learning program management skills to its partners.

Another risk, therefore, lies in assigning a single value creation logic to an alliance when the logic seen by its partners differs substantially or when a robust alliance creates value in multiple ways. GE and SNECMA, for instance, collaborated to improve their competitive positions against Pratt & Whitney and Rolls-Royce; to bring together complementary, nontradable, nonsubstitutable, firm-specific resources such as their privileged relationships with their home governments; and to learn capabilities and skills from each other. GE saw the alliance more from the co-option perspective, and SNECMA from the learning perspective, but both firms pursued all these logics. Most of the successful and resilient alliances we have observed have this multidimensional but precise fit between partners, creating value in multiple ways. The partners' roles complement each other. Each partner leads in some areas and lags in others.

Shifting positions. A third risk in analyzing how the competitive positions of partners influence their cooperation is to assume that their positions will be stable over time. This condition may not hold. The relative positions of the partners may change; as they do, they will challenge the stability of the alliance and create tension.

Shifts in the relative position of partners are most clear-cut in learning-based alliances whose partners learn at different rates. When Honda and Rover, for example, first entered into a collaborative agreement in 1978, each had a range of very cospecialized, ownership-specific resources. Rover was able to provide Honda with shared European manufacturing volume (an advantage in the event that local content requirements became an obstacle), access to a supplier base, and, as described earlier, design and engineering expertise for the large, fast sedans suited to European drivers and road conditions. Rover, for its part, expected to learn several key skills from Honda: new manufacturing processes, better ways to design new products, and faster development cycle time. Rover would also be allowed to use Honda-designed cars not marketed in Europe to plug holes in its product line and to access Honda's wide range of engines and other subsystems.

Over the first years of the alliance, Honda developed its competencies faster than Rover and successfully avoided dependence on Rover for European market access and learning. Once Honda had learned what it needed to know about design and engineering, the relationship became increasingly unbalanced. Honda had metamorphosed from newcomer to the car industry to powerful challenger. By the 1990s, its Accord model was the best-selling car in the U.S. market, and it remained so for several years.

Rover, on the other hand, continued as an automotive laggard. Despite quantum improvements in product quality and costs and substantial market share gains in Europe, it made no great strides in unit volume and developed no presence outside Europe. It continued to rely on Honda's major subsystems (for example, the Rover 800 Stirling engine) and car models (for example, the Rover 600 series). The net result was three unappealing choices: continuing to depend on Honda and losing strategic autonomy, tolerating inferior economic performance caused by low model volume, or seeking out another partner. Honda, of course, had fewer and fewer opportunities to learn from Rover. At the same time, the volume benefits it sought in the alliance had become less critical as its own worldwide system of production and supplier network grew.

As the Rover–Honda arrangement makes clear, the initial positions of the partners matters less than what happens over time, given differential rates of learning and different capabilities to accumulate competencies and build strong positions. Resources, capabilities, and ambitions matter more in anticipating alliance evolution than the initial positions of the partners. Thus, although starting positions do matter, an analysis exclusively drawn from them would be incomplete and potentially misleading.

Emerging industries. Clear industry leadership assumes an established industry. Leaders in such industries rarely collaborate with one another. When an industry is taking shape, however, potential leaders are more likely to collaborate with other potential leaders. As the shape of the industry becomes clear, though, collaboration is likely to break down. Collaboration is also imperiled as leadership within the alliance becomes more clear. In alliances aimed at creating opportunities, leadership within the alliance and within the new industry can thus become a bone of contention, as we saw in the Iridium case. The potential for conflict centering around issues of relative strength within the alliance versus the competitiveness of the alliance itself is magnified. Each partner must be strong enough to contribute its share toward establishing competitive leadership in the new industry, yet each would like to be stronger than its partners to secure alliance leadership and the lion's share of alliance benefits. Potential leaders cooperating closely with one another may also "take out" other potential competitors, both by discouraging competition and by co-opting these potential rivals.

The alliance between Dreamworks and Microsoft may be of the type just described. No one can predict where the movie and image entertainment industry will go, but combining the strongest "content" team (at least according to the track record of Dreamworks' three founders) with Microsoft's software product expertise is almost bound to make for a winning coalition. Whether Dreamworks, Microsoft, or some other partner will assume leadership within the alliance is less clear than the nature of the opportunity being pursued. But what can be safely predicted is that over time the interests of the partners will shift from value creation to value capture, and tensions will therefore shift from who contributes what to who gets what.

Likely Evolution of the Alliance

Despite thorough assessment of partner compatibility, alliances often unfold in unpredictable ways. Thus the process of evaluating and choosing partners must consider an alliance's potential evolution, not only the partners' initial strategic compatibility. A good starting point for that task is assessment of the strategic ambition of each partner. Ambitions are often more predictive of alliance evolution than are the starting positions of the partners, and the failure of one partner to comprehend the ambitions of the other often leads to conflict. In this, the alliance between JVC and Thomson is instructive.

Thomson was driven in its alliance with JVC by a desire to master mass-produced micromechanics, a technology that the French electronics group saw as a gateway to many new products. It had changed its strategic course to develop a deeper commitment to consumer electronics and had embarked on an expansion strategy with its takeover of Ferguson in the United Kingdom and of GE-RCA consumer electronics in North America and the Far East. Thomson was to manufacture VCR tape drums, a nonthreatening activity from JVC's perspective. Given JVC's misunderstanding of its partner's larger ambitions, Thomson's learning efforts were surprising; they appeared misguided and wasteful when viewed only within the context of the alliance rather than that of Thomson's broader aspirations. Thomson's desire to learn to manufacture the mechanical components of VCRs did not seem sensible to JVC, given its weak starting position. Indeed, Thomson's learning agenda made no sense unless one understood its larger ambition; once that ambition was understood, micromechanics competencies acquired through the alliance could be seen for what they were: a key enabler of Thomson's global strategy.

Compatibility between partners obviously shifts as their individual strategic priorities shift. Compatibility is also affected by what we see as evolutionary stages in the life cycle of an alliance. Alliances fulfill very different roles at various stages in the development of a market opportunity. Figure 4-5 depicts typical partnership objectives at various stages

FIGURE 4-5 *Typical Partnership Objectives along the Life Cycle of a Business*

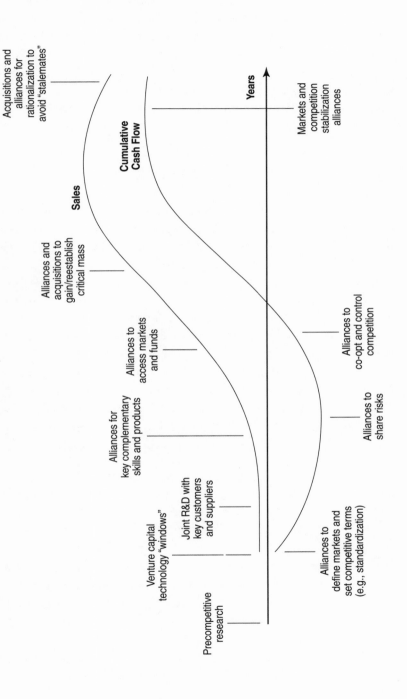

of the development and evolution of an opportunity. (Perhaps the race to the future or to the world requires different partners at different stages rather than a single team for the entire race.) Although not all situations follow the neat sequence hypothesized in the figure, the key implication of any sequence is that strategic compatibility will be periodically challenged by the very success of the alliance at pursuing its opportunity. In this sense, alliances can be victims of their own success.

Exogenous Factors

Finally, it is important to recognize that strategic compatibility can be challenged by macroeconomic, regulatory, technological, and competitive forces that originate outside the alliance, forces that cannot be controlled by the partners. For example, shifts in the relative value of the U.S. dollar and European currencies, and between these currencies and the yen, have threatened the stability of many transnational alliances as the relative costs and benefits to partners changed.

Technology changes, or mere technological maturity, may also affect the value creation potential of a partnership or a particular partner's need to remain in the alliance. Corning, for instance, sold its share in Videocolor, its joint venture with Thomson in TV bulbs, to its partner once the technology matured and margins contracted. Corning's needs for either joint learning or economic benefits from the alliance decreased, and the company began the search for more attractive opportunities.

Summary

In this chapter, we have argued that the relative competitive position of a company in its industry, or in a particular domain of competencies, is a good predictor of the types of benefits it is most likely to seek from an alliance and the kinds of partners it is most likely to join in an alliance.

We have reviewed a few of the commonly observed alliance configurations: leaders collaborating with newcomers to limit new competition and weaken other coalitions; followers or newcomers join-ing forces to challenge leaders; newcomers using laggards for market entry and learning or wrestling advantages from leaders in exchange for markets.

The strategic ambitions served by an alliance of a particular con-figuration are conditioned by the starting position of the partners in their industry. Even more important than starting positions, but harder to gauge, are the ambitions of the partners, the external forces that may affect the alliance value and/or the priorities of the partners toward it, and what they learn in the alliance and from each other. All of these factors may enhance or compromise strategic compati-bility between partners over time, creating a need to reassess strate-gic compatibility periodically. Such an assessment ought to address a few major points:

- the partner's relative position, present, past, and future
- the partner's strategic ambition, strategic scope, and specific goals for the alliance
- external forces (macroeconomy and geopolitical, technological, customer-driven, regulatory, and competitor driven) that shift value creation and strategic compatibility over time
- the contributions that the life cycle of the opportunity addressed by the alliance will require from the partner

Strategic compatibility between partners, then, must be reassessed periodically, as it is affected by several changes:

1. The strategic priorities of the partners shift independently of the alliance.
2. The alliance fulfills different needs at various stages in the opportunity life cycle as the most critical contributions shift over time.
3. Exogenous factors that partners cannot control induce change in the alliance relationship.

We have also pointed out the patterns associated with opportunities in emerging industries; here, potential leaders are likely to collabo-rate, but that collaboration is likely to break down as the industry takes shape, or as one of the partners assumes industry leadership .

In sum, all potential sources of value creation should be considered from the standpoint of all partners. The more ways in which an alliance creates value, in total and for each partner, the more robust it is likely to be. The more the alliance satisfies the value creation needs of the various partners, the more robust it is also likely to be, provided that the value creation logics of the partners are mutually acceptable and that their strategic ambitions remain compatible.

Alliances therefore remain vulnerable to all sorts of destabilizing factors, no matter how well conceived they are strategically. Hence an alliance cannot be fully designed at the start; we must expect that it will evolve over time. A strategically robust design, one that accommodates the value creation logic of the partners and alliance evolution, is a prerequisite for success. How the collaboration is started, its design and early process, is at least as important as the strength of the strategic premises on which it is based.

5

❖

DESIGNING
FOR COOPERATION

IN THE FIELD OF MANUFACTURING, most product quality and cost factors can be directly attributed to product and process design. Get the design right and most problems in assembly, reliability, cost, and customer satisfaction take care of themselves. Design plays a similar role in the success or failure of alliances. Assuming that an alliance is built on a foundation of strategic compatibility and a robust value creation logic, good design can prevent conflicts from jeopardizing an otherwise sound relationship.

In this chapter, we explain how alliance design, over which managers have substantial control, can be used to prevent needless conflict and foster cooperation. Design can be part of the problem, breeding and exacerbating needless conflicts, or it can be part of the solution, containing and minimizing tensions.

Alliance design is the set of features managers can choose that define where and how an alliance operates. Of these features, four are key to preventing avoidable conflicts and fostering cooperation. The first two address alliance configuration; the second two relate to coordination.

1. *Operational scope.* Operational scope defines the activities and tasks jointly performed by the partners in the alliance. While the strategic scope of an alliance is a "given" for each partner, the operational scope can be drawn to foster cooperation.

2. *Configuration and valuation of contributions.* How well, or poorly, the alliance design addresses the valuation conundra discussed in Chapter 3 enables or undermines alliance success. Contributions may involve products, technologies, know-how, information, or management practices. Trade between alliance partners, and between them and the alliance when it takes the form of a joint venture, directly influences, and often reflects, the partners' perceptions of their relative contributions and benefits. Differences in perception around the nature and value of contributions often undermine alliance success.

3. *Alliance governance.* Alliance governance defines how an alliance is managed, how it is organized and regulated by agreements and processes, and how the partners control and influence its evolution and performance over time.

4. *Alliance interface.* The interface of an alliance describes how day-to-day interactions and exchanges between partners are managed, the extent to which their respective contributions are commingled or kept separate, and the operational linkages between them. If the configuration of contributions (number 2 above) defines *what* trade will take place between the partners, the interface determines *how* that trade is accomplished. Practically speaking, the interface consists of exchanges of information, meetings, joint task forces, common teams, sharing of progress reports, and the like.

Management can use each of these design features to facilitate cooperation and to prevent or minimize conflicts. Operational scope can be made wider or narrower, and the interactions between strategic, economic, and operational scopes can be optimized and discrepancies limited. Decisions on scope can be made to include activities that would become sources of conflict if left within the partner organizations; these same decisions may narrow the operational scope of the alliance to activities that can be isolated from potential sources of interpartner conflicts. Partners' contributions can be positioned and configured, and trade managed across the resulting boundaries to minimize tensions.

In general, configuration choices can limit conflicts, and coordination mechanisms can address what conflicts emerge. Forms of governance can be chosen in terms of their ability to foster cooperation, and interfaces can be structured and managed to allow any remaining tensions to be handled constructively and to increase opportunities for learning and alliance evolution.

Although it is conceptually and practically useful to consider each design feature separately, they obviously interact. Solutions to a problem arising from one design feature often require adjustments to several others. Thus, managers should see the four types of design features listed above as complementary tools to be used together.

While every alliance requires a unique design, all alliances share some basic design rules. We'll examine these and our four design features through a number of cases. But first, two caveats:

1. Design features cannot solve all partner conflicts; clever design is no substitute for strategic compatibility. While design features may paper over strategic differences, unresolved strategic conflicts sooner or later break through.

2. Conflict is not always bad; partners can often learn and benefit from the different perspectives and priorities that exist between them. Suppressed conflict usually leads to failure. As we will see in Chapter 8, alliances with the least visible conflicts are not necessary the most successful.

Varying Operational Scope to Prevent Conflicts

While the strategic interests and potential benefits of each partner are largely determined by the individual partner's position, and usually set the strategic and economic scopes of the alliance, the operational scope of the alliance is a conscious joint decision of the partners. By expanding or shrinking the territory covered by the alliance's joint activities—typically in terms of products, functions, steps in the value chain, and geography—it may be possible to prevent or minimize conflicts. For instance, once Boeing recognized JADC's interest in learning about program management and the incorporation of airline needs into its planning, it let JADC's members participate in development meetings. It saw that some JADC familiarity with marketing issues was likely to contribute to the overall success of future collaboration and not compromise Boeing's leadership in the alliance or in the industry.

The simplest and most effective operational scope is one that is fully aligned with the economic scope of the alliance. Thus, Airbus partners are now bringing their plants and engineering centers into the alliance as it shifts from being an economic interest group, in which partners coordinate but retain separate ownership of their respective activities, to being a separate company.

When many valuable interdependencies exist between partnered and nonpartnered activities, making the alignment of operational and economic scopes impractical and costly, interdependencies can be managed so as to minimize conflicts. The GE–SNECMA alliance illustrates this principle. Even though GE and SNECMA do not share economic performance data about their contributions to the CFM joint venture and are in principle indifferent to each other's performance—as each separately makes or loses money on its 50 percent contribution—each company knows that the other would not let economic performance get too far out of balance.

If GE were to see SNECMA lose money on its contribution, GE would try to redress the balance, as would SNECMA if the situation were reversed. GE's assistance would not be motivated by altruism but by its understanding that divergent economic performance would compromise agreement on key issues, such as pricing policies. Indifference to each other's performance thus extends only to small variations and spares them the haggling over transfer prices, and each partner is encouraged to support the other should their performance diverge too much. Conflicts are minimized and incentives for mutual support provided.

When testing the limits of this simple approach, GE and SNECMA made adjustments to their respective economic scopes via side payments. For instance, GE shared with SNECMA its profits on the sale of spare parts since its "half" of the engine generated more sales of spare parts than SNECMA's "half." When the stakes are even bigger than for spares, they may extend the operational scope of their alliance. For example, as maintenance services came to constitute a bigger and bigger profit stream in the mid-1990s, they became candidates for entry into the operational scope of the alliance. (Not surprisingly, at the time of this writing, SNECMA wanted to include them, while GE was reluctant to share its highly profitable service activities.)

A few broad guidelines can be proposed for setting operational scope:

1. Seek to fully understand each partner's definition of the three scopes: strategic, economic, and operational.

2. Define operational scope in ways that minimize conflict. (In principle, aligning the strategic, economic, and operational scopes of the alliance minimizes conflicts. Achieving complete alignment of all three, however, would likely defeat the purpose of the alliance. Short of this, the operational scope can be narrowed or expanded so as to minimize conflicts.)

3. Make trade at the boundaries of the operational scope as frictionless as possible.

Clarifying Contributions and Benefits

A second key element of design is the specification of what goes into and out of the joint activities: flows of know-how, products, and money as well as less tangible trade between partners, such as the use of a brand, the borrowing of a corporate reputation, or even the reduction of uncertainties through better information. Most alliances have some dependence on activities performed separately by the partners on behalf of the alliance. The J2T alliance between JVC and Thomson provides a typical illustration, as shown in Figure 5-1.

In J2T, the partners jointly assembled VCRs. Nonassembly tasks were kept separate. Each partner supplied some components and was able to provide complete product designs for assembly in the joint venture (although, in practice, JVC was virtually the only source of original product types). Each partner also committed itself to purchasing part of the venture's production and to selling the jointly produced VCRs under its own brand name(s) in its own distribution channels. Obviously, the joint venture produced a relatively narrow range of basic product types but a wide range of product faces.

FIGURE 5-1 *Essentials of the J2T Alliance*

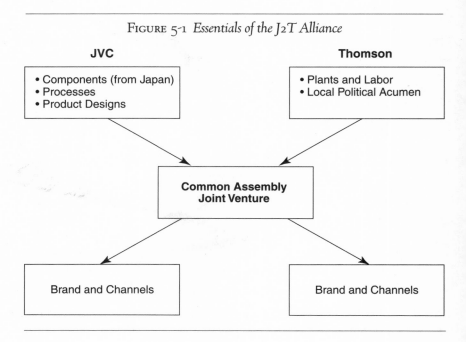

We have already noted in Chapter 3 the valuation difficulties created by "embedded" contributions and benefits, by unequal distribution of information among partners, and by the lack of transparency
about the benefits obtained and costs incurred in the J2T alliance,
particularly Thomson's lack of understanding of JVC's economics in
Japan and JVC's lack of awareness of Thomson's broader learning
ambitions. Not all alliances can have the elegant simplicity of GE
and SNECMA's 50/50 work share and revenue sharing.

A first approach, then, is to gain experience in evaluating each
partner's contributions, as did SNECMA and GE. In that case, each
partner could credibly evaluate the other's contribution, since each
knew roughly how to perform the other's tasks. This clarity was
lacking in J2T and was only resolved between JVC and Thomson
when Thomson was able to find realistic component pricing benchmarks from Toshiba and others. Finding external benchmarks, as
Thomson did, to more realistically assess the partner's performance
and evaluate its contributions is critical in assessing the true value of
a partner's contributions (components made by JVC in our example).

When valuation conflicts are many and where no benchmarks are available, the only solution may be to reduce the range of interdependencies between the alliance and the activities performed separately by each partner. This was the choice made by ICI and Enichem in letting their joint venture, EVC, procure its raw materials independently rather than exclusively from them, on terms set by the parents.[1]

Finally, adjusting the valuation of contributions over time, occasionally after the fact, may be necessary; short-term reactions, however, should be minimized. Partners are less well served by real-time scorekeeping than by attention to cumulative contributions over time. When some level of mutual trust is achieved between partners, ex-post adjustments and balancing of side payments between partners become possible; GE and SNECMA do this for spare parts. Fuji-Xerox has also demonstrated a remarkable ability to adjust to shifting contribution values over time.

Agreement on the sharing of contributions and tasks is not always easy, as being in charge of the more unique tasks may give a partner more influence over the alliance and may lead that partner to bargain for a higher share of benefits. The sharing of tasks in an alliance thus often becomes a source of conflict. At least initially, JVC controlled the trump cards in the J2T alliance, in particular once the European partners had dedicated plants to the production of VCRs designed by JVC.

Not all tasks, however, imply the same commitment to cospecialization. Some tasks are more easily substituted, imitated, and traded through other channels and with nonalliance companies. One source of tension in Airbus, for example, has been the German partner's perception that its British and French counterparts have confined its contributions to resources and skills less unique than theirs and used this difference to keep the German partner in a more dependent and vulnerable position (in particular to the subcontracting of the work it currently performs as offsets for export sales in countries aspiring to develop an aerospace industry). More generally, a high level of task cospecialization leads, over time, to a high level of mutual dependence. And partners are often wary of being left with the less strategic, less valuable, and less unique contribution.

The sharing of tasks, then, often becomes a bone of contention in the negotiation of complementariness. Fear of dependence has led many partners, particularly in defense systems, to apportion tasks so as to maintain a balanced pattern of mutual dependence—a condition in which each partner is hostage to the others. For instance, SNECMA insisted on a sharing of sales and support between GE and SNECMA, for both airlines and aircraft makers, splitting the world into marketing zones to create a high level of geographic cospecialization in market access between the two firms. In this case, SNECMA, the weaker partner, wanted a high level of cospecialization as a safeguard against GE's abandoning the alliance or encroaching into SNECMA's tasks and capabilities.

Not all alliances come to such a simple arrangement of complementation. Work-sharing agreements can be highly inefficient, with an overly extensive sharing of tasks, so as to exclude no partner from involvement in the most critical technologies. Perhaps instructed by its experience with Airbus, for instance, Daimler-Benz Aerospace insisted on a leading role in the development of the flight control system in the fighter plane it developed with British Aerospace and others, a task for which it had few skills. Such a pattern of task allocation negates cospecialization and often decreases the value creation potential of the alliance.

The trade-off between alliance efficiency and the risks of task cospecialization leading to one-sided dependency is not an easy one for most partners to accept.[2] Where external competition is high (as for Airbus), the need for efficient cospecialization prevails and tends to override concerns about dependence and unequal task sharing; where competition is less intense (as for fighter planes), partners may accept a much less efficient pattern of task sharing to preserve their independence in key tasks.[3]

Once partners have found workable solutions to the taxing problems just described, the design of the alliance provisions becomes possible. In particular, one can play at the margins with all kinds of "offset trades" that align partners' benefits with their acknowledged contributions. These include:

- equity sharing in a joint venture (this can be a rather rigid solution if conditions change).
- royalties and fees, some of a limited but renewable duration for intellectual property and management contributions.

- agreements and profit-sharing formulas that may depart from equity sharing and be variable over time.
- transfer pricing rules and benchmarks.

We cannot explore these many tools in detail. Driven by the imaginations of lawyers, accountants, and managers, their variety is almost endless and their specific arrangement in any alliance is bound to be idiosyncratic. The use of these tools should be driven by a concern for aligning the motives and incentives of the partners with the value creation profile of the alliance and should not be subject to constant haggling and divisive arguments between the partners.[4]

In sum, we suggest four broad design guidelines in clarifying contributions:

1. Avoid approaches that result in predictable haggling between partners about very limited issues, such as transfer prices.

2. Strive for designs that encompass both some mutual stimulation to excel independently and to support each other (à la GE–SNECMA).

3. Be ready to adjust the valuation of contributions over time as the external environment changes and as partners learn more about one another's contributions and benefits.

4. Acknowledge that the same contributions may be assessed differently from an economic standpoint (efficiency) and from a strategic one (risk of dependence), sometimes leading to less than economically optimal patterns of cospecialization.

Designing Governance Mechanisms for Effective Coordination

Governance is another key element of design. The central issue in governance design is the choice between contractual and institutional forms of governance. Should the alliance be defined through a set of contracts or as a separate institution, such as a joint venture? The institutional form does not exclude contractual arrangements, such as shareholders' agreements between joint venture partners, but it provides an institutional context for these contracts.

Contractual forms of organization imply legal agreements on contributions and benefits such as technology transfers, the use of brands, and distribution channels. Institutional forms typically involve the creation of a legally separate corporate entity, usually in the shape of an equity joint venture.

What factors should determine the best form of alliance governance? Economists and legal specialists would argue that the choice hinges largely on whether a "complete" contract can be drawn up. In other words, can a legal agreement among the partners account for specific future events and contingencies? Contracts, in principle, can be made contingent. But too many hard-to-specify contingencies complicate contracts to the point where they cease to be useful. When contingencies are many and complex, an institutional form of organization is preferable.[5]

Practically speaking, three kinds of contingencies make the crafting of alliance contracts difficult and ineffective, lending weight to the argument for more institutional forms of collaboration. These three contingencies are task integration, economic uncertainty, and the need to make decisions quickly.

Task Integration

Task integration, as we define it, implies process integration, not just output coordination. It requires working together on common tasks, not just passing on the results of one's work to the partner. Working together does not always require a separate institution, but a separate institution makes working together considerably easier.

Joint Optimization against Uncertainty

The more uncertain the nature and value of future trade between partners, the more difficult it is to govern through ex-ante contracts. As we argued in our discussion of scope and boundaries, the simplest solution to this problem is to put more rather than less in the "common pot." GE and SNECMA could hold to a work- and revenue-sharing arrangement and eliminate transfer pricing problems because once the joint engine was designed, economic risks (how many would sell at what price) were simple, and the partners shared enough of the same experience and skill to assess each other's contribution and to avoid the need for task integration. Had these conditions been otherwise, a wider joint venture might have become necessary.

An institutional form will not guarantee that an alliance can handle long-term uncertainty. However, when change occurs, an institutional arrangement may be easier to revise than one based on contracts. This is particularly true when the three scopes—strategic, economic, and operational—cover roughly the same territory.

URGENCY OF DECISION MAKING

A third factor in the choice between contractual and institutional forms of collaboration is the need to make decisions quickly. When CFM needs to grant a price concession to an airline on a newly developed version of its jet engine, it often must do so quickly or risk seeing the sale go to rival Pratt & Whitney. There is no time for a lengthy approval process conducted by the parents' corporate hierarchies. The fact that the key joint venture managers enjoy autonomy in decision making and also hold key positions in their parent companies makes quick decision making possible. Contractual arrangements between partners would not be supportive of such quick, unplanned decisions.

Alliances that require little task integration, face little uncertainty, and have no need for quick decision making can rely on simple contractual arrangements for their governance. Task integration, on the other hand, calls for a stronger interaction between partners. This is most easily achieved through an independent entity with its own identity, shared work space, and common management. Similarly, outcome uncertainty calls for a common pool of contributions and benefits, which is most easily achieved via an equity arrangement and profit-sharing plan rather than transfer pricing schemes. Finally, fast decision making calls for an autonomous alliance management team empowered to make key decisions without constant referrals back to the parent firms.

In sum, as any of these three dimensions of an alliance—task integration, outcome uncertainty, and speed of decision making—expands, the need for institutional forms of governance become more compelling. Conversely, when task integration is limited, when decision making lacks urgency, and when the outcomes of alliance activities are

FIGURE 5-2 *Factors Influencing Forms of Collaboration*

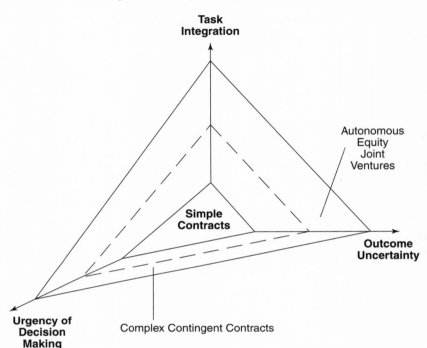

more certain, then contractual approaches to governance are more feasible. The interrelationships between these dimensions and the different forms of governance are illustrated in Figure 5-2.

While the three dimensions depicted in the figure deserve major consideration in the choice of alliance governance design, other factors also play a role. One in particular is the level of preexisting trust between partners. Partners who already trust each other will find it easier to handle high levels of uncertainty in an informal way; trust makes it possible for them to reach mutually agreeable ex-post adjustments in the sharing of alliance benefits. Indeed, we have observed some partners abandon formal joint ventures after a few years and replace them with informal arrangements.

The desire for strategic control may also influence the choice of alliance design. The power of joint-venture shareholders may give partners more direct control over one another's decisions than a contractual arrangement alone. This may make institutional governance preferable—other things being equal—to a contractual design. As they grow and mature, however, joint ventures may escape their parents' control and eventually provide them with less strategic control than contractual governance. Further, as we have argued already, a joint venture often assumes limited or no interdependence between what is pooled and what is not.

Managers should not overplay the design differences between contractual and institutional forms. Thanks to developments in contract law, it is possible to "nest" institutional governance within a contractual design built around shareholder pacts. It is possible to simulate an equity joint venture's performance and its governance mechanisms through a set of contracts, blurring the distinction between contractual and institutional governance forms. Finally, one should always bear in mind that contracts and the shareholders' pact provide a framework of safeguards within which to *start* the alliance. Any evoking of their specific provisions, in particular when they call for external arbitration, undermines the very process of collaboration.

Designing the Interface to Handle Conflicts

A fourth cluster of design parameters concerns partner interactions, both in the governance process and in the day-to-day performance of joint tasks. Here it is important to understand whether the partners' respective tasks need to be integrated through a true melding of cospecialized skills or merely coordinated, with each partner making its contribution separately and handing it over to the other partner(s).

To better understand these distinctions, consider the example of MATRA, a diversified engineering and technology-intensive firm. MATRA designed and developed the "Espace" multipurpose vehicle in the 1970s and convinced Renault to market, distribute, and service it. With the sales success of the Espace, this relationship developed into a very successful alliance. Operational coordination requirements were low: the Espace incorporated major power train subsystems from Renault, but there was little need for joint operation. Coordination was based on output, not process.

The GE–SNECMA alliance likewise began with output coordination. GE worked on the "core" of the engine, SNECMA on the fan, and each could bolt engines together from the subsystems both had made. There was no joint product development once the technical specifications of each subsystem had been set.[6] Once the not-so-joint engine entered service, though, output coordination had to give way to process coordination. It was no longer possible to keep each partner's work so separate. Improvement in performance relied on in-flight experience gained by complete engines, not by subsystems, and improving the performance of these engines called for interdependent optimization efforts involving the entire engine. Thus, over a period of a few years in the early 1980s, GE and SNECMA shifted at least partly from output coordination to process integration; that is, they worked together much more closely.

Airbus, too, incorporates both output coordination and process integration. There is some output coordination: for example, Daimler-Benz Aerospace, in Hamburg, does all of the internal cabin work and, until the introduction of the A320 in the early 1990s, only Aérospatiale in Toulouse did final airframe assembly. The partners and their many subcontractors work on various segments of the airframes. Finally, the development tasks require some amount of process integration, and flight testing is performed in an integrated fashion by Airbus teams representing all major partners. The current shift of Airbus from consortium to corporation is likely to lead to even more process integration between the partners over time.

Conflict can also arise when output complementation is the rule and when customers experience each partner's contribution separately. If coordination is not seamless, or if partners do not work to the same standards, then the product will fail to meet customer expectations and partners will bicker about who's to blame. This form of conflict plagues many service alliances with detrimental effects on customer retention.[7]

In sum, for managers, the more interesting question may be this: "Given the tasks we need to perform, where can each partner take full responsibility and where must we work together closely?" The need to work together stems from the nature of the task and its value creation logic. When shared learning or learning exchange drives value creation, working closely together is paramount. In cospecialization alliances, the nature of the task needs to drive how closely the partners need to work together, in particular whether output coordination will suffice or process integration is needed. When process integration is called for, the partners also need to work closely together. There may be several reasons for this. One is the need for hard-to-plan joint problem solving. For instance, it became clear in retrospect that Ciba-Geigy and Alza had limited their cooperation to output coordination. Alza would develop systems and hand them over to Ciba-Geigy for registration, manufacturing, and marketing, where process and task integration (for example, joint teams for specific product development projects) would have been necessary at least for some products. Without task integration, mobilization of the partners' skills and their creative combination would have been impossible.

More generally, the need for task integration tends to be highest in the early stages of the development of new opportunities, before the value chain structure becomes clear, before the required competencies are all identified, and before knowledge of how to combine them has become known. Task integration also becomes necessary when partners want to learn from each other or to learn jointly. It is therefore not surprising to find that task integration alliances are most prevalent in R&D where both of these motives are present.

An interesting example of achieving task integration in R&D through a flexible interface is provided by the design of the Japanese Very Large Scale Integration (VLSI) research cooperative—one of the first successful research cooperatives.[8] The VLSI project involved five semiconductor manufacturers: Fujitsu, Hitachi, Mistubishi Electric, NEC, and Toshiba. The most interesting aspect of this collaboration from the standpoint of task integration was the organization of the cooperative project in a common research laboratory. How could alliance architects induce five firms to work closely and cooperatively in this lab while they continued to compete in the marketplace? (Earlier cooperation efforts had merely led to complementary but quite separate research in each partner firm.) The answer was in the leadership and integration of research teams. Each of the five key research teams was headed by a manager from a different company (a sixth team being headed by a representative of a government research center) and staffed by researchers from all of the partner firms. A majority of each team's members came from the same company as did the team leader, providing unity, but members from the other partners participated in each team.

VLSI's staffing arrangement facilitated joint learning while avoiding the need to construct a new team hierarchy from scratch. Interteam cooperation was facilitated by the choice of overlapping research areas: several teams worked on the same types of topics, but in slightly differentiated ways, providing for original contributions from each team. After a slow start, and much encouragement from the Ministry of International Trade and Industry (MITI), interteam meetings became frequent, and informal interactions were fostered. For the four-year duration of the project, the cooperative lab developed its own identity as a social unit and functioned with a high level of cooperation and interteam competition. Multicompany teams created their own identities while providing each of the partner firms with complete first-hand exposure to all aspects of the task. Overall project leadership was vested with the Electro Technology lab of MITI, and particularly with two of its credible and neutral research managers.

The important point in the VLSI story is that the ability to transcend the "value creation versus value capture" and "cooperation versus competition" dilemmas is anchored in the design of complementation and interfaces between partners. How the tasks of subteams are defined, how these teams are constituted, by whom they are led, how horizontal communication across teams is achieved, and how a temporary system and a temporary identity are built are key to the ability to move beyond these dilemmas.

Interfaces that don't measure up to the requirements of the tasks at hand can wreak havoc with otherwise well-conceived alliances. We have already observed how the arm's-length interface between Alza and Ciba-Geigy failed to provide for the level of exchange and interaction necessary for success. We have also noted how the minimal interface between AT&T and Olivetti led to recurring squabbles in price negotiations that carried over to and polluted other parts of their relationship.

Contrast these failures with the more integrative approach being followed today by Motorola's Iridium space-based communication network. Motorola established a separate unit dedicated to the Iridium project. This new satellite communication division (SATCOM) was organized as a project with teams deployed according to processes and tasks. SATCOM very quickly integrated its corporate partners into these teams. In addition, an executive steering committee comprised of all the major partners met at least every second week to communicate progress between teams, resolve conflicts, and keep all key partners on the same track. According to a Motorola executive from SATCOM: "Motorolans tend to be a preachy lot. Sometimes we spend too much time talking and not enough time listening. It is absolutely foolish for us to expect to change another organization. Instead we need to do a lot of work on values and communication. We recognize that it can be very hard for our partners. Lockheed's employees have to be bilingual, they have to speak Motorolian and Lockheedian!"[9]

From the start, Motorola recognized that success would require a high level of quality communication between partners. Thus, each Iridium team was trained in transcultural and interorganizational skills.

Matching the Interface to the Task

Interface design begins with the tasks to be performed in the alliance. These can be many, diverse, and unpredictable, and the interactions between partners with different skills is often the source of greatest difficulty. It is not surprising, then, that GE and SNECMA were able to work together more easily than did Ciba-Geigy and Alza: the task demands of their alliance were less challenging and the partners were better matched in skills. Ciba-Geigy's formal, sequential, explicit, and mostly individual action process could not effectively connect or commingle with Alza's collective, interactive, and largely tacit and emergent know-how. Neither approach was better nor even more suitable to the alliance situation; they were simply incompatible. Nor were they easy to change or transcend, as each reflected the technical domain each partner was coming from: the chemistry of new drug discovery for Ciba-Geigy (which needs to be very structured and disciplined); the blend of many physical and chemical technologies for Alza (which needs to be adaptive, flexible, and innovative and to bring many disciplines and technologies together).

What can be done in the face of such difficulties? Two approaches can be considered: (1) decrease task demands and (2) improve the interface. Some situations demand both.

Decreasing task demands on the interface typically calls for breaking down task know-how into smaller, independent pieces, making it more explicit, better codified, and more mobile. This requires shifting the nature of the knowledge used in the alliance to knowledge that requires less interface between partners. This is easier to do with some technologies than others. With the exception of some very complex projects, most software development can be broken down into modules that can be developed separately and then reassembled with little interactive development. Output coordination rather than process integration is sufficient. Similarly, both GE and SNECMA could work separately on their respective "halves" of their aircraft engines.

Improving the interface usually involves increasing its "bandwidth," as Motorola attempted to do with its Iridium partners. Bandwidth can be increased in various ways: (1) through joint teams trained in cross-organizational processes, (2) through shared facilities and collocated team processes, (3) through organizational support for personnel working at the interface, and (4) through bridge building at multiple levels. The first two of these approaches have been explained already; the last two merit further discussion.

Supporting personnel at the interface. The interface issue concerns not just what to do at the interface proper but what each partner should do to support the people who work at the interface—where allegiances, authority, and personal self-interest are often unclear. When managers from Company A, which has a weak commitment and ambiguous goals, are thrown in with personnel from Company B, which has high commitment and clear goals, the managers from Company A are at a disadvantage. They are unsure of their authority, their parent company's expectations of them, and possibly the health of their careers. People who are excessively concerned with their own careers are rarely reliable alliance partners. The interface should be designed to ensure relative symmetry of authority; reassuring employees of the relative safety of organizational roles can solve this problem.

In some situations, buffering the interface by means of a small, shared organization can be effective in supporting personnel. The small CFM staff based in Evendale (the Cincinnati suburb where GE's jet engine operations are headquartered) originally played this role. As that joint venture matured, and as more managers in each organization gained the experience with the joint venture and personnel from the other partner, the need for buffering faded. The cadre of experienced managers and specialists who could interface directly between GE and SNECMA grew in size and self-confidence.

Building bridges. The interface is made easier by building bridges at multiple levels and ensuring alignment within and between partners on positions taken at various levels. Although the exact types of bridges and the levels at which they connect the partner organizations are bound to be specific to individual partnerships, we observed that bridges are needed at least at three levels:

1. At the operational level, where the detailed knowledge of the alliance tasks resides and where specialists can communicate with specialists. This bridge is essentially the operational interface between partners.

2. At the strategic level between CEOs or senior executives. A bridge here helps executives to understand and share the value creation logic of the alliance, to put valuation conflicts and operational problems into a broader strategic context, and to set a tone for cooperation at lower levels.

3. At the middle-manager level to bring operating personnel together on operational and strategic issues; typically, these managers are the ones most able to get things done.

In nearly all the alliances we observed, failures to build bridges at any of these three levels cost alliance partners dearly. For instance, Alza interacted almost exclusively with very senior Ciba-Geigy executives and with lab scientists, bypassing the intermediate personnel, the very people who might have crafted a more productive interface.

The most effective bridges we have observed were also social bridges, involving managers from the partners in nonprofessional activities and allowing them to understand and experience each other's culture and implicit norms and values. ICL's personnel, for instance, invited Fujitsu's executives to badminton and cricket games!

RECONCILING CONTROL WITH LEARNING

Efficiency and effectiveness in value creation should not be the exclusive drivers of interface design. Concerns for value capture sometimes drive one to knowingly choose a suboptimal complementation pattern.

Alza's reluctance to work more closely with Ciba-Geigy lest its technological know-how be transferred to a partner whose motives it did not
trust is an example. Where learning plays a key role, the partner who
wants to learn in a particular area will typically try to structure the
interface in that area with minimal constraints; the other partner(s)
will attempt to structure the same interface so as to minimize learning
opportunities. The tensions that arise from the control versus learning
conflict are evident in the early history of the ICL–Fujitsu alliance.[10]

To better develop point-of-sales terminals for ICL, Fujitsu's managers argued, its design engineers should accompany ICL's sales personnel to customer sites in the U.K. retailing industry. Logically, this
would give the engineers a better grasp of the real needs of customers and a practical understanding of how their products would
be used. ICL's management, however, wanted to keep Fujitsu personnel in Japan, where they would develop the terminals from
detailed technical specifications provided by ICL. In other words,
the interface may be made wider or narrower, and more or less
structured, depending on the partners' learning goals and concerns.

As will become clearer in the analysis of alliance processes over
time (Chapter 7), interface design of the alliance is not a static concept.
On the contrary, initial interface should be seen as something to be
perfected with time and experience. Partners need to continually ask:
Does the interface facilitate mutual understanding and trust? Does it
allow us to share enough information to make the alliance work? Will
it become broader and more open as collaboration develops?

In sum, the design of the day-to-day interface should be set by
the demands of the tasks, output coordination, and/or process integration, and should attempt to transcend the value creation versus
value capture trade-off by providing a high quality of ongoing interactions through multiple bridges.

Summary

In this chapter we have argued that the design of an alliance needs
to take into account four related issues:

1. The operational scope, that is, the activities, tasks, and operational domains that are combined in the alliance and the way

they relate to the economic and strategic scopes within which the partnered activities fit.

2. The configuration and evaluation of ongoing contributions and benefits, taking into account the economic and strategic scopes of the partners and their learning from each other.

3. The need for joint work, joint optimization, and speedy joint decision making as the key determinant of the governance form, structure, and process of the alliance.

4. The design of the interface, as a function of task demands and partners' interests, in establishing how coordination and integration are achieved, concretely, day to day, between the partners.

In considering these issues, partners must keep both value creation and value capture in mind. In particular, insofar as sustained value creation depends on the continued goodwill and forbearance of the partners, building into the design not so much safeguards as incentives to help each other perform is key. GE–SNECMA's work-sharing arrangement provided incentives for each partner to perform separately as well as incentives for the best performing partner to help the lagging partner. The blending of incentives to perform with incentives to help should drive the design of all alliances. As very aptly put by one of our Japanese interviewees: "An alliance, after all, is a commitment to enter a mutually stimulating relationship, and to be constantly improved upon over time in a way that makes it more beneficial to all partners."

Tension and conflict, and how to minimize them, must also be part of alliance design. We have noted in alliance after alliance how the recurrence of rather minor conflicts can make partner relationships more fragile and less trustful. Crafty design cannot paper over deep strategic divergences, but it can eliminate needless friction. In this, designers should not look for the "perfect" deal but for one that makes it possible for partners to start working together in constructive ways. They should try to project the design into the future, against future scenarios of alliance evolution: "If this happens, how will our design work in four years?" Equally important: "What inducement does it provide so that managers will make their best efforts?"

As obvious as it may seem, the architects of alliances should never forget that the success of alliances depends on people. After the "deal" is signed, and after the corporate chieftains have all given their uplifting speeches, success will depend on the people who do the work of the alliance. They must be confident that the alliance is capable of creating value for *them* as well as their employers. Often, what is seen as very worthwhile from a corporate perspective may be viewed as a career killer by operating managers. Alliance design, therefore, must include a structure of incentives for the individuals involved.

In the next chapter we explore the gaps that separate people in an alliance, how those gaps make cooperation difficult, and how they can be bridged.

6

❖

Initiating Cooperation

TWO CORPORATIONS have agreed to work together. They have assessed the value creation potential of their alliance and their own strategic compatibility. And they have decided on a design that promises to enhance collaboration and minimize tension. Everything looks good. Yet the fledgling partners find themselves unable to move from planning to implementation. Why?

These two are discovering what many others have found in the initial stage of collaboration. Between a well-designed and strategically sound alliance concept and its successful implementation lie several gaps that partners often find difficult to bridge. Indeed, a sad paradox of many alliance situations is that strategic complementarity and potential benefits from cospecialization accrue to partners who are so distant and so deeply different as to make actual cooperation between them all the more difficult. Deep gaps separate the potential partners. We find these gaps in the strategic and organizational *context* of the alliance, in the *content* on which cooperation must focus, and in the *processes* through which cooperation must be achieved. This chapter investigates each in detail. But, first, an overview.

Enablers of Cooperation

The strategic context of the alliance allows, or prevents, the partners' wholehearted, fully committed cooperation by shaping the strategic significance and scope each partner assigns to the alliance, by setting the tone of the relationship, and by setting each partner's expectations about the outcome. The organizational context of the alliance is shaped by the partners' preexisting ways of doing things and their compatibility, or lack thereof. The organizational context also conditions whether and how mutual trust and self-confidence develop between the individuals involved in making the alliance work. The concrete task and work content of what the partners undertake to accomplish also affects their ability to cooperate. Finally, the communications processes they establish and the norms they apply to their interactions also play a role.

CONTEXT

Each partner brings both a strategic and an organizational context to the initial stage of an alliance.[1] The strategic context of an alliance combines three elements:

1. the strategic scope the partner sees in the alliance
2. the way the partner frames the alliance
3. the ambitions the partner hopes to fulfill within that scope

Strategic context places the alliance within the partner's broader corporate strategy, giving the alliance its strategic scope. For example, SNECMA wanted to decrease its dependence on the French military market and on Dassault, the French fighter plane maker. Ciba-Geigy saw in Alza's advanced drug delivery systems a way to offset its lack of success in conventional drug research by turning well-known but hard to administer generic active substances, such as nitroglycerin, into patented, proprietary products. Thus both SNECMA and Ciba-Geigy found that their alliances fit well with larger corporate strategies. Strategic scope derived from that fit.

Strategic context also allows partners to place the alliance in one or another category of relationships, setting the tone, a priori, for partners' interactions and providing assumptions about their appropriate nature. AT&T's management, for instance, saw the relationship with Olivetti as a first step toward an acquisition, while Olivetti saw it as a minority equity investment and a source of supply contracts—two very different categories of relationships that set very discrepant tones in the alliance.

Finally, the strategic context within which partners place the relationship also sets their expectations about its benefits. Some expectations are explicit and shared; these revealed themselves during the negotiation stage of the alliance and provided the common basis for its start. For example, Ciba-Geigy and Alza were explicit in their expectations with respect to developing and marketing products based on Alza's drug-delivery technologies. When GE and SNECMA joined forces, they expected their midrange engine to power a new generation of narrow-body airliners.

In addition to explicit and shared expectations, most partners probably harbor private expectations that they do not share with their allies—revealing them could damage the cooperative relationship. These may concern the end state of the relationship. For instance, AT&T managers believed that their alliance with Olivetti would lead to an acquisition; some within Ciba-Geigy expected to learn important drug delivery technologies from Alza and to be able to do without the partner after a few years.

Secret thoughts or wishes about end states between allies are not the only unshared expectations. The full nature of the expected exchange between partners may not be explicit. For instance, some of SNECMA's managers expected to trade on GE's credibility and technical reputation in selling to airlines. Similarly, Alza's top management expected that Ciba-Geigy's reputation would enhance the credibility of its drug delivery technologies and help it negotiate lucrative R&D contracts with other pharmaceutical companies.[2]

Organizational context is as important as strategic context in an alliance. Each partner projects onto the alliance its "way of doing things," a set of tacit and accepted behaviors, norms, procedures, and routines. This includes not only the strategic decision-making processes but also day-to-day work routines. How each partner's organization works, independent from the alliance, is important insofar as its usual procedures and informal ways are most likely to be applied tacitly by the partner within the alliance.

The organizational context of each partner also defines roles and "anchors" for the managers and professionals who interact with members of the partner's organization. Visible and well-defined organizational roles communicate expectations of behavior to the partner's staff. Put differently, if we collaborate with a partner we do not yet know well, and may not necessarily trust, we will expect its managers and staff to behave according to our understanding of their organizational roles. If they do not behave according to these roles, or if these roles appear very unclear to us, we will be disoriented by their behavior and grow suspicious of their motives and of our ability to work with them constructively. Projecting predictable "in role" behaviors through the alliance is thus an important step in building early confidence.[3] Very independent joint ventures may give management "carte blanche" in defining new roles, processes, and ways of working from scratch. In most strategic alliances, on the other hand, managers and professionals at the interface keep at least one foot—if not two—in their home organization and tend to follow its rules.

Self-confidence is as important as confidence between partners in the beginning of an alliance. Again, organizational roles provide safety. If a company's managers have confidence in their roles within their own organization, they can comfortably reach out to the partners' managers. Personal safety and self-confidence allow them to both perform "in role" and know when to step "out of role" when the success of the alliance requires them to do so.[4] As we will see in more detail below, this duality between "in-role" safety and "out-of-role" risk taking helps make the alliance work.

CONTENT

Collaboration feasibility is also affected by the extent to which partners share a common understanding of the *content* of the alliance—that is, the task they will perform jointly. GE and SNECMA found collaboration relatively easy because the two organizations shared the same knowledge base in developing and building jet engines. Ciba-Geigy and Alza found it difficult to collaborate, partly because the technical aspects of their daily work were so very different. The overlap between their bases of knowledge and technology were so limited that attempts to bring the two organizations together bred frustration.

Sensitive to those differences, Alex Zaffaroni (founder and CEO of Alza) and Gaudenz Staehlin (head of Ciba-Geigy's pharmaceutical division) had agreed to minimize required interaction between the two companies: Alza would do the advanced development of their oral slow release technologies (OROS), full development of transdermal technologies (TTS), and "hand over" the results to Ciba-Geigy for OROS clinical tests and for production and marketing of both product types. Ciba-Geigy would do further development of OROS as well. Although this arrangement was simple and acknowledged the organizational context differences between the two companies by not requiring them to work closely together, it was not up to the task. OROS technologies in particular required more interdependence between system development (what Alza did) and application development (what Ciba-Geigy did). The process of collaboration, as drawn up by the agreement, did not allow for this. Worse, the skill overlap between the two companies was too small and their organizational routines too different to accommodate interdependence and closer collaboration.

The problems of the Alza–Ciba-Geigy alliance underscore our broader observations about how allies with partial content overlap and very different contributions work together. If the contents of what partners bring to the alliance—skills in particular—are too different, overlap too little, or share too little a priori understanding, collaboration is bound to be difficult and unproductive.

PROCESS AND NORMS OF INTERACTION

The process and norms of interaction between partners also determine alliance success. Intentions are converted into real cooperation through interactions. Let's illustrate the difficulties of this conversion by revisiting the experience of Alza and Ciba-Geigy. In that relationship, the intensity of the interface between partners was designed to be minimal, reflecting Staehlin's desire to protect Alza's entrepreneurial spirit and Zaffaroni's desire to maintain Alza's integrity and autonomy. Thus, the initial interface was limited to a "research conference" at which personnel from the two firms could become acquainted and alliance priorities could be set. Progress would be monitored and priorities would be reassessed at periodic meetings of a research board.

Frustrated with what they saw as Ciba-Geigy's sluggishness in developing and introducing their products, and with formal and infrequent interactions with their Ciba-Geigy counterparts, Alza's scientists and managers spent more time in Basel, Switzerland, at Ciba-Geigy headquarters, where they attempted, informally and single-handedly, to play the role of coordinator. In this they experienced high doses of organizational culture shock. Being used to easy access to people at all levels of their own organization, the Californians from Alza quickly ran afoul of their partner's typically Swiss formality and its staid management and scientific hierarchies. Knowing that the shortest distance between two points is a straight line, Alza researchers went directly to the managers most likely to give them an immediate (and favorable) answer or to the scientists most able to provide effective help; in most cases, these were very senior managers or lab scientists.

Their habit of bypassing the middle layers of their ally's hierarchy did not endear Alza personnel to the Ciba-Geigy people most able to get things done. Senior Ciba-Geigy managers were too far removed from day-to-day work to be helpful, and the potential conflict between their roles as investors and as partners made them extremely cautious in their interactions with Alza employees. Individual scientists, and even team managers, had little latitude in resource allocation, and despite their potential enthusiasm for advanced drug delivery systems (ADDS), saw little to gain from close involvement with Alza. In the end, the would-be coordinators from Alza found it extremely difficult to mobilize support within Ciba-Geigy. Alza's norms and processes of interaction were counterproductive in the relationship with Ciba-Geigy; Ciba-Geigy's were not suited to developing advanced drug delivery systems.

Let us now look more closely at how gaps in context, content, and process, such as the ones faced by Alza and Ciba-Geigy, can be bridged.

The Context of Cooperation

The initial context of an alliance seldom encourages cooperation: the partners generally lack mutual familiarity, understanding, and trust, and the absence of these can easily lead to an adversarial relationship. There are bound to be "gaps" between allies' expectations and initial results. Partners may differ on which rules and behaviors will lead to success. Such differences lead to a *frame gap* in which each partner's assumptions about the alliance may be quite different. Partners may also harbor different or unrealistic expectations, leading to an *expectations gap* between plans and results. Differences in styles, values, beliefs, and approaches to decision making likewise set allied firms apart—what we call the *organizational context gap*. There is also bound to be what we call *a confidence gap* between partners who may have doubts about their ability to make the alliance work and their private fears about their roles in it.

Let's consider each of these difficult gaps and then outline what can be done to close them.

THE FRAME GAP

Framing is an essential element of context that influences collaboration directly. A frame provides a consistent set of definitions, perspectives, rules, and assumptions for managers. Hence it is useful for guiding "sense making," for quickly coming to grips with a situation, and for accumulating some forms of learning and excluding others. At the same time, and precisely because it provides a structured receptacle for experience, an inappropriate frame is pernicious.

The problem of inappropriate framing is enhanced by the fact that every manager today has had some experience with acquisitions, alliances, or some other form of cooperation between companies. Few come to the table without a set of experience-shaped prejudices about what alliances are for and what makes them either successful or problematic. Past experience leads managers and their companies to *frame* their relationships with partners in unique ways, and these may be inappropriate for the new situation. There are several possible variants of this problem:

1. the wrong frame for the situation (for instance, an acquisition frame for an alliance)
2. different meanings given to similarly labeled frames between partners (for instance, one treating an alliance like an acquisition and the other an acquisition like an alliance)
3. different frames coexisting within the same partner organization
4. a frame borrowed from an old context applied in a new one

Perhaps the single most problematic frame gap stems from partners not recognizing the true nature of their partnership, that is, applying to a partnership assumptions borrowed from another type of relationship, such as an acquisition or a supplier agreement.[5] Such a frame gap is bound to create tensions. For example, most acquiring companies, rightly or wrongly, expect the acquired company to act like a "conquered nation" and adjust to the acquirer's way of doing things. A large company with many acquisitions under its belt often brings such a frame to alliances with smaller companies. This frame clearly violates the spirit of partnership, where each partner travels part of the way to meet the other.

A supplier agreement frame raises different problems. Supplier agreements generally entail contractual negotiations on specific commitments (prices, quantities, product specs, and the like), a modus operandi that hardly suits the uncertainty and complexity faced by partnerships that aim to reach new markets or develop new opportunities.

Frame gaps pose even greater problems when each partner frames the alliance differently. Different frames create ambiguity for managers about the true nature of the relationship and its likely evolution. The AT&T–Olivetti relationship described earlier underscores this point. Cooperation is particularly undermined when one partner—but not the other—frames the relationship as a prelude to possible acquisition. The potential acquirer has every excuse for not actively seeking cooperation while the other partner has every reason to be defensive. It is no coincidence that some of the more problematic relationships we have studied, such as AT&T–Olivetti and Alza–Ciba-Geigy, fell prey to these tensions, while the more successful relationships were free of them. Perhaps the greatest achievement of the Fujitsu–ICL relationship was that ICL's management welcomed its evolution from alliance to acquisition. Fujitsu had exercised such forbearance and restraint in its handling of the relationship that ICL's managers trusted it to manage the acquisition as an alliance, not as a takeover.

In general, too many managers treat alliances as acquisitions, and too few treat acquisitions as alliances. Culture plays a role in this. Japanese companies are more likely, for instance, to treat an acquisition as a partnership than are American companies. This cultural difference may explain why Fujitsu was so much more successful in acquiring different parts of the STC-ICL group in the United Kingdom than was Northern Telecom (now Nortel), particularly when it came to retaining key managers who were critical to maintaining an "insider" position in Britain. Northern Telecom should have treated its acquisition more as a partnership, in particular as it sought access to the British market for telecom systems. There, retaining managers with strong relationships in the United Kingdom was essential—something that Northern Telecom found difficult to do. It weakened its position in Britain and Fujitsu strengthened its own largely because of these differences.

There is even more confusion when different employees of the same partner company use different frames. For example, Ciba-Geigy's top management understood the need to preserve Alza's autonomy and identity and to interact with Alza with restraint. This understanding was not shared by everyone in Ciba-Geigy's pharmaceuticals division, where many framed the relationship as a potential acquisition opportunity. With the scent of a takeover in the air, Alza's scientists and managers, whose cooperation was essential to the success of the partnership, were understandably guarded in their interactions with counterparts at Ciba-Geigy.

Frames may also become obsolete, particularly when partners move from traditional joint ventures, or consortia, to new partnership forms. We have observed this development not only when partners transfer the same logic from one context to another (for example, from extractive industry joint ventures to information technology alliances) but also when the rules of the game shift over time within the same industry context. Table 6-1 contrasts old and new patterns of cooperation in the European aerospace industry from traditional program consortia, in which cooperation took place around one defense program at a time, to more permanent, rationalization-driven alliances. Clearly, transferring the lessons learned from past joint programs to the partnerships of the future would be both inappropriate and dangerous.

Recognizing the need for new frames for new alliances, and unlearning the frames inherited from previous collaborations, is perhaps the most demanding challenge facing managers as they enter new forms of collaboration. Managers underestimate the differences between their past experiences and their new situations. They can avoid this problem by developing frames that adequately recognize

TABLE 6-1 *Patterns and Characteristics of Cooperation in the European Aerospace Industry*

OLD RULES	NEW RULES
• Cooperation is externally imposed by governments as a function of joint programs pursued by military purchasing agencies.	• Cooperation is sought (or feared) as part of corporate strategy.
• Performance benchmark is "easy" (an inefficient alliance is still better than no alliance at all).	• Competitiveness against U.S. firms provides the benchmark.
• *Juste retour* (fair return) principle: work is shared in proportion to government funding.	• Efficiency principle: work is shared according to economic performance.
• Juxtaposition, but no cospecialization: each company/nation protects a complete range of skills.	• Efficiency calls for cospecialization: each partner specializes in some technologies and abandons others.
• External control on "balance" in the alliance as a function of government funding and orders.	• Internal alliance dynamics drive balance.
• "Keep a finger in all pies" is the guiding principle, leading to inefficient work-share allocation and redundancies.	• Irreversible choices of mutual dependence.
• Alliances "one at a time," typically on a program-by-program basis, easily reversible, with no long-term commitments.	• Alliance network as part of overall long-term corporate strategy.

the complexity and uniqueness of the new partnerships. The danger, of course, is shifting to the other extreme: the view that every partnership is so unique that lessons from other alliances cannot be applied. Each alliance is indeed unique, but the principles that contribute to successful collaboration are robust and highly generalizable.

How can the frame gap be bridged? The first step is to see the venture through the eyes of one's partners: seeing the value creation logic(s), the priorities, and the strategic intent that motivate them; learning about past collaborations that may color their view of future ones. Sharing past alliance experiences with new partners is an important element of bridging the frame gap. Because the past often forms expectations of the future, partners should share their experiences with past alliances and their views on what accounted for their success or failure, and compare their situation to past experiences.

As a second step, each partner should tell the other why it believes the other party is in the alliance. For example, Firm A should tell Firm B: "We believe that you joined the alliance to learn the new XYZ technology and expect to incorporate that technology in your new product families." Although this sharing of impressions will not reveal or eliminate hidden agendas, it will nonetheless help circumscribe them. Joint seminars, training workshops, and the like can also play a useful role.

The gap-closing that takes place between partners should also take place *within* partner organizations. Many frame gaps originate in poor internal communication, as we observed in the Alza–Ciba-Geigy case. Maintaining a common frame for a given alliance, across levels and subunits, is key to being consistent in behavior toward a partner. In its absence, partners received mixed signals. Top management has a key role to play in ensuring that everyone involved in the alliance shares a common frame.[6]

THE EXPECTATIONS GAP

High expectations are a common source of problems. To make the alliance more palatable to executives and line employees, future alliance benefits are often overstated. Successful negotiations between partners also contribute to inflated expectations. At the conclusion of the deal, commitment is made to what is usually an overly optimistic view of the future. Companies may overestimate the expected contributions of their partners. Each partner may also knowingly overestimate its own contribution. Did Olivetti's management really expect to sell several thousand AT&T minicomputers? Was it realistic to expect AT&T to adapt its product to the European market and to develop the applications software required for broad-based distribution? In retrospect, the partnership's sales forecasts for these minicomputers turned out to be wildly optimistic. If partners fall prey to unjustified optimism, disappointment is bound to follow. Excessively sanguine expectations set a nearly inescapable trap for the partners: as alliance performance is judged against initial expectations, plan and reality won't match and the alliance may well be terminated prematurely for no other reason than its overly rosy initial expectations.

Beyond pleading for realism in the initial assessment of an alliance, it is difficult to prescribe methods for avoiding the expectations gap. The quality of the initial assessment is the best guarantee that expectations will be in line with future outcomes. The more robust the value creation logic, and the more compatible the long-term strategic interests of the partners, the less likely they are to embrace unrealistic expectations. Top management can play a role here by remaining temperate in its representation of alliance benefits, and by reminding everyone of the effort required to obtain them. Overselling the gains and understating the pain is usually a recipe for disaster.

Another way to temper undue enthusiasm is to create substantial overlap between those who negotiate the alliance and those charged with implementing it. Operational managers who know that they will have to live up to alliance commitments are less likely to allow these commitments to escalate.

The Organizational Context Gap

Organizational dissimilarity between partners constitutes yet another gap that alliances must overcome. Although cultural and organizational differences are obvious sources of tension, partners may still cooperate successfully if those differences are acknowledged and constructively overcome.

We find that differences in organizational context, often stemming from differences in the size of the partners, do more to undermine alliances than do differences in national culture, hampering joint decision-making processes, making joint work difficult, and blocking joint learning. Table 6-2 summarizes the contrasts we often observe in

TABLE 6-2   *Decision-Making Styles of Large and Small Organizations*

BIGGER, MORE BUREAUCRATIC PARTNER (A)	SMALLER, MORE ENTREPRENEURIAL PARTNER (B)
• Formal, explicit decisions	• Informal, tacit, shared decisions
• Periodic, scheduled plans	• Continuous, unscheduled planning
• Low contextual embeddedness	• High contextual embeddedness
• Slow, sequential inputs to decisions	• Fast, simultaneous inputs to decisions
• Analytical choices	• Intuitive judgments
• Aggregation, consolidation of data	• Real-time immersion in data

the ways that partners of different size make decisions, the first cause of difficulty created by difference in organizational context.

Such differences in decision-making style are the source of numerous difficulties in alliances. In cases we have observed, Partner B is capable of making decisions much faster than Partner A but cannot explain its rationale for reaching a quick decision to its partner. Partner A must either take Partner B on trust, thereby accepting its recommendations without fully grasping its rationale, or require a more time-consuming approach to decision making at the risk of stalling the collaborative process. In neither case are the partners likely to be satisfied with each other. If Partner A simply accepts B's recommendations, it will feel "railroaded" into decisions that it does not understand; if it does not accept B's recommendations, Partner B will be frustrated by A's slowness and apparent lack of trust. Joint decisions are unlikely because the decision-making mechanisms of the partners operate at different speeds.

Differences in work routine between partners also make collaboration difficult. Managers who are baffled by their partner's work routines are unlikely to collaborate easily. This was clear in the Alza and Ciba-Geigy alliance. Alza worked in a "here, now, together" mode, with self-structuring problem-solving teams; in contrast, Ciba-Geigy worked in a "there, later, separately" mode, with sequential hand-offs between functional experts. Attempts by these firms to cobble together joint teams typically faltered on misunderstandings and behavioral frictions. These differences were difficult to resolve in that they emerged from fundamental differences in how the partners organized work.

Differences in organizational context can also block learning or lead to the *wrong* learning. Managers who feel uncomfortable with the operating practices of a partner may cling even more tightly to their own practices, abandoning attempts to adjust to their partner's ways. For instance, Ciba-Geigy's top managers thought that their company was learning to be more entrepreneurial through the Alza alliance; at the operating level, however, the alliance was having the opposite effect. With only a few exceptions, Ciba-Geigy's scientists saw the Alza model as threateningly different. Rather than embracing Alza's ways, Ciba-Geigy reinforced its own. The fact that Alza's financial and technical track record was nonstellar and that it did research in a field—pharmacology—that did not elicit much respect from researchers in other disciplines was used by Ciba-Geigy's scientists to dismiss its different practices. To a lesser extent, the same thing happened in the AT&T–Olivetti relationship: instead of providing a challenge that stimulated learning, the partnership reinforced each partner's sense of superiority. In each of the cases cited, managers confronted with threatening differences were less apt to learn than to revert to type.

One of the big problems of bridging differences in organizational context is that so few managers understand their own organizational culture. As one of our colleagues puts it: "The most difficult culture to know is your own." Managers who have grown up in a particular context seldom understand how idiosyncratic it may be. In that sense, it may help to appoint alliance managers who can distance themselves from the deterministic powers of their own corporate culture and collaborate with others with some measure of cultural neutrality. Managers whose careers have spanned two or more different corporate cultures may be the best candidates for these assignments.

Finally, and perhaps most alarming, is the fact that the difficulties we have described quickly lead managers to be critical and dismissive of their partners. The comments listed in Table 6-3 are fairly representative of those made by managers in floundering alliances. Notice the difference in tone between Tables 6-2 and 6-3.

Bridging the organizational context gap is thus no small task, and

TABLE 6-3 *When Organizational Differences Confound Partners*

BIGGER, MORE BUREAUCRATIC PARTNER AS SEEN BY THE SMALLER ENTREPRENEURIAL FIRM	SMALLER, MORE ENTREPRENEURIAL PARTNER AS SEEN BY THE LARGER FIRM
• Ponderous, slow, and stupid	• A bunch of cowboys
• Preoccupied with reviewing everything to death	• Shooting from the hip
• Awash in mindless procedures	• Disorganized, slippery
• Risk averse, procrastinating	• Going off in all directions, unfocused
• Characterized by paralysis through analysis	• Characterized by sloppy work
• Divided, fragmented	• Exclusive, clannish, hostile

it requires several steps. Recognizing the importance of cultural and organizational compatibility is an obvious first step. Taking the time and showing the openness of mind necessary to learn how the partner organization operates is essential. Participants must refrain from assigning their own values to the partner organization and the way it operates. Judgments about the relative effectiveness of the respective organizations must be deferred.

Some companies explicitly allocate time to learning about their partner's ways of functioning. In the wake of its experience with Ciba-Geigy, for example, Alza required that its people and personnel from new allies participate in introduction workshops intended to familiarize each firm with the culture and real operating procedures of the other. In other cases, executives from each partner organization participate in the other's executive development seminars. These exchanges have been practiced extensively by AT&T and Olivetti and by GE and SNECMA. Because these seminars provide an environment free of high-stakes business issues, executives are less guarded in their interactions. Participating managers have found that these sessions provide an invaluable "window" on the ways of the partner.

Using interactions with the partner to extract organizational process information and integrating that information across contact points are also fundamental to bridging the organizational context gap. Although each interaction is only fragmentary, the aggregate of these experiences forms a model of how a partner organization really operates. To benefit from these interactions, managers recognize the importance of learning how the partner operates and how to adjust to the differences they discover.

The exchange of managers and specialized personnel for more than short visits is even more helpful in bridging the gap. Over the thirty years of their alliance, for example, Fuji-Xerox has sent Xerox more than one thousand managerial and professional employees on assignments averaging about three years. This massive flow of personnel has provided Fuji-Xerox and its Japanese parent, Fuji Photo Film, with substantial insights into Xerox operations and business culture, greatly facilitating the interface between the Japanese partnership and its U.S. parent.[7]

More than understanding, however, is required to bridge the organizational gap. The design of the interface between partners must take organizational differences into account. In the most troubled partnerships we have studied, interface design failed to recognize organizational differences; in these cases, the partner organizations interacted with little mutual understanding and with no buffers between them. The results were uniformly poor: arm's length relationships that were sufficient for some alliance tasks but not others, and bungled attempts at collaboration that did more harm than good.

For instance, although both Ciba-Geigy and AT&T placed "liaison desks" on each other's premises, neither functioned effectively as either "gatekeeper" or "guide" with respect to the other organization. In contrast, Fujitsu's "collaboration office," a corporate staff group, served as a central contact point and repository of company-wide experience in managing strategic alliances and as a provider of expertise and alliance management training for the entire company. It also built a reservoir of managers with substantial cross-cultural experience who participated in meetings between Fujitsu and partner managers to facilitate cultural bridge building.

Using stronger buffers and liaison managers may indeed help, in particular if these buffers can be cross-cultural integrators. Eurovynil Corporation (EVC), a joint venture between ICI in the United Kingdom and Enichem in Italy, for example, used a British chartered accountant with years of experience in the Italian state-owned sector (a rare bird, indeed) to dispel potential misunderstandings related to the two companies' accounting practices. Buffering structures, such as the program management joint venture set up between GE and SNECMA, also help. In that case, promising younger managers were selected, signaling that the alliance had commitment at the top and that it was a fast track to senior positions. Over time, this structure developed a cadre of senior managers, both at GE and SNECMA, who were committed to the alliance, familiar with its operations, and knowledgeable about their allied counterparts.

Here again we observe that how organizations treat their own managers has an impact on the ability of those managers to overcome organizational context gaps. Managers who are at ease in their own organization have the confidence to reach out to the partner organization and do what the success of the alliance requires rather than stick to preexisting roles. Managers who are insecure in their own organizations are demonstrably less able to do so.

The Confidence Gap

The act of allying does not always generate confidence on the part of those managers who have to make it work. Employees may see entering the alliance as a threat, especially when the partnership is a result of the firm's having failed to deliver on its own. This clearly was a problem for Ciba-Geigy in its collaboration with Alza; its researchers had been unable to develop slow-release technologies. The feelings of failure or inadequacy the formation of a partnership triggers in such circumstances profoundly challenges the people involved. Emotions are only exacerbated when a company is or will be a competitor of its partner and fears that its key skills may be compromised.

Some see alliances as job threatening. Cospecialization is, after all, a form of business rationalization; duplications may be eliminated and activities moved from one geographic location to another. Fear of such developments has slowed the implementation of some potentially effective alliances, such as Eurocopter (the joint venture between Aérospatiale and Daimler-Benz in the helicopter business), or EVC, when key implementers dragged their feet and sought support from local politicians and governments. Observing the difficulties that rationalization poses and the way it can undermine cooperation, some alliance partners (British Aerospace and MATRA in their missile business, for example) have separately undertaken rationalization and employment downsizing before combining their operations.

Alliance cospecialization also requires a "giving up" of corporate autonomy and, potentially, valuable competencies. Thus, companies and individual employees fear that they may become too dependent on their new ally. An alliance may thus create a confidence gap: replacing self-confidence with doubts, pride with embarrassment, personal security with insecurity, and perceived self-reliance with dependence. This gap must be closed if partners hope to cooperate successfully.

The confidence gap raises a difficult dilemma: the level of commitment and cooperation required to get an alliance up and running may not be sufficient to carry the partnership through to completion.[8] The individuals involved must achieve higher and higher levels of cooperation, reflected in growing commitments to cospecialization. Unfortunately, the confidence gap often undermines these levels of commitment. At the same time, if commitments remain at the same low initial level, cooperation may be doomed to failure.

The Content of Cooperation

Once partners have committed to an alliance with the purpose of cospecialization or shared learning, individual managers and technical specialists should begin working together very soon on concrete tasks that combine their skills and competencies. But moving from the broad strategic concept that launched the alliance to the nitty-gritty of real work is not easy. Some early value creation assumptions may dissolve when examined more closely. New task requirements may appear unexpectedly and challenge the initial design of the alliance. In short, partners may not be able to begin collaborating until they have bridged two other gaps: one involving skill understanding, and another involving task definition.

THE SKILLS UNDERSTANDING GAP

Within a few months of beginning to work with a partner company, many managers complain that their partner's skills are not what they had supposed: we term this a "skills understanding gap." In their view, the partner's skills fail to match up to earlier assumptions. This disappointment leads managers to believe that the partner had overstated its capabilities in earlier negotiation (an attitude that questions the integrity of the partner). These complaints, however, are often groundless. The real problem in many cases is not the meagerness of the partner's skills but one's own ability to understand those skills.

While optimism, inflated expectations, and outright misrepresentation may play a role in the skills gap, disappointment also stems from the difficulty of combining disparate skills. To combine skills, you need to understand them, and we have observed several alliances where key managers and specialists did not! For example, Alza's ADDS development skills involved working in small teams, bringing multiple disciplines into close informal cooperation around specific problems in an ad-hoc way. While Ciba-Geigy's scientists understood these skills intellectually, they found it extremely difficult to participate effectively. Similarly, AT&T's executives could understand the importance of strategic marketing at Olivetti, but could not contribute much to it. They were too distant from these skills.

Bridging skills understanding gaps requires familiarity with the partner's skill base; short of this, skill combination may be impossible. This is particularly true when the organizational context was shaped by the partner's skill base and technologies, over time. Ciba-Geigy's organization, for instance, was keyed to the development of new active ingredients, not the requirements of delivery system development. Because what Ciba-Geigy did and how it did it was so tightly intertwined, the company could not understand how to adapt to the requirements of delivery systems innovation. Hence, it was difficult for Ciba-Geigy to understand and fully value Alza's contributions.

Gaining familiarity with new skills does not take place overnight, in particular where skills are tacit and their use emergent. It was, for instance, relatively easy for Alza's scientists to understand the highly formalized processes at Ciba-Geigy. The reverse, however, was not true. It was more difficult for Ciba-Geigy to understand Alza's skills, and even more difficult to figure out how to connect to them.

Closing the skills understanding gap begins with an assessment of the partner's skills and of the distance between those skills and one's own. This is obviously easier when the skills of the partners overlap, or when they are similar. Paradoxically, several alliances we observed had problems because the partners believed they shared skills when they did not, or used their skills in ways that made them difficult for others to understand. GM, for instance, in its alliance with Toyota, faced both issues: on first seeing the technical systems at work in the joint plant, GM managers thought they could be easily imitated. After all, Kanban and other lean manufacturing skills are simple. Only after technical imitation failed to deliver expected results did GM's managers become fully aware of the shop floor management social processes that enabled results: these were much less visible than the technical systems themselves.

Taking the time to understand each other's skills, including the less immediately visible ones, is critical to an effective definition of joint or coordinated tasks. A first approach is to codify each partner's skills, for instance, through detailed documentation of procedures. Very often, the basic tools that support a skill are accessible, but learning how to use them effectively is difficult. Not every licensee of American Airlines' yield management software will achieve the same results as American Airlines, although they have the same system. Indeed, the most valuable skills that alliances seek may not be amenable to documentation. For example, high-quality airlines have discovered that they need to (re)train the crews of their less service-oriented partners and have them work as "apprentices" on their own flights.

The Task Definition Gap

However desirable in principle, it is seldom possible at a partnership's inception to have a precise operational definition of the tasks to be carried out. A task definition gap thus stands in the way of initiating cooperation. While partners know broadly what they want to accomplish together, they seldom know how to do it.

Partners must work together to define joint tasks with precision. Here are a few suggestions for making the job of task definition more effective:

- Share operating information about skills, not just descriptions.
- Make task definition an iterative process over time, not a one-shot affair.
- Sequence tasks so that early tasks inform the definition of subsequent ones.
- Refine initial definitions of tasks at an early stage, before irreversible commitments are made.
- Find early objects of cooperation to learn from, and do not try to outline the full details of the task agenda at the outset.

The merits of quickly finding and acting on points of early collaboration are substantial. Tasks that seem vague and daunting at the start of an alliance often seem clearer and less formidable as the work proceeds. As in mountain climbing, the way forward may become steeper as one proceeds, but self-confidence and momentum also increase: a climber becomes more fit as he gets accustomed to altitude and more willing to trust his life to his teammates as they tackle more challenges together. Mountains are climbed one step at a time. Value is created in alliances in the same manner.

This suggests that the beginnings of the cooperation process can and should be used to broaden and validate the value creation assumptions of the alliance and thus to sharpen the definition of what needs to be accomplished and what benefits are expected. We have observed that while many successful alliances start by aiming for specific benefits, they also have ambitions for their alliances that extend beyond initial cooperation along some sort of alliance growth path. Some of the more resilient and robust alliances we have studied benefited greatly from a preplanned, albeit tentative, growth path. The GE–SNECMA alliance, for instance, went from a small subcontracting arrangement back in the 1960s to a quasi-merger of GE's and SNECMA's civilian jet engine activities in the 1980s. One can adopt such an approach to future growth paths even in the negotiation phase, using an existing agreement as the basis for improvements over time. In other words, the existing agreement can be a starting point for future improvements.

Fast-feedback tasks are also useful at an early stage. They provide experience in actual collaboration and help close the task definition gap one step at a time. Here it is useful to contrast the approaches taken by AT&T and Olivetti in two different businesses: one approach successfully closed the definition gap; the other did not.

For private branch exchange systems (PABX), the partners started by jointly commissioning market research to arrive at a common set of market development assumptions. They then scheduled a series of working sessions, the first focusing on getting to know each other. The partners paced the definition of the joint task to their own learning about markets, technologies, and one another. For minicomputers, on the other hand, these same two partners took a much less realistic approach. They organized a task force of engineers and specialists from both partners to define the entire alliance task precisely and accurately in one "standing conference." This was clearly impossible. Although they did develop a new product line plan, the plan lacked credibility, and neither key managers nor technical personnel were committed to its implementation. The realism of the plan was untested and thus its precision could not be trusted. Needless to say, the plan did not materialize, and its abandonment was an early sign of the alliance's failure.

In sum, the first steps in working together should typically be small ones, no matter how grand the ultimate goals for the alliance.

These small steps can be used for early confidence building between partners and for the sharpening of skills understanding and task definitions between partners.

The Process of Cooperation

The process of cooperation is challenging for even the most willing allies. Since each must look first to its own interests, a natural guardedness is bound to exist. In the sphere of military alliances, even long-standing alliances contain elements of distrust. In the 1980s, for example, an individual was caught and convicted of channeling classified U.S. military secrets to the Israelis. Despite decades of collaboration and sharing of defense technology and military intelligence, these two allies could not entirely trust each other. The same holds true in the realm of commerce. Even the most collaborative partners pursue their own interests.

The first difficult hurdle is the shift from negotiation to collaboration. By definition, negotiators are careful and guarded in what they say and what they share. They play their cards carefully, hoping, as every skillful negotiator must, to see more of the other party's hand than they must reveal of their own. Thus, when they finally move from negotiating together to working together, each party confronts an information gap—a gap between what it knows about the partner and what it *must* know to work in a collaborative manner.

Negotiations create an expectations gap that widens if the parties' anticipated costs of and benefits from the alliance differ widely over time. This difficulty is compounded by the fact that problems are encountered *before* the promised benefits are obtained, meaning that partners confront an alliance-straining time gap.

THE INFORMATION GAP

Alliances depend on the sharing of information. Collaboration typically starts at the end of a negotiation session, once the "deal" has been closed, yet negotiations seldom prepare partners for collaboration. Information is not shared openly in negotiations: a shrewd negotiator tries to obtain as much information as possible and to release no more than is necessary. Some types of information, such as that concerning technologies, would lose their transaction value if shared openly. If the provider of technology were to furnish all the information necessary for the recipient to precisely assess the value of the transferred technology, he would have already given away the store. In technology- or skill-intensive partnerships, then, information is bound to be asymmetric at the start of the relationship.

Information asymmetry thus creates a gap at the outset of an alliance. And given the existence of intra-alliance rivalry, information asymmetry is likely to continue throughout the course of the relationship. Power in an alliance depends partly on who controls, and who uses, proprietary information. Thus, despite the best of intentions, an enduring information gap exists in most alliances. To argue for more "disclosure" or greater openness, then, is probably naive. Still, if partners share information on a reciprocal basis in the early phases of an alliance, they are more likely to volunteer information unilaterally and perhaps keep a less precise balance of information exchanges. As one of the key managers in an alliance we studied put it:

> When we started taking stock of each other, we told each other, "Show us what you can do." But nothing happened! Slowly, as people became frustrated, things changed to "If you show us this, we will show you that." This worked but left a feeling of "us" versus "them." Then we realized we had to show them first, and we started to overcome the feeling of belonging to different camps. Everyone finally started to see the value of sharing information.

Obviously, the greater the value creation potential and the stronger the cospecialization between the partners, the easier it is to convince allies to unilaterally provide information.

Commitments that indicate trust in the other partner's judgment ("I'll send you my ten best engineers. You decide how to use them") also help to bridge the information gap.[9] As long as the alliance has built enough flexibility into the renegotiation process and the sharing of its benefits to adjust to such improved information and assessment, bridging the information gap is likely to contribute to alliance success.

THE TIME GAP

The time gap is caused by a difference in the partners' timing of the costs and benefits of collaboration: pain before gain, more for one side than for the other. The wider the time gap, the more difficult and problematic collaboration is bound to be. The first years of the Eurocopter alliance, for example, were periodically shaken by the possible loss of commitment from its major military customers, first in Germany, then in France, and by uncertainties associated with export sales. These losses undermined the very logic of the enterprise, which was critically dependent on these markets, and threw the balance of contributions and benefits between partners into question. In spite of the uncertainties looming over their future benefits, however, Eurocopter managers nonetheless had to make courageous decisions on rationalization, cospecialization, and downsizing.

The time gap between contributions and benefits may differ between partners by design. One partner may, for instance, trade access to a "safe," relatively immediate opportunity in return for a bigger but more uncertain one in the future. Pharmaceutical companies, for example, have sometimes traded comarketing of existing products for access to the future "research pipeline" of a partner. In these situations, one partner obtains certain short-term benefits, while the other makes short-term commitments in exchange for the possibility of larger, longer-term benefits. With respect to the time gap, however, these trade-offs may undermine the level of trust between partners by creating incentives for defection.

Bringing a sense of timing to an alliance, as well as scheduling both commitments and expected benefits (through milestones and contingent contracts or commitments), can help make the interests of partners more resilient in the face of the time gap. Awareness of the time dimension is half of the solution to the problems it causes.

Summary

Table 6-4 recaps the significance of the gaps we have identified in this chapter and reasons they may block cooperation from the start, their likely sources, and our suggestions for ameliorating them. As the middle column of the table indicates, gaps are likely to be severe at the beginning of the cooperation, as interpartner distance in strategic and organizational contexts, in skills and ways of doing things, and in management processes goes hand in hand with complementarity. Wide gaps often separate the more complementary partners. Unplugged, they would lead to early demise of the alliance. The "What to Do about It" column in the table summarizes our recommendations on how the gaps can be closed.

A common theme runs through our recommendations: companies should invest in their understanding of the situation and gather intelligence about their partners. They should view the inception of the partner relationship as an opportunity to learn and to improve. This may be more important than blindly rushing into implementation of joint tasks. The actual learning processes are analyzed in the next chapter.

TABLE 6-4 *Closing Interpartner Gaps to Initiate Cooperation*

TYPES OF GAP	WHY THE GAP MATTERS	WHAT ARE ITS LIKELY SOURCES	WHAT TO DO ABOUT IT
FRAME GAP C O N T E X T	• Perspective and definition for understanding the relationship and heuristic gap rules for behaving within it, driving day-to-day interaction.	• Wrong frame, not matching actual situation. • Irreconcilably different frames between partners. • Same label, different actual frames. • Different frames in the same organization. • Obsolete frames as wider context changes.	• Select a frame appropriate to the true nature of the alliance. • Ensure frame compatibility through joint sense making and sharing of assumed frames. • Communicate within own organization. • Discard inappropriate frames. • Unlearn own frames when obsolete.
EXPECTATIONS GAP C O N T E X T	• Benchmark against which the actual performance (or the strength of early signals alerting to performance difficulties) is to be assessed.	• Results from negotiation process; may lead to overly optimistic and sanguine expectations through mutual overselling between partners.	• Contain early escalation, do not over promise. • Prepare managers for the possibility of lowering their expectations; make the implementers part of the alliance negotiation team.
ORGANIZATIONAL CONTEXT GAP C O N T E X T	• Structure and process for decision making, work, organization and performance, and organizational learning may be more or less compatible between partners.	• Discrepancy in organization size and style. Intuitive and analytical styles make sharing frames and expectations difficult. • Differences in handling knowledge, between tacit and explicit speed and rhythms of decision making, prevent joint decision making from taking place between partners. • Projection of own organizational routines makes joint work hard.	• Recognize the importance of organizational and cultural compatibility between partners. • Refrain from judging partner's context from one's own context. • Learn about partner's organization, milieu, and origins. • Adjust to each other, using buffers and gatekeepers.

TABLE 6-4 (continued)

TYPES OF GAP	WHY THE GAP MATTERS	WHAT ARE ITS LIKELY SOURCES	WHAT TO DO ABOUT IT
CONFIDENCE GAP	• Self-confidence allows strong personal commitments and personal risk taking in cooperation; lack of confidence makes wholehearted cooperation difficult.	• Threat of losing face, because of the alliance creation and within the alliance. • Fear of losing influence and position. • Threat of unfavorable cospecialization and need for "giving up" to the partner, reluctance to accept mutual dependence.	• Avoid trying to resolve all tough issues up front. • Balance the need for "giving up." • Foster loyalty to alliance or/and to partners, depending on the type of collaboration. • Understand and accept individual feelings. • Provide space and time for "giving up."
SKILL UNDERSTANDING GAP	• Need to combine and blend differentiated skills between partners, in particular where process integration is required.	• Distant and differentiated skill bases do not connect easily. • Skill bases reflected in different organizational "ways," making connections between partners difficult.	• Gain familiarity with partner's skills. • Understand their nature. • Assess their distance.
TASK DEFINITION GAP	• Need to define a concrete set of tasks in order to start operational and tangible cooperation.	• Lack of accurate and precise task definition; need to define and revise the tasks to be performed.	• Recognize task definition as an iterative process over time. • Sequence tasks for fast feedback.
INFORMATION GAP	• Need to share information.	• Information and knowledge asymmetry resulting from negotiation. • Rivalry in the alliance may further the information asymmetry.	• Shift to an attitude of unilateral commitments and contributions. • Reassert value creation potential and need for combining information.
TIME GAP	• Need to keep balance of costs and benefits in perspective over time, for each partner and between partners.	• Different planned or unforeseen timing of when costs are incurred and benefits obtained between partners over time.	• Structure timing so there is a commitment schedule over time to use as reference point; keep long memories.

(Left margin labels: C O N T E X T for CONFIDENCE GAP; C O N T E X T for SKILL UNDERSTANDING GAP; E N T for TASK DEFINITION GAP; P R O C for INFORMATION GAP; E S S for TIME GAP)

7

❖

MANAGING LEARNING AND ADJUSTMENT OVER TIME

IN THIS CHAPTER we turn from issues of strategy, planning, and initial design to the evolution of an alliance and how learning through collaboration contributes to success or failure. How alliance partners learn and adjust to each other over time, as we will see, is as important as planning and design.

The natural clarification of alliance objectives, value creation logics, and the evolution of interpartner relationships dictate that few alliances can succeed by holding fast to their initial plans. Indeed, what separates alliances that last long enough to fulfill their aspirations from those that break apart at the first difficulty is their capacity for learning and adjustment. Yet, as Chapter 6 made clear, the initial partners' positions are seldom conducive to easy adaptation. Initially, most partners are distant, often suspicious of each other, and may not yet share a deep sense of the opportunity before them or of how to capture it. This is when partners are *least* ready to work

This chapter draws on and extends the research presented in Yves Doz, "The Evolution of Cooperation in Strategic Alliances: Initial Conditions or Learning Processes?" *Strategic Management Journal* Special Issue, 17 (Summer 1996): 55–84. Copyright John Wiley & Sons Limited. Reproduced with permission.

together. The "same bed, different dreams" metaphor often applies here. Nevertheless, it is in this early stage that they must learn to work together, to trust each other, and to reexamine early assumptions and expectations: they must close the gaps described in the previous chapter and improve on the imperfection of their initial design. Learning is thus at the heart of successful alliances.

Not all alliances, unfortunately, learn and evolve. Indeed, most alliances enter a deep crisis within their first three years. While we have argued that longevity is not, in itself, a measure of success, there is no compelling reason for premature death! Some early failures occur for the right reasons: weak value creation potential, irreconcilable strategic conflicts between partners, and so forth. But other alliances seem to die by accident.

The key to longevity and accident avoidance, in our experience, is learning and adjustment, first to each other, then to changed circumstances, if required. Alliances that succeed go through cycles of learning, reevaluation, and readjustment over time. Through these adjustments, commitments increase in size and in scope, allowing the alliance to create more and more value. The perception of greater value justifies still deeper commitments.

In this chapter, we review what partners must learn to initiate cycles of success and growth. We then discuss how partners can put that learning to use in a cycle of reevaluation and readjustment (see Figure 7-1). Briefly put, the initial conditions of the alliance either facilitate or hamper learning along a number of dimensions: the environment of the alliance and how it changes; the tasks to be performed; the process of collaboration itself; the skills of the partner; and partnership goals. As the partners begin learning from their cooperation, they begin to reevaluate the following:

1. the potential of the alliance to create value

2. the expected balance and equity of value capture among partners

3. their ability and their commitment to adjust the existing conditions of the alliance

Positive reevaluations on these three points, in turn, may lead to important revisions in the partnership, in shared expectations, shared tasks, governance, and interfaces.

FIGURE 7-1 *Cycle of Learning, Reevaluating, and Readjusting*

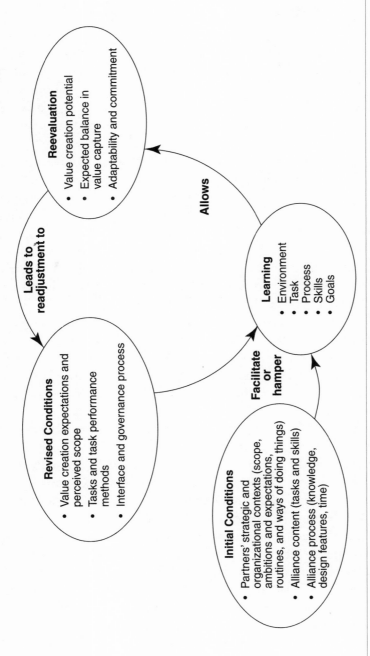

Source: Adapted from Yves Doz, "The Evolution of Cooperation in Strategic Alliances: Initial Conditions or Learning Processes?" *Strategic Management Journal* Special Issue, 17 (Summer 1996): 64. Copyright John Wiley & Sons Limited. Reproduced with permission.

What Partners Need to Learn

To sustain successful cooperation, partners typically need to learn in five key areas: the environment in which the alliance will operate, the tasks to be performed, the process of collaboration, the partners' skills, and their intended and emerging goals. We'll introduce the terms here before entering a complete discussion on each one.

To make their alliance more robust in the face of uncertainty and more resilient to changing circumstances, partners benefit from learning together about their alliance's *current environment* and about its likely *future environment*. The alternative—each partner making its own observations, drawing its own conclusions, and making its own predictions—is bound to push the partners further apart. A *joint* effort at learning about the competitive, technological, and market environment helps partners develop mutual trust and shared understanding and reduces the risk of framing gaps.

The *tasks* that partners recognize as essential to their mutual success in the beginning are likely to evolve as the partnership changes and matures, and as they learn about how to perform the partnership tasks. Partners thus need to learn how to improve the initial definition of the work they need to perform jointly and of how to perform such work successfully.

The *process of collaboration* can be surmised in the planning stage, but the best-suited one is only fully discovered by doing and then fine-tuned by the partners, who must be willing to transcend the decision-making and business processes of their own organizations.

Some amount of learning is required to commingle and meld *skills.* Yet despite the obvious merits of each partner learning about the skills of the other, rivalry often makes such learning difficult for reasons already cited.

Collaboration is bound to be difficult if any partner fails to understand the *goals* of its allies. This is particularly true when a high level of rivalry exists. Suspicion and mistrust will fill any vacuum of knowledge or certainty about partner goals.

To make each of these learning priorities more clear, let's consider them in terms of some by now familiar cases.

About the Alliance Environment

Learning about the environment of an alliance is fundamental. The more the alliance aims to access new markets and create new opportunities, the taller the learning agenda with respect to the environment.

Creating a joint "sense making" process to refine early assumptions about the environment makes it possible for partners to transcend starting conditions and to avoid being locked into divergent viewpoints. This is far from easy, as Ciba-Geigy and Alza discovered. There was little for them to learn, at least initially, since there were no ADDS products and little competition to provide information and feedback. The few signals available were read differently by the two companies. As the main proponent of ADDS for years, Alza was prone to read the environment optimistically. Conversely, many at Ciba-Geigy remained skeptical, despite positive assessments of ADDS by its own staff. They and Alza "read" the same information quite differently. For example, an announcement that a potential competitor had stopped research on OROS was seen by Alza as a reason to redouble its efforts; Ciba-Geigy viewed the same announcement as a signal to curtail its efforts.

GE and SNECMA provide a stark contrast in joint sense making of the environment. Disappointed in the late 1970s by the nondevelopment of the midrange airliner market they had targeted, these allies began looking for other markets. Together they identified an opportunity to retrofit existing aircraft with their new, more fuel-efficient engine. Through years of difficulties and delays, the two partners jointly gained a far richer understanding of the airline markets. They also learned about each other's governmental constraints and understood better what was required to maintain government support for the alliance on both sides of the Atlantic. Through a series of early market setbacks the two companies remained committed to joint learning. Had this not been the case, the partners might simply have blamed each other for the failure to realize their initial plans.

AT&T and Olivetti offer an interesting example of how well, or how poorly, partners learn about the environment depending on their level of collaboration. In private telephone exchange systems (PABX), the two firms carried out joint market research to better understand the structure of the industry. In minicomputers, however, the preconceived views of each firm prevented learning. AT&T's views had been shaped by its experience with protected and proprietary systems. Olivetti's views, on the other hand, had been shaped by experience in the intensely competitive IBM-compatible world. These very different viewpoints made joint learning difficult.

It is paradoxical that partners are often *least* likely to learn in the very areas that interest them most intensely. Why this happens is not difficult to understand. These areas are likely to have been central to internal debate about whether to create an alliance, and with whom; they are central to the alliance's a priori logic. By the time the alliance is formed, each partner's assumptions about the environment are strongly held and difficult to modify.

An explicit joint learning effort about the environment, therefore, has two merits: it provides a realistic basis for steering the alliance, and it helps partners to build common ground, to build trust, and to bridge expectations gaps. Part of the brittleness of the Alza–Ciba-Geigy alliance stemmed from the expectations gap that opened between the partners: Alza grew more enthusiastic as its ally grew increasingly skeptical. Joint learning might have closed or at least narrowed that gap.

What can partners do to jointly learn about the environment? Our research suggests several approaches:

1. *Find and use new common data.* Joint learning is more likely if partners seek out new data. The neutrality of new common data helps each partner shed its preconceptions.

2. *Clarify and debate assumptions.* Shared understandings are more likely when partners stop debating conclusions and instead sort out what they see as assumptions, constraints, and variables.

3. *Share the "whys."* Each partner should keep asking itself and its allies, "Why do we/you see the world this way?" This is an effective way to expose the root causes of the partners' different assumptions and force them to challenge their own thinking.

4. *Contain personal risks.* In nearly all the alliances we have observed, the most learning was done by what we call "secure mavericks," individuals who were safe enough in their own organizations not to be hostage to its preconceptions. When confronted by new facts, they had no trouble changing. Appointees to alliance

positions thus need to be self-confident individuals who aren't afraid of arrows in their backs.

5. *Be patient.* Joint learning takes time. It requires listening, sharing, and reflection. These are unnatural acts for many action-oriented managers, but they are essential when two or more companies want to learn about the environment together.

6. *Do not assume that views of the environment will automatically converge.* We have observed alliances in which deep differences in environmental perceptions have endured for some time—to the detriment of the alliance. This suggests that convergence of understanding cannot be taken for granted. Convergence only occurs in the presence of a structured process for joint learning.

About Alliance Tasks

Early in the relationship, partners must learn to better define, or to redefine, their joint tasks. This requires an appropriate level of interaction. As we saw, the arm's-length relationship of Ciba-Geigy and Alza made joint task definition unduly difficult. Problems with OROS, for example, caused Ciba-Geigy's technical managers to question the potential of OROS rather than the way they interacted with Alza to exploit that potential. GE and SNECMA, on the other hand, succeeded despite the restrictions the U.S. Department of Defense imposed on them. These firms quickly saw the costs of such restrictions and decided to interact more closely through joint staffing of the program coordination team, the exchange of managers, and joint training and development. This allowed them to learn together how to best perform joint tasks. SNECMA had learned from its disappointing experience with Rolls-Royce in building Concorde engines that it needed a novel, more integrated, approach to managing its relationship with GE. That approach worked: the partners learned both about the content of their tasks and the conditions under which they could be performed successfully.

We recommend these four guidelines for task learning:

1. *Simplify joint tasks by making the knowledge to be shared more explicit.* Typically, this means that the knowledge to be exchanged must be articulated and codified. This is possible in certain well-planned engineering tasks (such as the development of a jet

engine) but not always in innovative tasks (as in the development of OROS applications). The extent to which partners will permit their knowledge contribution to be made explicit, codified, and transferable is highly variable. Some partners resist this to maintain advantage and bargaining power. Intel, for instance, found its Japanese partners in several development alliances reluctant to make their know-how explicit.

2. *Increase the "bandwidth" of interpartner communication.* Task learning is facilitated, as we argued in Chapter 5, by an interface design that allows intense, relatively informal communication between partners. Communication over the task itself, however, may not be enough. Those involved need to consider how the task can best be *performed*, that is, they need to think about how to improve the interface and make their day-to-day task performance routines and processes more compatible. Improving both organizations and their "plug-compatibility" was a secondary objective of GE's and SNECMA's early learning efforts. They may also need some skills overlaps. ICL and Fujitsu accomplished this when they developed elaborate guidelines about knowledge-sharing procedures; they also maximized the time available for their managers to interact outside the formal workplace and to learn about each other's culture.

3. *Limit the number of sites, groups, and teams interacting but improve coordination between them.* Many cooks working independently in the kitchen rarely produce as good a meal as a few cooks working closely together. Alza had multiple links to the major units of Ciba-Geigy but not particularly well-coordinated ones between units. The two partners did not exchange personnel or set up common work teams. The fact that the parties were often at odds did not make task learning any easier. Conversely, in its Iridium project, Motorola took great care to coordinate the work of the various partners and their interactions. Keeping the number of partners—and partner subunits—to a minimum is an obvious advantage in learning. Collocation of people into fewer sites makes informal learning easier.

4. *Enhance the cooperation of managers and specialized personnel.* The people assigned to alliance activities can make or break the entire effort. Their cooperation is essential. Yet these same people may

lack enthusiasm for the project. Some may view the alliance as an admission of their own weakness; others may be threatened by it. Thus, both *who* is selected to work in the alliance and *how* the alliance is presented to them is key. Thomson's collaboration with JVC was positioned as an opportunity to learn something new, not as an admission that its personnel had failed to learn on their own. ICL's collaboration with Fujitsu was positioned as a way to secure the long-term future of an otherwise vulnerable company and to concentrate on ICL's areas of strength.

About the Collaborative Process

As they learn about the conditions that facilitate performance of their joint tasks, partners must also learn about the "process" of collaboration itself. Understanding the process makes partners more effective in their joint tasks and better able to adjust as those tasks evolve over time.

Learning about the collaboration process goes beyond the tasks to be performed to what makes each partner tick and how members of the partner organizations approach the process of cooperation. Alza personnel, for example, learned that rivalry between Ciba-Geigy's Basel headquarters and its U.S. subsidiary, as well as conflicts between pharmacology (Alza's main interface) and other functions and disciplines, made a consistent effort toward ADDS unlikely. To an extent, the aims of the alliance became hostage to a wider debate on the global organization of Ciba-Geigy R&D. Alza also learned that some of Ciba-Geigy's key operating procedures were not conducive to alliance success. In other words, Alza learned how its partner's organizational issues would affect its collaborative process on ADDS.

A number of things can be done to learn about the process of collaboration:

1. *Step outside the process for a better view.* Personnel who participate in a dysfunctional business process can feel in their bones that it is not working, but they may not understand how to fix it because they are too close to it. They need to step outside the process to learn what makes it work and what makes it fail. Efforts to develop process maps and process indicators—focusing on how well the cooperation starts—and to use them to monitor process

changes over time are forms of process learning. Quarterly process reviews are also effective.

2. *Let objective parties observe the process.* The process needs to be observed, and the players are not always the best observers. Here internal facilitators and/or consultants can play a useful role: observing and analyzing the process and feeding back their results to the participants. Neutral third parties may also fill the role of process architects more easily than anyone in the partner organizations.

3. *Stimulate collaboration.* The collaboration process must be actively pursued; it will not simply happen. But who should take the first move? Unilateral commitments are often needed to get things moving. When one partner gives another the tokens of trust and opportunities to show itself trustworthy, it stimulates collaboration. A unilateral commitment signals the other partner that a reciprocal move is appropriate.

4. *Work on misunderstandings.* Left untended, small misunderstandings fester and grow into major differences. Partners need to identify and address misunderstandings as they occur. Mutual "playbacks" of what each partner believes about the other can be very useful.

About a Partner's Skills

As we argued earlier, though cospecialization of diverse skills is the raison d'être for most alliances, major skill differences may inhibit the successful combination of partner skills. In these cases, partners must work diligently to learn about each other's skills. The same is true when the organizational routines that embody those skills are very different—as they were between Alza and Ciba-Geigy. It was not the difficulties of ADDS technologies per se that blocked the larger company's learning but Alza's rather opaque approach to product development.

An important distinction needs to be made between the skill *familiarity* needed to combine skills successfully—a requirement for value creation in many cospecialization alliances—and skill *mastery*, a threat to cospecialization and alliance value creation. (We deal with the latter in the next chapter.) By *familiarity* we mean learning enough about the partner's skills to commingle them successfully.

Managers can do a number of things to enhance skill familiarity:

1. *Do your homework.* Managers should do as much as possible to understand their own skills and those of any potential ally. While this seems obvious, it is actually rather difficult: the most valuable competencies are often the most tacit and least understood. Although some skill sharing can be done as a pre-amble to forming the alliance, much more remains to be learned.

2. *Understand how the partner's skills, organizations, and procedures interact.* Collaboration connects skills via organizations and action proce-dures. As the Alza–Ciba-Geigy case illustrates, there is a risk in connecting to skill bases that are more tacit and more embedded than one's own. The two skill bases may never "connect." Skills that manifest themselves through informal collective behaviors are hard for outsiders to fathom. Competence emerges from a well-honed pattern of relationships, but no one has the map—and even less the causality links—of that pattern. As we saw, for instance, Toyota's technical skills were relatively easy for GM to grasp; Toyota's skills at managing people and social systems in plants were harder to comprehend.

3. *Aim for "plug compatibility" between skills.* One way to achieve skill connection in the absence of skill mastery is for partners to articulate the work routines and process implications of their own skill bases to make them more "plug-compatible" with each other. *Plug compatibility* usually requires active work on the design of the interface so as to adjust each partner's work routines to interface more easily. GE and SNECMA, for instance, worked together to develop the procedures and processes each would use to perform new activities, such as customer service, quality control, and spare parts logistics.

About Goals and Expectations

Once cooperation gets underway, partners watch each other care-fully, looking for indications that a partner has a hidden agenda. Alza, for example, was surprised by Ciba-Geigy's "reinventing the wheel" in manufacturing ADDS, a signal that Ciba-Geigy did not wish to remain permanently dependent on Alza's know-how and manufacturing capacity, at least for ADDS. As we saw earlier, the initial phases of cooperation may also lead each partner to clarify its own goals and expectations.

Several approaches are useful in learning about a partner's goals and in clarifying one's own.

1. *Observe the partner's pattern of behavior in the alliance.* Behaviors of the partner that do not appear consistent with shared expectations, or are at odds with earlier public statements, may indicate a hidden agenda. In one of the few areas of tension between them, SNECMA saw GE's retention of spare parts supply and exclusion of service activities from the alliance scope as a desire by GE to maximize its economic benefits from the alliance in a way that SNECMA might not fully measure.

2. *Watch for related actions around the alliance.* Check, for instance, the willingness of partners to make hard-to-reverse cospecialization commitments, a proxy for the partner's real willingness to accept a degree of dependence. The quality of people seconded to the alliance, and hirings of specialists in fields related to the alliance, may reveal the partner's true goals. For instance, when Thomson started working with JVC on VCR manufacturing in Europe, it replaced existing audio product supervisory personnel with recently hired former watchmakers, a move that should have given JVC a clue about Thomson's learning and internalization intent.

3. *Analyze how separate but related alliances might be used together by a partner.* In the 1980s, some American and European aerospace companies became concerned when they observed that the Mitsubishi group was apparently developing a capability to design and build an advanced aircraft piece by piece through a network of alliances. Each alliance was by itself innocuous. Together, they had the potential to rival the Western companies.

4. *Discuss interests rather than positions in the evolution of the alliance.* Being explicit about one's true interests rather than hiding them behind negotiation positions will encourage other partners to put their interests on the table. Putting forward negotiating positions one has to retreat from feeds doubts about the extent of hidden agendas.

From Learning to Reevaluation

Learning along the five paths—environment, task, process, skills, and goals—provides partners with the insights they need to improve on the initial conditions of their alliance. This learning is a precondition to successful adjustment, even when it reveals the limits of cooperation.

Ideally, learning leads us back to the conditions and design issues that prevailed at the beginning of the alliance, helping us to reevaluate each with the benefit of greater perspective. As shown in Figure 7-2, progress on each of the learning paths provides the material needed to build a more successful alliance.

THE REEVALUATION METERS

Partners should ask themselves three questions when they evaluate an ongoing alliance:

1. How much value remains to be created?

2. Is that value likely to be appropriated equitably between partners?

FIGURE 7-2 *Learning Returns Partners to Issues at the Heart of the Alliance*

3. Given uncertainties and needs for change, how capable and willing to make adjustments are the partners likely to be?

These three questions are the basic "meters" according to which the evolution of an alliance should be assessed. Each of the learning paths outlined earlier feeds into one or more of these meters.

Learning about the environment allows partners to better assess what value can actually be created and to build a sense of equity in sharing it. Learning about the alliance task reinforces confidence that value will be created and, if adjustments to initial practices are required, allows the partners to test their ability and willingness to make these adjustments constructively. Learning about the collaboration process itself also contributes to testing adjustment capabilities. Learning about each other's skills enhances the assessment of value creation if that learning is done in the spirit of facilitating complementation; if, however, the partners are perceived as encroaching upon each other's skills sets, the learning may undermine the equity assessment. Goal learning also feeds the equity and potential value creation meters.

In sum, the learnings in each of the five key dimensions jointly feed the three meters by which partners typically gauge the alliance's progress. We can contrast the Alza–Ciba-Geigy and GE–SNECMA relationships to make this point concrete.

The Alza–Ciba-Geigy Alliance

In the Alza–Ciba-Geigy relationship, negative assessment on all three dimensions surfaced rapidly. As time passed, Alza's managers saw less and less value in the relationship. They perceived their partner as slow to market, even in TTS, where good progress was being made. In this business, first to market with an FDA-approved product was key.

Alza's assessment of future potential deteriorated when TTS encountered manufacturing problems. It attributed these problems to poor coordination within Ciba-Geigy and to Ciba-Geigy's misplaced desire to "reinvent the wheel" rather than rely on Alza's manufacturing experience. This was a warning signal on both adjustment capability and the possible presence of hidden agendas.

As for OROS, Alza's managers were baffled by what they saw as slow progress by their partner, which they attributed to the "not-invented-here" syndrome, Ciba-Geigy infighting, and plain passivity. In other words, Alza did not fault the interface, which would have been easier to change. Instead, it saw the trouble within the larger partner. This criticism placed the blame where things would be most difficult to remedy. Reforming Ciba-Geigy as a whole was out of the question.

As Alza's confidence in the relationship waned, ADDS became increasingly well accepted in the pharmaceutical industry. This had two further consequences for Alza's assessment of the alliance's potential. First, acceptance by the industry introduced a sense of urgency: if Alza did not capitalize on ADDS technologies quickly, someone else would. Second, Alza began to see viable alternatives to its relationship with Ciba-Geigy; its partnership with the larger firm was turning into a liability.

Alza's assessment of the alliance's adaptability also deteriorated over time. As its managers discovered how their partner operated and how it reacted to their prodding, they lost faith in their ability to make Ciba-Geigy operate to their liking. They would never teach the elephant to dance. Also, certain developments caused them to question Ciba-Geigy's motives: Ciba-Geigy's independent work on TTS and OROS; investments in manufacturing; and discreet efforts to recruit key Alza scientists. Did Ciba-Geigy ultimately want to do without Alza?

Alza's diminishing expectations were matched by its partner's. Alza's perceived lack of commitment raised suspicions. And problems encountered with the technology under development further dampened Ciba-Geigy's interest. Its scientists and managers concluded that the difficulties they encountered in developing OROS were inherent in the technology—not a result of their own organizational processes. Thus, Ciba-Geigy drew away from OROS.

Nor was the long-term horizon abundant with promise. TTS technology had potential, but the other technologies addressed by the alliance were too undeveloped to offer clear value, leading Ciba-Geigy personnel to ask "After TTS, what?" With nothing of tangible value on the horizon, many took a "get TTS and get out" attitude toward the alliance.

Could this alliance have been saved? It seems unlikely, given the positions of the two partners. Unresolved framing and organizational context gaps plagued the relationship from the start. The task requirements and the process of cooperation, at least for OROS, did not match, and attempts to improve the relationship and to reform the interface were ineffectual and too late. The initial "separateness" of tasks between the partners impaired recognition of the task performance needs, particularly in that these called for a level of task interdependence that Ciba-Geigy did not know how to handle.

Fundamental differences in organizational routines also undermined task coordination. Alza's attempts to do things its way within Ciba-Geigy only created friction and alienated the larger company's middle managers. Working together created more frustration than learning. Attempts to strengthen this working relationship through "liaison desks" and other fixes were greeted cynically as bureaucratic responses that caused more problems than they solved.

Three years into the alliance, both partners were determined not to develop the relationship further. Alza was looking for third-party deals, and Ciba-Geigy was searching for ways to benefit from TTS and limit its subsequent commitments. Both partners' reassessment of efficiency, capacity to adjust, and equity had proven negative. Trust evaporated, and the partners lost hope of building a longer-term relationship.

Lessons in Learning

The Alza–Ciba-Geigy experience provides a number of practical lessons for alliance builders:

1. *Initial conditions can block learning.* As we observed, if serious gaps exist in the initial state of collaboration, partners may fail to identify what to learn, fail to define tasks clearly, and fail to communicate. Suspicions and misunderstandings will become entrenched and cooperation will languish. Bridging gaps early is key to alliance evolution and adjustment.

2. *When learning does take place, it may be misguided or incomplete.* Alza and Ciba-Geigy stumbled with OROS by not tackling the interface, where improvement could have made a difference. Instead, they blamed either the technology of the innovator (Alza) or the organization of the developer/marketer (Ciba-Geigy). It is interesting to observe here that somehow the interface was not part of the explicit scope of attention shared by the partners; neither paid much attention to it. Instead, they suffered from a confirmatory bias: some at Ciba-Geigy, in particular among those who

had worked on ADDS prior to the agreement with Alza, vindicated their doubts about the Alza technologies and acted out their "not invented here" syndrome by quickly downgrading OROS's potential. Rather than learn that they were mismanaging the relationship, they "learned" about their partner's shortcomings. Some at Alza vindicated their fear about Ciba-Geigy's bureaucratic, hierarchical, and political character by assigning failure to those traits. In other words, people were learning selectively whatever suited their earlier prejudices. As managers became more aware of what had to be done, they felt less and less capable of doing it.

3. *Alliances can fail when partners are unhappy with what they learn.* To some extent the Alza–Ciba-Geigy alliance fell victim to what each partner learned about the other and their relationship. What managers on both sides learned caused them to doubt the longer-term value of the relationship, the standards of equity, and the adaptability of the partner organization to the alliance requirements. Rather than use their learning to make adjustments, both partners simply "gave up."

The GE–SNECMA alliance presents an instructive contrast to Alza–Ciba-Geigy and its set of lessons. Without revisiting all the details of the case, we can recall that all elements of context, content, and process—the initial conditions—were much more favorable to learning. The engine-making partners saw the strategic context of the alliance in the same way, they shared a common ambition, and they jointly sought the right organizational context for their civilian activities. Their skill and experience bases, as well as the nature of the task, made interdependent development work possible.

The gaps between partners did not block joint learning. That learning, in turn, led each partner to see the positive aspects of the alliance, its potential, and how it could be improved through periodic adjustments.

The collaboration process of the two engine makers also went through a series of constructive phases, initial commitments being deepened and widened over time. This evolution illustrates some more general points:

1. *Do not create conflicts of interest for the involved managers.* In the GE–SNECMA alliance, managers saw themselves as working both

for the alliance and for their own firm without conflicts, whereas Ciba-Geigy's delegates at Alza were both investors in Alza and business partners at Ciba-Geigy.

2. *Do not hold the partner at arm's length.* It is impossible to learn from a partner kept at a distance.

3. *Make commitments to the interface.* Explicit attention, managerial time, and adjustment efforts are needed.

Into, Around, and Out of Death Valley

Learning is seldom easy. Even successful learners may go through a period of crisis—"Death Valley," as we call it. Since pain comes before gain, those involved in day-to-day alliance activities during this period may lose sight of long-term benefits and focus myopically on their difficulties. Indeed, most of the alliances we have observed entered a crisis as the initial learning cycle came to a conclusion—usually two to three years into the alliance.

What triggers the crisis is a negative evaluation of the alliance. That negative evaluation is often rooted in an incomplete learning cycle: partners discover all the difficulties in their alliance before they see the benefits, and they give way to discouragement prematurely. In some cases a negative evaluation is justified, but in many others the failure to bridge the gaps described in Chapter 6, to avoid excessive expectations, or to trigger healthy learning is to blame rather than a genuine lack of value creation potential.

When a healthy learning process is absent, partners cannot discuss the difficulties of cooperation. Early warning signals of this problem include decreased communication and socialization between the partners,[1] dissatisfaction and frustration on the part of those involved, and persistent unresolved issues. These signals turn into acute symptoms as the situation worsens, as listed in Table 7-1. Typically, members of the partner organizations start to blame difficulties on cultural differences, *national* cultural differences in particular. This form of blame has psychological utility. When the French start to blame the Swedes because they are Swedes, for example, they are assigning blame to something they have no ability to

TABLE 7-1 *Signs and Symptoms of a Poor Learning Situation*

EARLY WARNING SIGNS	SERIOUS SYMPTOMS
• Growing frustrations	• Cultural scapegoats
• Decreasing communications	• Breakdown of communication
• Declining personal satisfaction	• Resignations
• Persistent unresolved issues	• Enduring open conflicts
• Lack of socialization	• Segregation
• Personnel turnover	• Requests for transfers back to parent partner organization

change. Making culture the culprit exonerates all involved from responsibility for the alliance's failure.

When the blame game reaches this low ebb, watch for the Death Valley vultures to start circling. Few alliances survive this condition without a major relationship transformation.

The best way to survive Death Valley is to avoid it entirely. Earlier discussion of the importance of starting off on the right foot is pertinent here. Managers should:

1. *Bridge the gaps.* Bridging the context, content, and process gaps that separate partners *early on* is obviously helpful, since these gaps are the major barriers to learning.

2. *Monitor the process of collaboration, not just the results.* Managers should focus on the quality of the interaction process. It is the process, after all, that produces the results.

3. *Be realistic in your expectations.* Some unrealistic expectations are unavoidable in the beginning. A completely realistic view at the beginning would dampen the enthusiasm required to get the alliance into play. Here, jointly mapping the alliance growth path can be helpful. This activity allows a conditional sequence of benefits and commitments to be drawn, with the early benefits defined modestly. A series of scenarios with a gradation of expected benefits may also help temper excessive optimism.

If an alliance cannot bypass Death Valley, it should be prepared to cross it. This is easier when the alliance is set up as a separate business. Here the alliance managers can forge a common and unique identity, separate from the parents, and affirm a shared desire for autonomy and respon-sibility. Being alone in the wagon together, they recognize the relation-ship between effective collaboration and their own survival.

When the alliance is not set up as a separate entity, or when that entity is simply a coordination body (as in the case of GE and SNECMA), this approach is not feasible. In these situations, we have observed that only a deep transformation of the alliance will get it out of trouble, and even then only when the situation has not dete-riorated too badly.

Transformation has a greater chance of success when participants do two things well: (1) shift from organizational to interpersonal role relationships and (2) build bridges at different levels.

Transformation requires a shift from organizational role relation-ships to interpersonal ones, from playing as members of a partner firm "by the book" to playing together, as members of the alliance, for its success. Organizational role relationships between allies have certain benefits for individual participants early in the cooperation process: they provide both personal safety and predictability of behavior. Individuals can avoid personal exposure by behaving according to the prescribed norms of their own organizations. At the same time, members of one partner organization use these norms to predict the behavior of those employed by the other partner(s). "Because Steven works for XYZ Corporation, we can predict how he will behave in our joint task." Useful as this appearance of pre-dictability may be, however, organizationally defined norms of behavior eventually get in the way of successful cooperation when the partner organizations are distant in terms of how they function and when gaps between partners are not bridged.

Organizationally prescribed roles are helpful early in the relation-ship. They help to reduce some of the uncertainty, ambiguity, and fear people associate with alliance interactions. They can become straitjackets later, however, when learning indicates that people must change their behavior to make cooperation more effective.[2] In these cases, personnel at the interface must be able to break the rules of their own organizations. If they cannot, collaboration will stall. They must be able to look at their behavior objectively and consider how to change it for the good of the alliance. Obviously, this requires a joint commitment to value creation and trust in the judg-ment of individual employees.

The Alza–Ciba-Geigy case provides a striking contrast in organizational and individual behaviors. While people involved in OROS mostly played "by the book," their colleagues working on TTS were able to put their organizational roles on the shelf and do what was right for the project. For example, Ciba-Geigy scientists involved in TTS bypassed some of their company's usual drug development procedures to move the process more rapidly. Two things encouraged this flexibility: commitment to TTS by Ciba-Geigy, and the personally secure positions of its TTS personnel. Among the "doers" who made TTS move forward at Ciba-Geigy were a well-respected scientist with a strong social role in Basel, a well-regarded manager who was close to retirement, and a young research scientist who shared Alza's dreams for ADDS.

We have seen alliances become stranded in Death Valley because of communication failures and loss of perspective at both operational and top management levels. In these cases, operational managers immersed in day-to-day problems lost sight of the benefits of the alliance and let their own frustrations overwhelm them. They forgot that pain comes before gain. Some asked for transfers to nonalliance operations. Others advocated an end to the partnership.

Top managers have their own ways of dealing with the knotty problems of alliances. Being far above the day-to-day conflicts, and often unaware of them, top managers' expectations remain pegged to the rosy expectations of initial negotiations. When they discover the magnitude of the problems going on in the trenches, these top managers are tempted to "pull the plug," in particular if they rely on disheartened operational managers for their information.

The antidote for these behaviors is a set of communication bridges between levels and between partners. Robust alliances exhibit both strong vertical communication patterns within each partner organization and strong multilevel communication linkages between partners, as depicted in Figure 7-3.

While good communication is no guarantee of success, it does limit the risk that partner expectations will suddenly collapse. Just as mapping an alliance growth path is a way to contain expectations inflation, strong communication is a damper on excessive deflation of expectations. Partners should not wait until they are bogged down in Death Valley to begin communicating intensely. Communications must be established early, as the initial difficulties tend to reduce rather than

FIGURE 7-3 *Communication Patterns and Alliance Strength*

Weak Alliances

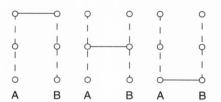

A   B   A   B   A   B

Strong Alliances

A   B

- Weak vertical communications in each partner organization (A + B)
- Strong linkage between partners at one level only

- Strong intrapartner vertical communications
- Strong interpartner horizontal communications at multiple levels

increase interpartner communication as middle managers shy away from close interactions and revert to type. Interpartner communication may also suffer in risk-averse cultures, where middle managers are tempted to try to find solutions by themselves.

Learning Cycles

In successful alliances, contrary to those which end in Death Valley, a series of learning cycles take place over time. These are shown in Figure 7-4. In the first cycle, the initial gaps are bridged successfully through the types of actions outlined in the previous chapter (in Table 6-4). These result in a clear understanding of value potential, a realistic set of expectations, trust built through early interactions, and willingness on the part of members of the partner organizations to go beyond organizationally prescribed roles.

During the first cycle of learning the partners also find that the learning process yields insights into how their interaction can be made more effective. They then improve on initial conditions, demonstrating their adaptability to each other and making the alliance more efficient. A positive assessment of all three dimensions—equity, adaptability, and efficiency—encourages the partners to begin making irreversible commitments and to increase their expec-

FIGURE 7-4 *Learning Cycles in Successful Alliances*

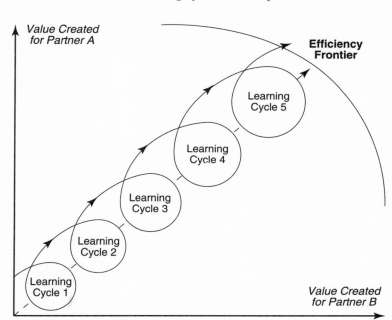

tations, as sketched in Figure 7-5. They are now willing to map the alliance growth path and engage in the race together. This is the point at which the alliance becomes real.

As the relationship demonstrably improves in efficiency over time, the partners are willing to make additional commitments that improve the efficiency of the relationship further. The relationship evolves into a positive spiral with widening and deepening commitments and scope.

For the successful alliance, one learning cycle leads to another, as shown in Figure 7-4. Each cycle results in a higher level of learning, reevaluation and readjustment, and higher expectations of value creation on the part of all partners. Theoretically, the final cycle reaches an "efficiency frontier," beyond which greater cospecialized commitment, learning, evaluation, and adjustment will produce no greater value.

In reality, even the best alliances can only approximate this level of efficiency. However, the more successful their experience of

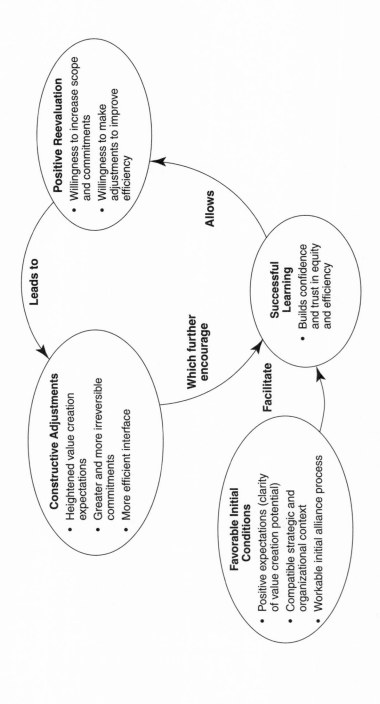

FIGURE 7-5 *A Typical Successful Learning Cycle*

Positive Reevaluation
- Willingness to increase scope and commitments
- Willingness to make adjustments to improve efficiency

Leads to

Constructive Adjustments
- Heightened value creation expectations
- Greater and more irreversible commitments
- More efficient interface

Which further encourage

Allows

Successful Learning
- Builds confidence and trust in equity and efficiency

Facilitate

Favorable Initial Conditions
- Positive expectations (clarity of value creation potential)
- Compatible strategic and organizational context
- Workable initial alliance process

working together, the greater the confidence that partners will have that continued effort will bring them closer to the efficiency frontier—that is, that continued effort will create greater value.

Summary

In this chapter, we have shown that the success of most alliances is contingent not only on the strength of their value creation logic and on the integrity of their design, but also on the effectiveness of each partner's learning about the others and of their joint learning about the environment, the task, and the cooperation processes of the alliance. While minimizing interpartner gaps, as recommended in Chapter 6, allows cooperation to start, what stimulates it to gain momentum is the partners' successful avoidance or overcoming of the "Death Valley" syndrome and completion of the first learning cycles in the evolution of the alliance.

The process of development can be likened to that of a mountain climbing team in which each climber learns to trust his equipment and teammates as they traverse and enjoy success traversing terrain at greater and greater levels of difficulty. As they progress together, the partners in the alliance keep watch on the equity of the partnership: Is each partner carrying its share of the load? Is the balance of commitments and benefits, actual and expected, appropriate for each?

Chapter 8 turns to a more thorough discussion of the issues surrounding the evolution of balance and perceived equity in alliances.

8

❖

MANAGING THE BALANCE OF POWER AND DEPENDENCE

A
S PARTNERS LEARN how to collaborate more effectively, and as their expectations of value creation increase apace, the issue of balance in the sharing of benefits becomes more important. Value capture isn't high on the agenda when allies are slogging through Death Valley and the rewards of successful collaboration are far beyond the horizon. But once those rewards come clearly into view, each starts thinking about getting a fair share.

Naturally, no two partners define "fair share" in the same way and, to some extent, there is competition for who will extract the most value relative to contributions. Even in alliances that benefit from very high complementarity and cospecialization, the issue of fairness in value capture is a bone of contention and a source of rivalry. Our purpose in this chapter is to consider how partners can both create and capture value in a way that uses such rivalry constructively.

What determines the ratio of partner benefits to partner contributions? Although the negotiating and bargaining savvy of the partners plays a role, we believe there is a more powerful arbiter of where that ratio settles: over the long run the ratio nearly always tips in favor of the partner who makes the most indispensable contributions.

In the hypothetical case of perfect cospecialization, the contribution of each partner is equally indispensable and the issue of relative influence fades. In the more usual case, where cospecialization is less than perfect, the partner that makes the most indispensable contributions quite logically gains the most influence and is in the best position to claim the larger share of the value created in the alliance. So long as the other partners still gain from the alliance relative to the alternatives available to them, they are likely to continue the relationship, despite one partner getting greater benefits.

In the competition for benefits, rivalry takes this form: each firm tries to (1) make itself indispensable, while (2) making its partner less indispensable. The relative emphasis on (1) versus (2) depends partly on whether a partner sees itself as potentially regaining full independence in the future. If future independence is a desired state, the firm will not so much emphasize its own uniqueness as it will seek to diminish its partner's uniqueness. If the partner's contributions are not unique, then substitutes can be found over time. If independence is *not* a firm's ambition, or a realistic alternative, then it will try to maintain its own uniqueness and hence its bargaining power within the alliance.

The relative uniqueness of partner contributions is not static. At any given point in time, it may appear that certain unique contributions are set and stable, in particular when a partner makes contributions that are not tradable, not easily substituted, and not easily developed alone. These characteristics, however, are not set in concrete. As a competence matures, it becomes accessible from other sources via contracts rather than alliances. Substitutes may appear, creating alternatives to a partner's contributions. And as one partner's own skills grow, dependence on the other's (perhaps no longer) unique skills may diminish. Hence, one can conceive of the balance of influence as ebbing and flowing over time as the relative uniqueness of each partner's contributions changes.

The important strategic question is: How can a partner increase the relative uniqueness of its contributions and, in so doing, increase its influence and share of alliance benefits? The most effective and usually most viable way is to increase the extent and scope of the skills and competencies of one's contribution to the alliance. Whoever provides the alliance with the most unique competencies and skills gains relative influence by making other partners more dependent. The importance of increasing one's skill and contribution has, in fact, set off a *race to learn* in many of the dynamic alliances we have observed.

This chapter begins with a review of what makes contributions most valuable in the three main value creation logics we developed in Chapter 3: co-option, cospecialization, and learning/internalization. Here we present analysis of how skill uniqueness affects bargaining power in all three value creation logics. We then review three major determinants of the ability of a partner to learn in an alliance and address the management implications of the learning and competence internalization processes.

How Contributions Yield Bargaining Power

Firms with unique capabilities are the most attractive alliance partners: the more unique and distinctive the potential contribution, the higher the value creation potential of an alliance. By *capabilities* we mean hard-to-imitate bundles of skills that a firm develops over time and that are intertwined with the way it works, with its organization, and with its business processes and culture. Paradoxically, although these capabilities are extremely valuable, they are typically hard to trade or even leverage except through an alliance in which the partners work closely together.

What constitutes a highly valued and unique contribution varies with the value creation logic of the alliance. For example, what is valued in a co-option alliance may not be the kind of capability most valued in a cospecialization alliance. In the former, the position of a company may well be more valuable than its capabilities. Therefore, we analyze the uniqueness of partner contributions, and their value as bargaining chips, in terms of the three logics of value creation: co-option, cospecialization, and learning/internalization.

CO-OPTION PARTNERS

Co-option partners need to be strong and/or numerous to build a winning coalition. JVC was quick to enlist the support of RCA, Thomson, Thorn, Telefunken, and others in its bid to establish the VHS standard. Likewise, Toshiba quickly grasped the importance of entertainment and computer industry support for the success of its digital video disk. The size of the partners, in market share terms, is a clear priority in standard-setting alliances, as the share of market the coalition can claim, at least for de facto standards, is key. Thus distribution power or access to a key strategic asset such as a library of movies is much desired.

Beyond size, differentiating capabilities and unique strategic assets also make co-option partners attractive. It is not simply Microsoft's size that makes it an attractive partner; its ability to differentiate and control the PC user interface through its Windows product, a unique proprietary operating system it licenses to others, gives it tremendous bargaining power in any collaboration.

Constant innovation is needed to sustain a position like the one Microsoft now enjoys. This requirement was painfully discovered by video game makers Sega and Nintendo, who saw their leadership diminished by video game newcomers such as Sony and by the increasing availability of personal computers. When the pace of innovation slowed at Sega and Nintendo and at their game development partners, Sony jumped in with a system exploiting the latest available technologies to carry innovative games.

Companies that have few strategic assets that yield differentiating power, such as IBM in PCs, and companies with little ability to build them, such as most European computer makers, are not sought-after partners. IBM still plays a key role in the PC industry because of its brand and distribution strength, but so do rivals like Compaq and Hewlett-Packard and a handful of others.

Differentiation is a valued contribution in co-option alliances when partners maximize their differentiating powers in ways that are useful to others, such as when one partner uses its lobbying power to create value for its alliance partners. Not all strategic assets are equally valuable over time. For instance, a partner that wins a one-time regulatory ruling in favor of its coalition may enjoy tremendous power in the alliance during the weeks or months prior to the ruling. Once the ruling is made, however, this partner may find that its value to the coalition has evaporated. A partner who brings differentiating contributions of a more sustainable nature—such as a leading brand—will enjoy a more sustained influence. Nestlé, for instance, brings the strength of its brand and distribution in Europe to General Mills in its breakfast cereals alliance, allowing General Mills to put precious competitive pressure on Kellogg in Europe, where General Mills was traditionally weak.

Cospecialization Partners

Bargaining power in cospecialization alliances stems from asymmetry in contribution uniqueness. Asymmetry creates unbalanced dependence among partners; if you make the most unique contribution, your partners need you more than you need them. As cospecialization grows, the dependent partners find it increasingly costly and difficult to terminate or exit the alliance even though conditions in the alliance are increasingly unfavorable to them. They are left with a choice between ineffectiveness on their own and lack of balance, or stature, in the alliance.

To maximize bargaining power in the alliance, the goal is to get the partner to make commitments that are less unique than yours but more specific to the relationship than yours.[1] This has several consequences. First, the partner bears more of the risks. Second, exit becomes more costly to the partner; by making commitments that are very specific to the relationship, the partner is locked in and becomes vulnerable to renegotiation and/or exit threats. The partner has more at stake in the continuation of the relationship. Third, by having your partners make the more specific commitments, you will be better able to pursue multiple opportunities and options more flexibly, since your commitments to the alliance will be less irreversible than your partner's. The trick here, as we will discuss more fully in Chapter 9, is to develop and use core competencies as well as other assets that can be deployed and leveraged across a whole range of businesses and partnerships and to have partners devote specialized resources exclusively to the alliance.

Contributing a narrowly focused but widely usable competence, such as wing aerodynamics for British Aerospace, provides the most "bang for the buck" in alliances. Bringing the "missing piece of the puzzle" yields the most value, in the form of partner dependence, from the smallest contribution—and even more so when that same piece can be used to create multiple puzzles.

The issue here is not to take asymmetric cospecialization as a stable given, which defines the relative uniqueness of contributions once and for all, but to see cospecialization asymmetry itself as a stake in a cooperation process that can be changed in one's favor over time. Starting positions may define an initial cospecialization pattern, but this pattern may not endure as partners strive to change it by making their own contributions more unique and less specialized or those of their partners less unique and more specialized.

Some of the changes in cospecialization may be caused by forces outside the alliance and outside the control of its members. For instance, when Eurocopter, the alliance between Aérospatiale and Daimler-Benz, was created, the initial balance of contributions and benefits and the respective roles granted to each partner reflected the anticipated balance of orders by the French and German armed forces.[2] Following German reunification in 1989 and the collapse of the Soviet Union in 1991, German orders plummeted, decreasing German influence on the alliance and creating tension between the initial design and the new, de facto balance. By 1995, French military orders also began to look shaky, reestablishing a balance of sorts. Cospecialization changes in this alliance also resulted from decisions of the partners themselves, and tensions rose as each partner sought to retain control over the same critical technologies, such as composite structures. The alliance suffered from the tension between the search for cospecialization and the desire of its partners for internalization, or at least protection, of the most critical technologies. Although the alliance was a merger of sorts at the operating level, each national entity—French and German—maintained its identity and used its domestic government as a source of bargaining power. For example, although its economics were hard to justify, Eurocopter Germany, at its government's insistence, kept its own flight-testing capacities.

Cospecialization assumes, almost by definition, some skills differentiation between partners. The key issue, though, is the degree to which each partner's contribution is indispensable to the alliance.

The tensions that surrounded task allocations within Airbus provide a tangible example of how partners sense their vulnerabilities and lobby to build protected cospecialized positions. We mentioned in an earlier chapter that DASA insisted on carrying out final assembly of certain Airbus types in Germany, even though this insistence was undermining the alliance. Why was DASA so determined to do this? Was it simply national pride? (When dignitaries visit an aerospace plant they want to see planes being built, not parts.) A more likely answer is that final assembly was one of the least likely tasks to be relocated or outsourced, whereas parts manufacturing or even "segment" assembly could easily be moved in

response to cost pressures or offset requirements by major customers. In other words, the absence of final assembly in Germany
would put DASA in an unfavorable cospecialization position; its
contribution could easily be outsourced, subcontracted, or substituted. Conceivably, most Airbus parts could be made in East Asia,
but a major final assembly site there would be politically unthink-
able, except to serve local markets.

While every alliance partner must look to its own interests, the
success and viability of the alliance requires that the balance of benefits and contributions is seen as relatively fair, especially as partners
are asked to increase their stakes in the alliance and make increasingly irreversible commitments. In other words, cospecialization
aimed at creating mutual dependence, that is, roughly equal dependence and benefits on all sides, is essential. The straight, diagonal
line in Figure 8-1 depicts the ideal condition.

This ideal does not necessarily prevail in practice, however. We
have observed situations in which the trade-offs are heavily skewed

---

FIGURE 8-1 *Effects of Balanced and Unbalanced Dependence on Value Creation*

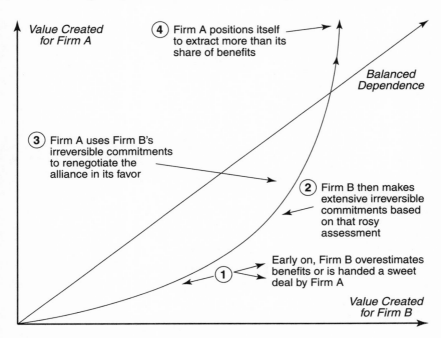

through accident (where external conditions alter the balance between partners in unforeseeable ways), through misunderstanding (when the yardsticks used to measure benefits are faulty), or through manipulation (when one partner uses a deal "sweetener" to lure another into a one-sided, irreversible commitment). The result generally follows the four stages shown in Figure 8-1. In stage 1, Firm A offers Firm B a deal sweetener to induce it to commit to the alliance. Initially, the deal gives B the larger share of the value created by the alliance. Encouraged by its prospects, B makes extensive and irreversible commitments (stage 2). Shortly thereafter (stage 3), Firm A uses its independence to renegotiate the terms of the alliance in its own favor, which begins to pay off in stage 4 and continues thereafter.

Obviously, this unbalanced situation cannot endure for long if good-willed cooperation is to continue. A dependent partner deprived of other options is unlikely to make a willing cooperator. Balance in the timing and in the emerging pattern of cospecialization is thus essential to maintain a workable alliance. Mutual forbearance, though sometimes required, is not a precondition for balance: two equally self-interested partners may each pull equally strongly for their own advantage but keep the alliance moving (close to the diagonal in Figure 8-1) and hold each other in check.

Learning/Internalization Partners

Internalization of new skills is the raison d'être of the learning alliance. Typically, one partner sees the skills to be learned as the cornerstone of a strategy for leveraging those skills across multiple business and/or product lines. J2T is a good example of this type of alliance. Whereas JVC sought international partners in its standards battle with Sony, Thomson—its most ambitious European partner—wanted to master micromechanical skills that could be used in a number of products worldwide. While JVC viewed J2T as a co-option alliance, Thomson viewed it as an internalization alliance.

Desirable partners for skills internalization are not necessarily industry leaders, as in co-option alliances, or the firms most likely to continually renew the skills they bring to the alliance. Desirable partners are those which are willing to exchange skills for other advantages, such as market access, or which are simply unlikely to be diligent in protecting their skills. They are likely to be challengers or to be laggards that still have some critical skills to contribute but that lack the competitive strength to exploit them on their own.

Partners in learning alliances have several important decisions to make:

1. What to internalize *from* the alliance. Although it is conceivable that one would want to learn from the partner just to tip the alliance in one's favor, the effort involved seldom makes this worthwhile, unless the partner contributes the "missing piece" of the puzzle. An internalization motivation is usually driven by the desire to leverage acquired skills.

2. What to develop independently and contribute *to* the alliance—both to allow the alliance to create more value and to gain bargaining power; in other words, what contributions to reserve for oneself.

3. What to rely on the partner for, that is, where to accept a dependence-creating pattern of cospecialization.

The risks of interpartner tension in learning alliances probably make partners at both extremes of the competitive spectrum most valuable for the company that seeks to learn. Undisputed leaders may not be concerned with others learning from them. They believe their leadership to be so unassailable that learning by weaker companies is no threat. Boeing's managers, for instance, appeared rather unconcerned with JADC's learning efforts and brushed off their results, arguing that many hurdles remained to be crossed before JADC could even dream of competing against Boeing. At the other end of the spectrum, hapless laggards may be all too ready to trade whatever skills they still have for cash. Laggards are usually willing to let the partner substitute for what they can no longer afford to do. They may well see an alliance in which they let their partner learn as a way to exit the alliance domain profitably and gracefully. Two ambitious newcomers, each eager to learn, seldom make good bedfellows. This is a reason that Korean and Japanese companies have often had problems in partnering.

Learning through Alliances

We discussed at great length in Chapter 7 how partners need to learn to work together to make cospecialization effective. Here, given the key role of contribution uniqueness, we focus on the narrower agenda of how a company can learn specific competencies and capabilities from its partner(s) through the alliance.

THE INTENT TO LEARN

Learning and internalization in a strategic alliance begin with a clear intent to learn; this intention drives the learning process. In alliances where one partner learns substantially more than the other, we have observed that the intentions of the partners have been substantially different. The partner with an internalization intent viewed collaboration as a low-cost route to acquiring critical skills. The other partner saw the same alliance as a low-cost alternative to acquiring or maintaining skills. For instance, some fear that American companies in U.S.–Japanese alliances have used these alliances to substitute their partners' competitiveness for their lack of competitiveness and, in so doing, have lost critical skills. The concern is not that the Japanese firms are using alliances to catch up, but that U.S. companies are using alliances to escape the relentless pressure for continuous improvement in core skills. Obviously, the skills of the U.S. companies would erode over time while those of the Japanese partners would move forward. Clearly, over many years the relationship between Honeywell and NEC in computers followed that pattern, with Honeywell putting its priorities elsewhere and letting itself lose ground to NEC.

Many also fear that these alliances induced Western firms to forgo investments in important areas. In supplying power trains to Ford, video recorders to RCA, aircraft wings to Boeing, computers to Siemens, and camcorders to Philips, the objective of Japanese partners may have been to induce Western firms to disinvest from these critical value-creating activities. Whether or not Japanese partners actually intended these consequences, asymmetries in intent may have produced, de facto, the same outcome: skills erosion on one side and skills enhancement on the other.

Once they are lost, critical skills are difficult to rebuild. U.S. consumer electronics companies that outsourced heavily to their Japanese suppliers have made this painful discovery. They now find it difficult to rebuild the competencies needed to develop and produce the next wave of household electronics: high-definition television products.

Competencies are complex bundles of constituent technologies. They are not built through sudden leaps of inventiveness but through patient and relentless innovation. Once these efforts are abandoned, it is extraordinarily difficult to jump back into the race with the fast leaders. Thus, where there is no intent to learn, substitution is possible, if not probable. Learning happens more by design than by default; substitution more by default than by design. When skills that erode through substitution are critical to continued participation in a business, substitution is a form of surrender.

It would be wrong to imply that every partner that lacks a strong learning intent is hopelessly myopic. An alliance may have no other purpose than to provide a graceful exit from an unattractive business. It may be that the areas in which the firm substitutes its partner's skills are not critical to long-term success in its business. The fact that, in entering an alliance, a firm makes a positive decision not to carry on with some activities does not automatically lead to decline; the firm may simply be redirecting its energies and capital into areas of far greater opportunity. Investment avoidance, in one form or another, is a motivation common to most alliance partners.[3] However, where there is substitution and no learning intent, the competitive balance between partners can be maintained only if the funds conserved through collaboration are invested in skill areas where the firm is able to outpace its partner and other competitors.

Learning Intent in the Trenches

The people at the top may identify learning as their strategic intent in the alliance. But to turn intentions into reality, they must make sure that (1) their strategic intent to learn and internalize new skills or knowledge is shared by those actually involved in the process of collaborative exchange and that (2) those directly and indirectly involved in the process of collaborative exchange are capable of protecting key skills from migrating to partners on one hand and fully exploiting opportunities to learn from those same partners on the other.

The interface where people, facilities, documentation, and knowledge move between alliance partners is usually only partially governed by the formal collaborative agreement. Just as the Ten Commandments do not provide detailed guidance on life's small ethical conundra, a collaborative agreement is only an imperfect arbiter of the day-by-day, week-by-week trades that take place between parties. What adjudicates most interactions are *microbargains* struck by employees on the different sides of an alliance. These bargains may not be so crude as "I'll show you this if you'll show me that," but bargaining in some form governs much of the exchange between partners. The cumulative impact of these microbargains to a large extent determines in whose favor future microbargains will be resolved.

Winning at the level of microbargains often means outlearning one's partner. A firm can "lose" at higher levels of bargaining, but it can outpace the learning of its partner in the end by striking a series of advantageous microbargains at the operational level, winning one little battle over accessibility and information sharing at a time. A clear learning intent, well communicated to all, puts pressure on frontline employees to "win" these microbargains.

For learning to take place, those who are most intimately involved in the process of collaborative exchange must share the internalization intent established by senior management. There must be a common definition of success up and down the organization. The bulk of learning will take place at the operational level, where the bulk of the firm's distinctive skills reside, where joint tasks are carried out and value created, and where contact between the partners is likely to be most intensive.

LEARNING PROCESSES

In all the alliances we observed in which competence learning took place, it did so through several key processes:

1. *Senior management communicated and reiterated the learning intent.* It communicated to everyone who interacted directly with the partner, both at the outset of cooperation and over time.

2. *Learning was disaggregated into a sequence of steps, arrayed in some logical order of growing complexity.* Table 8-1 summarizes Thomson's learning agenda in its VCR alliance with JVC. Its learning steps were sequenced into a calendar as a way to measure competence development over time.

3. *The interface was designed with learning in mind.* The alliance interface was structured to provide both a "window" on the skills underlying the required competencies and an opportunity to coprac-

Table 8-1 Thomson's Step-by-Step Agenda for Learning

1. Capability to assemble JVC-supplied subassemblies using JVC-supplied equipment and process controls.

2. Capability for autonomous improvements in assembly efficiency through improvements to JVC-specific assembly line layout and procedures.

3. Capability to specify and bring onstream European process equipment to supplant that supplied or specified by JVC.

4. Capability to develop advanced product features independently from JVC.

5. Capability for separate manufacture and assembly of precision components.

6. Capability for design and manufacture of a VCR independent of JVC.

7. Capability for simultaneous and closely coupled advances in both product design and product manufacturing processes, independent of J2T.

8. Design and manufacturing capability for next-generation product (for instance, handheld mini video camera).

tice these skills. For a while prior to Fujitsu's acquisition of ICL, the British computer maker wished it had been a bit less forthcoming in sharing its knowledge of the retailing computer market segment with its partner.

Transparency and Receptivity

The process of collaborative exchange is governed not only by intent but by the transparency and receptivity of each partner. *Transparency* refers to the learning opportunity that each partner affords the other, either intentionally or inadvertently. *Receptivity* refers to the capacity of each partner to absorb the other's know-how.

It is reasonable to expect that the degree of effort expended in limiting transparency and enhancing receptivity will be influenced by the strength of top management's intent. If senior management does not possess a strong learning intent—or fails to articulate it to employees—it is unlikely that employees involved in the alliance will see the partnership as a series of microbargains in which the goal is to learn more than their partner.

Understanding how transparency and receptivity influence learning outcomes requires a shift in perspective from top management's agenda to the operational interface.

The Learning Opportunity

A firm's intent determines the strength of its desire to learn from partners. But the desire to learn must be matched by opportunities to do so—by the ability to gain access to the skills of the partner. Transparency defines the opportunities available to internalize key skills. So while intent establishes the desire to learn, transparency determines the potential for learning.

There is always tension between providing learning opportunities for one's partner while protecting the core skills that provide bargaining power in the relationship. A firm must share enough information to make value creation possible, but it must also protect its bargaining power and competitive advantage by avoiding the wholesale transfer of key skills. Firms that manage their transparency well walk a fine line between openness and opaqueness.

Transparency and the Collaborative Agreement

As much as firms would like to "manage their transparency" through formal collaborative agreements, they should recognize that the migration of skills between partners will not always go according to plan. Skill transfer occurs both within the terms of the agreement and outside its terms. Transfers that take place outside the formal agreement, or in more depth than anticipated, are likely to be unintentional and may go unrecognized. It is these unintended and unsanctioned skill transfers that alter the balance of power and dependency in an alliance.

Executives new to the alliance game sometimes believe that the problems of unintended and unsanctioned skill transfers can be handled with the stroke of a pen—that is, by simply being more specific in the terms of the collaborative agreement. Experience shows this to be wishful thinking. However far-reaching and tightly written the agreement, the potential for unintended skills transfer remains, and for several reasons. If the restrictions placed on interorganizational contact are too onerous, joint tasks are impossible to carry out. Joint development and manufacturing projects (NUMMI, for instance) require intensive cross-organizational communication. If both partners are obsessed with the risk of unauthorized skill transfers, too much effort will go into protecting key skills and too little into creating value. A certain degree of skill "leakage" must be anticipated. It cannot be recognized in formal agreements.

So how should a firm approach the collaborative agreement? Should it seek a moderately tight agreement or one that is fairly open? The answer should be dictated by the firm's confidence in its learning abilities. If it believes that it can outlearn its partner, it has an incentive not to make transparency a central bargaining issue. Better to seek an open agreement that gives substantial scope for access to partner skills, then work to outlearn one's partner. The observed preference of Japanese partners for relatively ambiguous, open-ended agreements, for example, may reflect not only a cultural response to the problem of the future's indeterminateness but also the confidence these firms have in their ability to protect their key skills while quickly absorbing those of their Western partners.

Where the terms of the collaborative agreement are ambiguous, there is little to interfere with the opportunism of the more capable learner. On the other hand, the firm that has little confidence in its ability to learn but nevertheless recognizes the implications of asymmetric learning will most likely seek an agreement that limits its own transparency to the greatest possible extent. Limiting transparency, however, requires effort and may entail efficiency costs as joint tasks may be performed less well when access is denied and when employees of each parent adopt adversarial roles.

ESTIMATING THE VALUE OF SKILLS

The effort that goes into limiting transparency in a particular area must reflect a point of view about the partner's ultimate ambitions and its capacity for learning. It should also consider the value the partner would derive from learning those skills and the competitive consequences that would ensue from a leveling of relative capability.

The problem of uncovering a partner's real competitive goals has been noted earlier, but valuing the strategic importance of a set of skills to a partner is no less problematic. This is because the value of any particular skill to a partner will depend on what other complementary skills the partner possesses. The careless transfer to a partner of the "missing link" in that firm's skill set will lead to a more serious competitive consequence than transferring the same skill to a partner that has few of the other skills needed to prevail in future competitive contests, as Boeing reassured itself about JADC. It may also be difficult to judge the costs the partner would incur in building the capability independently.

Deciding how much effort to put into limiting transparency also requires an understanding of a partner's other options for skills acquisition (internal development, other partners, and so forth).

Placing a value on skills transferred is particularly difficult if the investment in building those skills has spanned several decades. There may be no easy way of calculating the total investment and effort that goes into building the skills. It may be difficult even to identify critical skills as such if over time they have simply become "the way we do things around here." Examples of such taken-for-granted knowledge include RCA's knowledge of distribution and merchandising practices in the U.S. consumer electronics market, Philips's understanding of the politics of European telecommunications procurement, and the practice of project management at Boeing.

To the extent that knowledge of the cost and effort invested in building capabilities is lost in time, a firm may underestimate the value a partner gains by avoiding, through learning, the need to reinvent the wheel. For example, Boeing has been careful to place some key technologies off-limits to its Japanese partners, but it has found it necessary for project management purposes to indoctrinate these same partners in the "Boeing Way."[4] One can only speculate as to how much Boeing's basic values and disciplines might be worth to its partners. In short, which skills get protected will depend on the firm's estimate of the strategic importance of those skills, both to itself and to its partner.[5]

PASSIVE METHODS FOR LIMITING TRANSPARENCY

What are the methods for managing transparency? At the broadest level, a distinction can be made between passive and active methods for limiting transparency. Passive methods rely on the inherent "unknowability" of certain skills. Some organizations are inherently less penetrable than others. Their skills and knowledge are highly contextual, that is, embedded in their social systems. In general, knowledge in East Asian cultures is more contextual than in Western cultures. Form and content, ritual and substance are not easily separated. Context-dependent knowledge (such as the principles of industrial relations in Japan) is inherently less transparent than context-free knowledge (such as the principles of the transistor). To open the door to context-dependent knowledge, the would-be learner must first understand the social system and cultural milieu in which it resides.

Another factor influencing the penetrability of an organization is the degree to which its members make a distinction between insiders and outsiders. Where there is a strong and unique process of socialization coupled with a high degree of goal congruence, a sense of clan prevails.[6] Where "clannishness" is high, opportunities for access are limited. The clan employee involved in a partnership identifies with the parent, not with the alliance or with the individuals with whom he or she works on a daily basis. When conflict arises, the clan member seeks solutions consistent with the parent's goals. In the case of Japanese firms, this tendency is reinforced by the parent-child quality of the relationship between sponsoring firm and joint venture; this relationship exists sometimes in law and almost always in attitude.[7]

If the problem of managing transparency falls largely on the shoulders of operatives who interact regularly with the partner's agents, loyalty and goal identification may be critical. Close identification with parent goals makes it more likely that a clan member will recognize which skills need to be protected from encroachment. In resisting a partner's entreaties for greater access and information, clan members suffer no contest of loyalties. When clan members relocate close to the partner and far from the parent, loyalty survives; they are unlikely to "go native."

Yet another factor influencing transparency is the internal complexity of the partner's organization. Outsiders typically have trouble getting to the source of information and knowledge in organizations with these characteristics:

- The allocation of decision-making power cannot be deduced from hierarchical structure.
- Functional roles and responsibilities overlap.
- Critical resources are shared by several units.
- Patterns of internal communication are dense and complex.
- Knowledge resides in groups, not in individuals.

Indeed, in a survey of international joint ventures located in Japan, "communication" was the problem mentioned most often by both expatriate and Japanese managers.[8] However, for expatriate managers, "difficulty in receiving exact information and data" from their Japanese partners ranked a close second, mentioned by 87 percent of U.S. expatriate respondents. The next most noted problems, "reluctance to report failure" and "no open discussion of problems," further reflected the frustration these managers felt in trying to extract information from their Japanese partners. No Japanese manager, on the other hand, mentioned access to information as a major annoyance in dealing with Western partners. From the perspective of those involved in U.S.–Japanese joint ventures, Western partners appear to be more transparent.

Another passive approach to transparency is the inherent capacity of the technology or skill itself to be appropriated. Laws governing patents and trade secrets make it easier to protect some forms of knowledge than others. So, too, does the systemic nature of certain skills. Skills are systemic when individual roles, routines, and data combine to yield results that cannot be achieved by a subset of those elements. An understanding, however deep, of a single subelement will not yield the benefits of the whole. The distinction between a technology and a competence is important here. A discrete, stand-alone technology is, by definition, more transparent, more easily understood and internalized than a competence deeply buried in the social fabric of a firm. Japan's prowess in auto manufacturing represents a competence that is both contextual and systemic. It is not surprising that the report of MIT's International Automobile Program concluded the following:

> *The difficulty with adopting individual Japanese practices is that the various features of an industrial-relations system interact with one another and may not be separable from other features of the total system. For instance, the method of setting pay interacts with the union representation structure (enterprise-based bonuses are supported by the system of enterprise-based unions in Japan) and also the form of worker participation. Even if they choose to, it may not be possible for Western producers and unions to adopt Japanese industrial-relations practices in a piecemeal fashion.*[9]

An attempt to extract a deeply embedded competence is often akin to pulling threads from a rug: the material may be the same but the pattern is lost. In Japan in particular, manufacturing excellence is a complex web of employee training, integration with suppliers, statistical process controls, problem solving in small groups, advanced process technology, value engineering, and design for ease of manufacturing. It is difficult to extract overarching competencies one skill at a time.

ACTIVE METHODS FOR LIMITING TRANSPARENCY

What range of active measures can be employed to limit transparency? Several methods come to mind. The most obvious of these, and one over which both partners have some influence, is the design of the task structure and the collaborative interface. Transparency in these terms is largely determined by the nature of the task at hand. When task complexity is high, as in the alliance between Ford and Mazda, organizational complexity is also likely to be high. This implies a high frequency of interaction between partners on both routine and nonroutine issues.[10] Likewise, where task and organizational complexity produce a multilevel, multifunctional, and multicountry interface, transparency will be higher than it would be in a simpler relationship.

Transparency can also be managed through the selection of individuals for partnership roles. Some individuals have a broader and deeper understanding of core skills than others. Limiting a partner's access to these individuals limits transparency. However, sending second-rate employees to the alliance may also limit opportunities to learn from one's partner. This seems to be the lesson that members of the Microelectronics and Computer Corporation, a U.S. research cooperative that initially faced difficulty drawing good researchers from its members, learned from their early attempts at collaboration.

Partner firms can also influence transparency through their decisions on process integration and output coordination. If extremely limited transparency is desirable, process integration and output coordination can be minimized. A partnership based on output dependence is the ideal form for this. The contributions of each partner occur at different stages of the value-adding process. For example, one partner manufactures the product and the other markets it. The work performed by one partner at one stage is "handed off" to the other partner at the next stage. In such cases it may be possible to partition quite precisely the contributions of each partner and thereby narrow the scope of interaction and potential skill transfer. The opposite occurs in alliances in which contributions require process integration; here, partners collaborate closely in the same value-creating activity (for example, joint product development). Process integration implies substantial interorganizational contact between employees with similar functional responsibilities, often in a common facility. Dialogue and opportunities to learn in these instances are abundant.

Partners can also manage transparency by designating "gatekeepers." Anyone who has been well briefed on which skills can and cannot be shared and who has the authority to deny access to those skills can serve as a gatekeeper. If gatekeepers are used, they should be backed up with a higher-level authority, and for two reasons. First, a gatekeeper at the operating level may know which technologies are off limits but is unlikely to know whether information about competitors and customers is considered confidential. Someone with a broader perspective must be available to handle these questions. Second, if operating employees bear the full responsibility for saying "no" to partner requests, their ability to maintain collegial working relationships with partner employees will be undermined. They need to off-load some of the gatekeeper functions to someone back at headquarters. Then they can honestly tell their collaborators, "Sorry, the decision is out of my hands."

There may be advantages in having a single gatekeeper consider all partner requests for access and information. Channeling a partner's access through a narrow aperture provides an opportunity to manage transparency in a consistent way. By processing all requests for access and by being present at most key meetings with the partner's agents, the gatekeeper can calibrate the breadth and depth of the partner's learning ambitions. By monitoring the many microbargains struck in the course of the partnership, the gatekeeper can ensure that core skills are not unintentionally transferred through small, incremental accommodations to the partner. The gatekeeper can also limit end runs by a partner seeking information from one unit that it had been denied by another. In other words, the gate-keeper can help to ensure that learning microbargains are resolved in favor of his or her own company.

The location of joint activities, another potential design parameter, is also a tool for managing transparency. When an activity is located in close proximity to the partner's facilities, opportunities to learn from that partner are likely to be heightened and one's own transparency lessened.

There is another active mechanism for limiting the unintended migration of core skills: controlling the learning ambitions of partners through fear of jeopardizing the whole relationship. When it was revealed that Israeli intelligence had accepted classified military secrets stolen from its most reliable ally, the United States, many in the Israeli government must have shivered. For a few bits of information, one of its agencies had threatened the country's most important alliance. Fear of dire consequences tempered Israeli interest in further encroachments on classified information (at least one must suspect as much). It had a huge investment in its alliance with the Americans, which it did not want to jeopardize.

Commercial alliances can also be influenced by fear. Partners who make large, irreversible investments in facilities and capabilities can be constrained from overstepping agreements on skill transfer if they know that doing so would undermine the alliance and their investments in it. Managing transparency at this level is obviously the business of senior executives.

Receptivity

Receptivity denotes the capacity of an organization to learn from its partners not just what they do but how they do it and why it works, so what they learn can be predictably repeated and even improved on independent of the relationship with the partner. Gaining such useful knowledge means having answers to two basic questions:

1. *Know-what.* What is the level of performance achieved by the partner? (For instance, a competitive benchmark, such as a lower defect rate.)

2. *Know-how. How* has the partner achieved this level of performance? (For instance, more stringent process controls.)

It is possible for a firm to gain know-what without gaining know-how.

ON BECOMING MORE RECEPTIVE

Firms can actively enhance their own receptivity by a number of means.

Translating learning intent into clear and actionable learning goals. Translating intentions into goals is the first step toward enhancing receptivity. To firmly establish learning as a goal, senior management must make operational employees aware of the competitive side of collaboration. The people most intimately engaged in the alliance must understand the imperative of the race to learn. By establishing learning as a fundamental goal, senior management can both spur and legitimize the efforts of employees to learn from their partners. Specific learning goals will determine the partner knowledge actively sought by operatives.

The extent to which top management is visibly concerned with the process of learning and rewards learning behavior will influence the degree to which its learning goals are pursued in the trenches. Specific steps it can take include:

- a regular review process in which operatives are asked to report what they have learned.
- face-to-face meetings between top management and the firm's alliance team.
- financial and career development rewards linked to learning outcomes.

Avenues of access. Having established clear learning goals and responsibility for competitiveness, it is the actual exposure of the firm vis-à-vis its partner that delimits the boundaries of receptivity. Exposure is an issue of access to people and facilities—who talks to whom on what issues, what degree of access is given to which facilities—and the extent to which the partner's suppliers, distributors, and customers can be interrogated.

To become more receptive, the firm must maximize the number of its potential access routes into its partner—just the opposite of what it would do to limit transparency. One would expect that access reciprocity would always be demanded by all parties to a collaborative agreement, but this is not necessarily case if there is an asymmetry in intent among the partners. Thus it is possible to imagine a situation in which a firm has gained entrée to its partner's skills through several approach routes (at different organizational levels, in different facilities, and across several divisions), while it has limited its partner's access to a single gateway.

The easiest organizations to penetrate:

- are internally fragmented.

- have poorly developed channels of communication.

- are hierarchically stratified.

- are partitioned by business, geography, or function.

These organizations are in a poor position to recognize the extent of a learning-driven partner's inroads or appetite for skill transfer. The voracious learner can seek out the most accessible routes to its partner's core skills without necessarily revealing the full extent of its own ambitions.

The importance of language. Receptivity may also be a function of the language and benchmarking skills of those who operate at the collaborative interface. If one partner is very familiar with the other's language, and the reverse is not true, asymmetry in receptivity is likely. Access to factories and laboratories, for example, is worth little without an ability to interrogate the partner's staff, to read its technical and marketing literature, to understand offhand remarks in joint meetings, and to fully exploit the opportunities social occasions provide for ad hoc discussions. Knowledge encoded in an unfamiliar language is, for practical purposes, inaccessible.

Learning as benchmarking. Learning from a partner requires many of the same skills used in competitive benchmarking: calibrating internal performance against an external standard; using rough estimates to determine where a competitor is better, faster, or cheaper; setting internal targets; and then recalibrating to establish the rate of improvement in a competitor's performance. Receptivity should be higher in companies where the benchmarking discipline is deeply ingrained.

Collaboration with a potential or actual competitor provides substantial opportunities for benchmarking, presenting a firm with the chance to internalize a partner's core skills in toto. Simply acquiring a new or more precise benchmark of a competitor/partner's performance may be of substantial value. A new benchmark might provoke a review of current performance levels and could spur a new round of innovation as the firm seeks to match its partner's performance level. Benchmarking a partner may help a firm answer difficult questions, such as, "Where should we put our development funds?" "At what level of performance should we work to achieve with this equipment or process?" or "Have we fully exhausted the limits of this particular technology?"

The value of parallelism. Our discussion of language and benchmarking skills suggests that good receptors must be competent learners. They must be capable of organizing and interpreting the fragments of knowledge garnered during the course of the partnership. They must also be prepared to make the most of their partnering experience. One way to do this is to make the training, operating experiences, and conceptual skills of alliance personnel as similar as possible to those of their counterparts in the partner firm. This will help them to make the most of their interactions.

The notion of parallelism as an aid to receptivity may also be applied to physical facilities: manufacturing equipment, laboratories,[11] and plant layout. In building a "shadow" capability the goal is to create a tight coupling between transmitter and receiver: the tighter the coupling, the clearer the signal. The more complex the skills being transferred, the more critical a close coupling. The investment required to prepare receptor sites may be substantial—as in the case of an automobile production line. The payoff from this investment will be a learning curve that is steeper than the partner's or the opportunity to acquire a competence unavailable by other means.

DIFFUSION OF LEARNING

Individual learning becomes organizational learning only when it is diffused throughout the receptor firm. Leveraging what is learned across business units and across geographical locations requires a process of diffusion. Diffusion, like learning, cannot be left to chance. It requires that those directly involved in the collaborative effort take responsibility for disseminating the knowledge they gain to those for whom it would have the greatest relevance, who in turn must share the enthusiasm for learning possessed by those more directly involved. In effect, the frontline learners should be viewed as a clearinghouse for information about the partner and its skills.

It is reasonable to expect that the diffusion of partner skills will be largely determined by preexisting patterns of interunit communication. Thus organizations that are tightly partitioned will experience less success with diffusion than will those characterized by effective patterns of two-way communication—horizontal and vertical, informal and formal.[12]

Diffusion can be aided by policies that increase the number of people who interface directly with the partner. This approach may entail a hidden cost, however, since stability in the membership of collaborative teams contributes to effectiveness in joint tasks.[13]

Moving Ahead

Skill and knowledge transfer from a partner as well as effective diffusion beyond the alliance interface are obvious goals for the firm bent on internalization. Less obvious is the need to regenerate those skills. In the last analysis, successful internalization requires that a firm be able to upgrade the skills acquired from a partner at the pace dictated by competition. Only if it is able to do this will it ultimately overcome or reverse the dependency that binds it to its partner.

Whether learning becomes self-sustaining or skills degrade when the partnership ends would seem to depend on two factors: the depth of learning that has taken place and the firm's capacity for continuous improvement. Whether learning is self-sustaining may also depend on whether the firm has sufficient scale to amortize its investments and make the most of its learning experience to match the development pace of competitors. If learning is superficial, and/or the firm lacks the discipline of continuous improvement, and/or the firm continues to operate at subcritical scale, skills gaps closed through collaboration are likely to reopen. On the other hand, if the firm has captured know-why, drives for continuous improvement, and is steadily expanding the scope of its operations, competitive collaboration will give it an opportunity to permanently outdistance its partner.

Summary

Value capture is equally important to value creation. What determines the respective value capture between partners is largely the relative uniqueness of their contributions. Preexisting market positions and other positional advantages, such as lobbying power, tend to drive uniqueness of contribution in co-option situations. Uniqueness in cospecialization hinges on who brings the rarest skills and the less duplicable or substitutable capabilities to the alliances. When learning and internalization are key value creation goals, which partner can learn the most from the other(s) typically determines the value capture shares. Interpartner skill learning, in turn, is determined by learning intents, receptivity of organizations, and relative transferability of contributions.

9

❖

MANAGING MULTIPLE
ALLIANCES

More and more firms are involved in multiple alliances, often
with multiple partners. Some alliances involve large numbers of firms, sometimes in a homogeneous network, such
as the many banks brought together by Visa International or Mon-
dex (now associated with Mastercard), sometimes in a more discrim-
inating way, such as the highly differentiated roles PixTech assigns to
its partners. Many firms are involved in several alliances, particularly
in information technology and health care. While some, such as
Corning, find ways to keep their alliances separate and run them as
portfolios of discrete bilateral relationships, others find themselves
entangled in a complex web of interdependent relationships that tax
their strategic cleverness and managerial skills.

Corning, Fujitsu, and PixTech thrive on these webs and networks
and extract competitive leverage from them; others, such as GEC in
the United Kingdom and many European aerospace companies, find
their complexity a true handicap to their strategic development and
assess their benefits as less than their costs.

For purposes of simplicity, previous chapters have focused
mainly on bilateral alliances. In this chapter we will consider what

happens as the number of alliance partners increases and as an individual firm becomes involved in several strategically related alliances. Forming and managing multilateral alliances is not easy, particularly when they include competitors. Participants must shift their perspectives from competition or from cooperation with a single partner to selective multilateral cooperation, from individual opportunism to shared interests and reciprocity.

Greater numbers of participants also complicate alliance design and governance. The management and maintenance functions of multilateral alliances must be effective and balanced for the alliance to bring enough value to each of its members.

Firms that participate in multiple alliances also face problems of strategic consistency. Maintaining strategic consistency when one is bound up in a web of relationships that involves firms that are now collaborators and now competitors is challenging for even the most savvy manager. The strategic "game" between participants in the web can be complex and ambiguous, and few managers are prepared by experience or training to play it.

Despite the difficulties, however, some companies gain strength from multipartner alliances and from multiple related alliances, achieving through them what would otherwise be impossible.

First, Some Definitions

Before going further, some definitions are in order. Both academics and practitioners use a number of terms to describe multipartner alliances, and not always with consistency. We use the terms *network*, *portfolio*, and *web* throughout this chapter to refer to different types of alliances:

- *Alliance network:* A set of linkages between many relatively comparable firms (for example, networks of accounting firms in various countries, such as Nexia) or an international network of independent local accounting firms or cooperative banks (such as Unico, the network of European agricultural cooperative banks).

- *Alliance portfolio:* A set of discrete bilateral alliances entered into by a firm (for example, Corning, which has many alliances but keeps them separate).

- *Alliance web:* A set of alliances that are more interdependent than a portfolio but less uniform than a network. The European aerospace industry can be seen as a web, but each alliance in the web involves a set of industry members in a particular project (for example, Airbus, Eurocopter, European Fighter Aircraft). The various alliances are operationally independent from each other but strategically interdependent for each partner involved.

One Alliance, Many Partners: The Alliance Network

Some multilateral alliances between many partners, and often the simplest networks to build and maintain, are merely information collection and exchange networks. SITA (Société Internationale des Télécommunications Aériennes), an alliance of airlines and air traffic control authorities that operates a worldwide data network for air navigation, is an example. Others go beyond merely putting information in common networks and provide norms and standards; Visa International has done this for credit card retail transactions, and SWIFT has done the same for interbank clearing.

Alliance networks also serve as conduits for the sharing of privileged information. The value here lies in content and credibility rather than in the mere infrastructure for sharing information. Network members bring "social capital" valuable to other members in the form of information, reputation, contacts, and referrals.[1] Networks bring not only information but also a priori trust, a key ingredient in alliance building. They also share expert interpretation of information. For example, stock market quotations are widely available in real time, but the insights of fund managers and securities analysts are not. Their interpretation of the volumes of public information spilling out the world's financial markets each day is more valuable than mere quotations. Thomson Financial Services makes these insights and real-time investment strategies available to its major customers through videoconferencing, thereby not merely distributing information but operating an information interpretation network shared by its major clients.

Other alliances bring many companies together for joint coordinated action, not just information exchange. The central purpose of these is to strengthen the competitive position of members against nonmembers. Co-option alliances with many members, such as the Time Warner–Toshiba Alliance in DVDs and the global HDTV alliance, fall into this category.

Beyond building and exploiting network externalities and first-mover advantages for new standards and technologies, many of these broad alliances aim to establish global market access and service or quality coverage and integration, a form of cospecialization between network members. National members of these networks rely on one another to achieve global market coverage, often to meet the needs of transnational customers. Nexia, an alliance of many national accounting firms, does this by providing referrals, handling transnational customers, and fostering collective learning between member firms.[2] UNICO, an alliance of cooperative banks in Europe, is built on a similar logic. Airline alliance networks, such as the "Star" alliance between Lufthansa, United, SAS, and Thai, are similar. In spirit and logic these alliances are no different from bilateral cospecialization alliances, except that many partners are needed to provide global coverage.

Broad multilateral alliances may also be created to perform a collective learning function for an industry, something that might be impossible without collaboration. SEMATECH, a research and development cooperative of fourteen firms accounting for about 80 percent of the U.S. semiconductor industry, is an example of such a multilateral learning alliance.[3] U.S. semiconductor companies were alarmed during the 1980s by what they saw as the increasing vulnerability of their equipment supplier base, mostly small independent firms, to competition from Japan. They knew that if these domestic companies were swept from the field, U.S. chipmakers would then be dependent on their competitors for manufacturing equipment. The prospect of this dependency was too perilous to even consider, both for the U.S. companies and for the U.S. government. The result was a multilateral alliance of U.S. companies whose goal was to strengthen the U.S. equipment supplier base.[4]

In summary, networks generally share the value creation logics of alliances with fewer partners. The real difference between bi- and trilateral and network alliances is the greater difficulty of management and maintenance. What can be assumed with few partners needs to be managed explicitly and actively with many. We now turn to these tasks.

Building the Multilateral Alliance

Information-sharing networks are easier to build than joint action networks such as SEMATECH. Their success hinges on a common language, rules for who is and who is not a member, and a sense of reciprocity among members. As in other alliances, inclusion rules for sharing networks should be based on a willingness to contribute value. Thus, free riders who capture benefits without reciprocating with contributions of their own are not accepted. Norms of reciprocity like those used in the scientific and intelligence-gathering communities make it clear that firms will not be given access to information or to the network members' deliberations unless they contribute both information and insight.

Norms of reciprocity do not require full disclosure as much as they do "balance." They echo the sentiment, "From those to whom much has been given, much is expected." This balance is easier to achieve if any given "trade" is relatively small and there is a strong assumption of continuity.

Joint action networks, that is, networks in which the participants engage in coordinated and collective action, are more difficult to initiate. Consider R&D cooperatives such as Japan's VLSI (Very Large Scale Integration) project, SEMATECH and MCC (the MicroElectronics and Computer Corporation) in the United States, or ESPRIT (European Science Policy Research in Information Technology) and JESSI (Joint European Silicon Structure Initiative) in Europe. All are complex multilateral alliance networks. Each was formed through a process that recognized the need to collaborate and then proceeded with several alliance-building steps.

RECOGNIZING THE NEED FOR COLLABORATION

Executives do not awake one morning with an unexplained urge to collaborate. It is not in their nature. Nor do nation-states. In the absence of some compelling reason, both steer their own courses and avoid entangling alliances. Something has to drive them to collaborate with other firms: typically an external threat or a compelling opportunity that can be addressed only with the help of others. For example, Japan's VLSI program was triggered in the 1970s in large part by the perceived threat of IBM's "Future System" announcement (which, ironically, was never developed). Similarly, as discussed earlier, SEMATECH was a defensive response on the part of the U.S. semiconductor industry to possible Japanese dominance of the semiconductor production process technologies and equipment suppliers. The same is true in the current American R&D initiative on flat screens and display technologies, a cooperative effort intended to prevent complete domination of that market by Asian suppliers.[5] A combination of potential crises and new opportunities may also be the catalyst, as in the German collaboration on adhesives for metal bonding (as an alternative to welding). That project brought together steel makers, adhesive and chemical firms, various research institutes, and a major potential user—the Volkswagen Audi Group (VAG).[6]

Identifying the benefits of joint work is a key step toward multilateral action. This is easier said than done, however, because the benefits of collaboration are not necessarily perceived until the inadequacy of the current situation is recognized and accepted, even in the face of a crisis or competitive threat.[7]

Most executives are action oriented by experience and disposition. This orientation usually serves them well, but not in the initial stages of an alliance. Their tendency is to move too quickly, restrict the network to a few participants, define the problem too narrowly, seek an immediate solution, and revert to autonomous—rather than joint—action. For instance, in the German adhesive project one of the first hurdles was to overcome VAG's natural impulse to consider the project from the standpoint of supplier selection and qualification and to look for a suboptimal quick fix.[8] Another hurdle was for all participants to recognize that the development of a new technical solution was likely to require the collaborative involvement of suppliers (for instance, steel makers and chemical companies), producers (the makers of adhesives), and customers (VAG). Positioning the project as new research rather than simply sharing existing knowledge was also a difficult but necessary precondition, both justifying the effort and making collaboration less threatening to the individual companies in the individual network.

Mobilizing Network Participants

Recognizing the need for collaboration is an important first step for building a multilateral alliance. But even firms that recognize a clear need will not automatically unite and begin working together. More likely, they will try to figure out how they can solve the problem unilaterally. What's needed is a "mobilizer"—either an institution or an individual—to get the ball rolling.

An effective mobilizer provides personal or institutional credibility and expertise, trustworthiness, and a sense of neutrality. The mobilizer also has access to influence: sources of funding; regulatory impact; an existing forum for the promotion of collaboration, such as a professional or industry association; connections to other alliances, and so on. In government-sponsored projects, a personally credible and institutionally supported individual can play this role.

The mobilizer also articulates a vision of how value can be created. In every R&D cooperative we examined, the emphasis was on the potential for new discoveries and new technologies—joint value creation. While some limited sharing of existing know-how was a precondition for joint value creation in each case, this was dwarfed by the potential for value creation in the minds of alliance participants.

An effective mobilizer works through other resources: bilateral contacts and preexisting networks of individuals. These network-building contacts facilitate buy-in to the problem and collaborative approaches to its solution; they are also effective selectors of alliance members. Two issues are central to this selection process: the *sequence* of member enlistment and the *inclusive nature* of membership. Successful alliance building seems to require both the right sequence of commitments (existing members facilitating the co-option of future members) and the inclusion of a large number of diverse participants to develop a common ground—one that does not reflect the perspective of a single participant or category of participants.[9]

Still, a convergence of interests is needed. The mobilizer must "compose" the alliance and decide when to move from private bilateral contacts and tentative commitments to a more public multilateral venue and binding commitments (such as a workshop, conference, joint announcement, or actual creation of the alliance).

Defining Common Ground

The next step in multilateral alliance building is to reach a definition of common ground that all participants can accept. In the successful alliances we have seen, common ground was defined ideologically and often at the initiative of the mobilizer. For SEMATECH, for example, the view that American technological independence was being threatened by encroachments from "Japan, Inc." was something that all participants could support. Charlie Sporck, then head of National Semiconductor and a well-respected defender of U.S. leadership in semiconductors, was a champion for this position. So was Robert Noyce, a founder of Intel and a highly regarded scientist and entrepreneur. Common ground only emerges over time, as it usually requires convergence and collective *sense making* among alliance participants. The Japanese VLSI project, for instance, took about a year to define its strategic objectives. Less successful collaborative networks often fail entirely to define a common strategy.

Common ground has a strong behavioral element based on norms of trust and reciprocity. Who will be part of the alliance and how participants will behave toward one another is determined by this common ground. Here again, the mobilizer may lead the way in establishing standards of behavior for potential alliance members.

Making Formal Mutual Commitments

Eventually, potential participants must either commit to the alliance and its members or sit on the sidelines. The mobilizer, again, can facilitate formal commitment. Japan's MITI did this in its role as mobilizer of the VLSI project. MITI experts created the clever design that prescribed that all other members would manage each project efficiently under the leadership of a single firm, but with participation. This design provided for firsthand learning and assured that some participants would not keep their best work proprietary. Without this assurance, few firms would have committed to VLSI.[10] Likewise, in SEMATECH, member firms were encouraged to delegate their best engineers to maximize the opportunity for all members to learn—however, not all did so.

Competent people are perhaps the most meaningful commitments that participant firms can make to an R&D alliance. In non-R&D situations, such as service-oriented alliances, commitment to "seamless" services of equal standards by all members and pledges not to bypass local partners may be the most critical commitments. In information networks, the commitment to full sharing of information may be the most critical.

Moving from Commitment to Process

As in bilateral alliances, the formal commitments made by multilateral alliance partners are superseded over time by informal arrangements that transfer commitments from the institutional to the individual level. If the collaboration process runs into difficulty, the alliance may turn back to the redefinition of common ground. For instance, the realization that a SEMATECH member would find it difficult to share manufacturing process technology—the alliance's initial objective—led them to search for a new common ground. Ensuing debate triggered a redefinition of SEMATECH's role in strengthening the domestic equipment supplier base. Three of the original members dropped out around that time, but the other eleven went along with the redefined priorities and made new commitments.[11]

The Evolution of Cooperation

The sequence of activities we have just described does not happen overnight. In the multilateral alliances we have studied, the "define common ground" step alone generally took about a year. We observed no shortcuts, and each step had to be taken in order. This sequence is sketched on Figure 9-1.

Eventually, cooperation stabilizes in a series of ongoing interpersonal commitments. If and when this process falters, as it did with SEMATECH's original plan, the partners must redefine their common ground. Redefinition may result in a change in the composition of the network. Some members may drop out and new ones, with new perspectives, may join. If the change in membership is substantial, then the initial attempt to build a network will have failed and what follows will be less a "corrective" action than a new start.

Obviously, networks built at the instigation of a leading firm within the context of well-defined competitive terms can bypass some of the steps described above or accelerate them considerably. A strong industry leader may find it possible to directly propose specific contractual commitments to potential partners. Microsoft does this today. If its power in the industry is unchallenged, a "take it or leave it" approach to potential partners may be possible; during its heyday, this was Nintendo's stance with video games. A strong but neutral power broker can also proceed more rapidly than can a

FIGURE 9-1 *Starting a Multilateral Alliance*

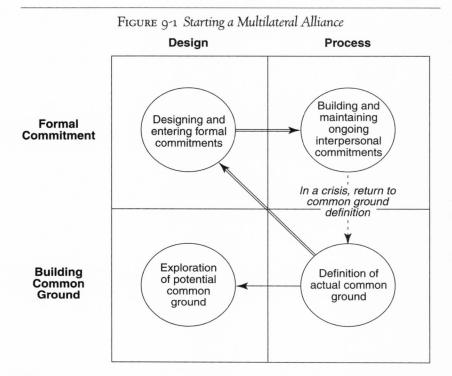

mobilizer faced with more diffused power. MITI's clout and credibility, as well as the negotiating skills of its officers, contributed to the relatively fast start of the VLSI project.

Maintaining the Network

Maintaining a network of allies can be daunting. Coordination difficulties, the state of norms of reciprocity, and conflict resolution (mainly in the balance of contributions and benefits) are among the issues that network managers must face. This is particularly true when joint work (for instance, R&D cooperatives), not simply shared positions (for example, an industry association or lobbying group), is involved. If that work is not dispersed as the network grows wider, common ground may have to be defined more narrowly for the network to retain coherence.

Clear benefits for members obviously make networks strong. The Visa credit card network demonstrates this principle: the benefits of membership are substantial, while the benefits of individual banks issuing their own cards are almost nonexistent. Keenly sensitive to the advantages and disadvantages of network membership, firms weigh them continually. Thus, they watch for "free riders" and question the value of membership when they find them.

Indeed, networks are weakened when members succumb to the temptation to contribute something less than their best efforts—for instance, by sending their second-tier technical personnel to work on common projects and keeping their star performers at home. Then, too, partners are often tempted to defect from the network by opportunities that are too good to share. A partner who sees a really lucrative opportunity may decide to pursue it alone rather than via the network. Presented with a business opportunity, one of Nexia's partners, for instance, decided to open its own branch office in a partner's territory rather than refer the opportunity to the appropriate network members.

The Network Manager

The need for both effective value creation and equitable value capture, in networks as in other forms of alliances, usually calls for active network management. When the members of the network are of relatively equal status, and the network is built as a federation of individual members, network management is usually entrusted to a specialized body. This body can be either an emanation of the network membership, like an association's secretariat, or a hired neutral third party. Conversely, when the network clearly includes a "primus interpares" firm, often the alliance mobilizer and the most influential network member, it is fairly natural for that firm to assume both a nodal position in the network and responsibility for its management. Let's briefly review both approaches.

Concerns for efficiency and equity often lead the partners in multilateral alliances to create a separate network operation and maintenance organization. Funding and supervision of this entity are usually shared by the partners. This network management entity provides a number of functions:

1. *A focal point for communication and exchange.* The network manager is at the hub of the alliance, with spokes connecting it to each partner organization. This structure facilitates member access to information and expertise.

2. *A watchdog for free riders.* As a neutral observer of contributions and benefits by members, the network manager can exclude free riders from the communication and exchange they seek.

3. *A central repository of information about member performance.* The network manager is in a position to identify and quickly disseminate information on best practices. It can also encourage and monitor selective experiments on the part of partner firms: new market approaches, innovative work practices, and so forth. This increases the feasibility of learning within the network while lowering the risks for individual member firms.

4. *A maintainer of behavior norms within the network.* It is much easier for a neutral coordination body to police member behavior than for the individual members.

Considerations of efficiency and equity have led some networks to turn to *third-party network managers.* These fulfill all the functions just described and bring specific expertise to the network. Many U.S. banks, for instance, now outsource critical information technology activities to consultants such as EDS and CSC-Index. Their expectation in doing so is that the consultant will accumulate learning and innovation from its many banking clients and diffuse it fairly across the industry.[12] The key network maintenance functions outlined above in points 1 through 4 are performed by the third-party consultant for the benefit of all network members.

Not all network members wield equal power and influence in a network. What we argued about sources of influence and interpartner power in the previous chapter also applies to networks: some network members may have a much bigger say than others. The *nodal* position is usually the most strategic position in a network. Like a military unit that occupies a key road junction, it can observe everything that passes through; it is able to direct traffic along different routes; and it has the power to impede traffic movement if it chooses. In fact, for these nodal firms, the network is precisely a way to increase their ratio of influence over size. PixTech, for instance, is quite influential in its network without being anywhere near the size of its partners, even if one considers only flat-panel displays. Microsoft has been able to enroll nearly the entire information technology industry in its alliance network. Such leading firms may also provide key alliance management functions and assume a day-to-day management role, in particular when ongoing joint operational action is required. Benetton in Europe is one example of a nodal firm that has built its network of producers and franchised distributors and plays the role of network manager. IKEA is another.

In other cases, a nodal firm emerges over time from the ranks of alliance members, or there may be different nodal firms for different issues or capabilities. In the UNICO alliance, for instance, Crédit Agricole and Rabobank became *de facto conodal* firms, but the Austrian partner was the nodal player in the network's development of opportunities in Eastern Europe.

ACHIEVEMENT AND MAINTENANCE OF THE NODAL POSITION

The advantages accruing to the nodal firm in a network raise two interesting questions:

- How are nodal positions earned and maintained over time?
- Are networks built around firms that aspire to be nodal players, or do nodal roles emerge in preexisting networks?

The experiences of some well-known firms can help us find the answers. Let's start with Benetton.

Benetton, the famous Italian knitwear manufacturer and distributor, is the nodal firm in its network of suppliers and distributors. It built this network for flexibility and speed and as a means of combining the virtues of being small and independently owned with the benefits of being part of a large entity. The key operating principle of the Benetton network is simple and "bottom-up": make product and stocking decisions at the local store level, and use those decisions to drive the supply chain. This devolution of decision making to the individual franchised store aims to stimulate autonomous learning and variations in practice where they matter most: close to the customer.

In this arrangement, network members are free to learn and to optimize their operations. Individual stores can use different approaches; the regional agents who franchise stores for Benetton can develop knowledge and skills about the best locations for new stores; and Benetton can focus on brand marketing and the systems and services needed to maintain the network. The company sees the transfer of expertise and know-how within the network as its key task; thus, it focuses on high-impact areas of promotion, merchandising, and the like.[13] Its system helps network members learn and improve, and at the same time increases cospecialization between it and its franchisees. Benetton alerts network members to information they would otherwise receive slowly or not at all.

In the Benetton-type network, the nodal firm does more than act as information clearinghouse; it also develops a vision and a business concept through which all partners can create value. IKEA, Nintendo, and several other nodal firms have done the same. The business concept provides a way to gain intellectual and market leadership and to sustain competitive advantage. Nodal companies that simply contribute a process concept—as Olivetti does with its marketing and distribution processes—are at a disadvantage in attracting partners since the logic for the selection and management of their relationships is less robust.

The nodal firm also provides guidance and legitimacy in assigning roles and in defining governance rules. Nintendo, for example, has an extremely precise and tightly enforced concept of how to "partner" with game developers and subcontractors to maintain a "closed" proprietary environment. Sun Microsystems has made the opposite choice for its workstation business, opening the standards around its products as widely as possible, beating competitors through speed and agility in new product development, and retaining leadership by means of technological excellence and continual innovation rather than monopoly market power.[14]

Once established, nodal positions are likely to benefit from self-perpetuating advantages that are strengthened as the nodal firm continues to contribute information and competencies generated outside the network itself. For example, many partners remain part of Sun's UNIX/Ethernet-based network not simply because of Sun's judicious early choices on technical standards but because of their confidence in Sun's ability to outpace its competitors in improved workstation design and performance.

Each of the nodal partners we have described has used its advantages to maintain a positive and disciplined relationship with network participants. Benetton, for example, deals primarily with small, labor-intensive knitting firms, but does not press them to the wall or play one against the others, as happens in many traditional customer-supplier relationships. Instead, it guarantees these firms margins on costs of at least 10 percent and keeps them operating at or near full capacity year-round. Rather than treating them as subcontractors and squeezing them on prices, Benetton treats them as partners that are due a fair return and that deserve periodic technical and financial assistance. Where Benetton provides inducements, Nintendo makes its partners hostages. The game developers who share in Nintendo's overall success are tightly controlled, in particular because Nintendo keeps the interface standards and the manufacture of the actual game cartridges proprietary.[5]

Each of our nodal firms exercises strong discipline over its network members, but each also provides support and some shelter from market forces that members would face on their own. This is part of the trade between the nodal firm and its partners.

In sum, nodal positions are built on the strength of three elements:

1. *An enticing and compelling vision.* This vision acts as the magnet that attracts other partners and legitimizes the need for a network.

2. *Unique resources and competencies.* These may be proprietary innovations or a willingness to assume risks for the entire network; they are the basis for influence and power.

3. *Negotiating skills and forbearance.* These are the glue that keeps the network together.

Once built, the nodal firm's speed of reaction to external changes affecting the value of the network to members as well as the continued exercise of leadership are keys to the maintenance of nodal positions. The network retains its value to members only insofar as it allows them to react more rapidly and more effectively to market changes than they would on their own. Unique resources and competencies need to remain with the nodal firm; thus the nodal firm must seek partners that bring equally unique competencies to pursue a complex opportunity. Competitive developments may also

---

TABLE 9-1 *Key Strategic Issues in Building a Multilateral Alliance*

1. Choosing the alliance composition

   - Cosuppliers
   - Users   } Assembling the needed capabilities and positions, and selecting exclusive partners
   - Complementers

2. Optimizing the alliance size (number of participants)

   - Creating and sharing enough value for all partners
   - Maintaining enough strategic consistency/compatibility between partners
   - Containing the complexity of managing (too) many relationships
   - Diminishing returns to extra/late membership

3. Selecting a growth path

   - Establish sequence of new partner participation: credibility, criticality, leverage
   - Surround but do not confront strongest established players
   - Recognize speed of growth, first-mover advantages
   - Avoid going for "missing links" late
   - Segment markets/applications first, "de-segment" later

4. Containing competition between members

   - Role differentiation/duplication/complementarity
   - Sustained leadership by nodal firm

5. Providing alliance governance

   - "Open" neutral (third party/association) governance
   - Management by nodal firms

6. Maintaining the nodal firm's advantage

   - Make enough knowledge and technology available, keep enough proprietary to maintain advantage
   - Be able to afford accelerated learning

---

place the value created by a network in doubt and entice members to either defect to rival coalitions or simply drop out altogether.

Table 9-1 summarizes the key strategic questions to be addressed in building a multilateral alliance.

DISTRIBUTED NODAL ROLES IN A PREEXISTING NETWORK

Nodal firms like Benetton and PixTech create a network to help implement their own strategic visions. One would think, however, that a nodal firm might emerge *from* the network itself and assume its leadership. UNICO and Nexia provide opportunities for this emergence. Yet in none of the cases we observed has this happened. More typically, different network members step forward to play a nodal role on different issues, each of which calls for different competencies. For instance, the Austrian partner in UNICO knew more about dealing with Eastern Europe than did the other partners; thus the leading role for UNICO's development in the East quite naturally fell to that partner. Likewise, the partner in Luxembourg had long experience in fund management and so took the nodal role for the development of UNICO investment funds. In this case, the various partners did not fear the leadership role assumed by different firms on different issues. Their concerns, as it happened, were that some partners were not assuming leadership on anything and were becoming free riders.

The process through which a firm develops a nodal role probably calls for specialization and balance, particularly within networks started by relatively comparable firms, where equality and balance are assumed and required for all members to stay committed. A single partner is unlikely to develop a leadership position on everything, in particular when competencies are the key to leadership; other partners might not accept its leadership in any case. Thus emerging nodal positions are likely to focus on specific competencies and nurture cospecialization between network members. This may explain why UNICO has been more successful than other interbank alliances. In general, those short-lived alliances have confined themselves to running collective utilities—such as clearinghouses—for their members, tasks that created little long-term commitment or mutual dependency between partners.

One Partner, Many Alliances: Managing a Portfolio of Alliances

In the first dimension of multilateral complexity, we considered a single alliance with many partners. There is a second dimension of complexity to consider: the single firm with many alliances. The information technology industry contains many of these. In the mid-1990s, IBM and Xerox were together involved in almost 300 significant linkages! Although not all would qualify as strategic alliances, the existence of so many points of cooperation came as a surprise to their own managers.

Obviously, when a single firm is linked to many alliances, confusion and conflict are constant dangers. Corning is perhaps the best example of a company that has faced this danger successfully—so successfully that more than half of its current revenues now come from its many joint ventures.

Over the years, Corning has formed joint ventures with partner companies with complementary technologies, skills, and marketing capabilities. In 1937 an alliance with Pittsburgh Plate Glass gave it access to the building industry. In 1938 an alliance with Owens-Illinois provided entry into glass fibers. Dow Corning was created in 1943 to develop applications for the silicon products invented by Corning. Many others have followed over the years. Today, Corning may be defined as a cluster of core competencies leveraged via a series of alliances into discrete business domains.[16] We observe that it follows a set of alliance operating principles:

- Seek complementarity and cospecialization.
- Favor bilateral alliances using the joint venture entity.
- Develop market applications.
- Minimize overlaps and risks of encroachment between the partner and Corning.

Following these principles, Corning has sought partners that provide a high degree of complementarity and cospecialization but that pose little threat of encroachment on Corning's unique core competencies and technologies. For example, in its alliance with Siemens to develop, manufacture, and sell optical communication fibers, Corning provided the fiber development and manufacturing skills but relied on Siemens's expertise in communications networks to develop the market and to help guide Corning's technology development. Corning was not about to develop expertise in communications systems, and Siemens was neither interested in contributing nor able to contribute much to the development and manufacturing of the fiber itself. The two firms were complementary and cospecialized; their overlap was limited to fiber connectors and splicers.

Corning's preference has been for equity joint ventures that pool its interests and those of its partners in single entities. These have clear initial cospecialization potential: Corning knows the material and process technologies, while the partner understands the market and customer characteristics. Corning has also shown its interest in combining its own technologies with those of its partners and with developing markets more rapidly than competitors. Its preference for stand-alone joint ventures has served it well in those instances in which it found itself under pressure to divest from certain businesses. The ownership simplicity of the joint venture made it possible to divest with a minimum of pain: save for ownership, little changed for either the employees of the venture or it customers.

Corning's heavy involvement with separate joint ventures, however, has not been problem-free. First, alliance partners have often pulled Corning in too many directions at once, creating the risk that the firm's limited R&D resources would be spread too thin. Its strategy of leveraging its competencies via a wide array of alliances made this risk all the more worrisome. To be an outstanding partner, Corning had to contribute a great deal to individual alliances, but it could only do so efficiently insofar as it achieved synergies across alliances. If each alliance had an independent technology base, economies of scale in core technologies and economies of scope across alliances would be lost, making Corning a much less attractive partner. In nearly all cases, Corning's value to its partner—and hence its main source of influence and bargaining power—was rooted in its technology leadership. Synergies were essential to maintaining that leadership and its affordability. When Corning was allied with partners of larger size or greater resources (such as Siemens or Asahi Glass), affordability remained essential, but was difficult to maintain.

Margins tend to decrease over time in mature businesses subject to intense competition, and the room for technology-based rejuvenation may not be found. So it is not surprising that Corning turned away from some of its more mature partnerships to pursue others. The television tube business provides an example. This had been a bonanza business for Corning for years. As one company executive put it, "The TV business was just raining money out of the sky."[17] But as that business and its technology stabilized, and as margins declined, it became less attractive for Corning, which divested its share in its joint venture with Thomson while keeping a technology-sharing agreement. In the United States, Corning sold part of its equity in the TV glass business to Asahi, keeping only 51 percent, a position cut further since.

Corning has been careful to keep its partners separate; it manages a portfolio of bilateral alliances but avoids being entangled in a multilateral web of relationships. An examination of Corning's joint ventures reveals that its involvements are in individual businesses and usually in separate geographical areas. Geographic boundaries, however, have posed difficulties. For instance, the relationship with Asahi Glass had begun as an alliance to gain access to the Japanese market. But Asahi's growth, and the success of Japanese TV makers in international arenas, made geographic spillover unavoidable. Likewise, Thomson outgrew its regional business and became a significant player in North America. The issue of how Corning's U.S. TV tube customers would react to its alliance with a rival put Corning in a tight spot.

Corning has dealt with the conflicts caused by its alliances on a case-by-case basis, looking for the most effective solution. Nevertheless, these conflicts have led Corning to keep partners separate by addressing widely different market areas in each alliance.

Finally, Corning's ability to maintain strategic control in a network of alliances with strong partners through clear technology leadership is constantly challenged. Its whole approach rests on the underlying principle of achieving synergies within itself, as the nodal company in the portfolio, rather than directly across the various joint ventures it co-runs. Corning has "internalized" the critical value-adding linkages in its portfolio of alliances.

Corning's experience helps us to summarize the critical issues of alliance portfolio management:

1. The broader the application of core competencies and technologies across the alliance portfolio, the stronger the nodal position. Related applications provide economies of scale and scope. An alliance portfolio with no synergies across the competencies and technologies required in each alliance is of limited value.

2. The nodal partner remains valuable to its partners only insofar as it maintains leadership in crucial areas of technology and/or competencies.

3. Keeping partners separate in terms of product and market positions facilitates the role of the nodal firm. By and large, Corning's partners have been in different "downstream" industries, and their offerings are not substitutes for each other. As a result, there are few interdependencies, if any, between that company's various partners.

4. The nodal partner can maintain its leadership position only insofar as it avoids stretching its technical and financial resources too thin. A firm cannot maintain leadership if it is incapable of matching the investments of its partners.

5. The managerial capability of the nodal partner must be up to the task.

Each alliance in a portfolio raises issues of partner compatibility and management process. Partner diversity is a source of both difficulty and potential learning, as diversity calls for more generalized alliance management skills. Originally, Corning treated each alliance separately. During the 1960s, it allowed the management of each alliance to adjust to the requirements of the task and of the partner organization. In the 1980s, Corning began to manage its many alliances strategically, and by the end of that decade it had developed sufficient expertise in alliance management to rein in its free-wheeling alliances without creating serious conflicts with its partners (except when conflicts originated in genuine differences of strategic priority).

A portfolio approach to alliances may also make sense for companies that are not technology powerhouses, like Corning, but probably only as a second-best option when faced with tight resource and competency limitations. Olivetti is a case in point. Over the years it transformed itself from typewriter maker to information technology network supplier and survived several deep technological discontinuities—from electromechanics to digital electronics, from stand-alone to networked products, from component boards to microprocessors, from hardware to software and services. During that period, Olivetti came to see itself as a "platform" organization that leveraged the technologies and products of partners with its own. Even as it built marketing competencies and channel capabilities, it relied increasingly on partners for the provision of technologies and products.[18] Yet marketing competencies were less of a source of influence and network glue than Corning's shared core competencies.

Similarly, British General Electric Company (GEC) entered a series of alliances in the 1980s under the leadership of Lord Weinstock, its long-time chairman, partly for defensive reasons (they made a takeover less likely), only to discover a general truth that led his successor, George Simpson, to begin dismantling them in 1997: Managing a broad portfolio of not so tightly related alliances is even more difficult than managing a broad portfolio of separate businesses. Indeed, independent partners exert even more centrifugal forces away from any common logic than do autonomous business unit managers. Just as there is a limit to top management's ability to create value from unrelated businesses, it is very difficult to add value from a portfolio of unrelated alliances.

In contrast to GEC's alliances, the logic of which was mainly financial and defensive, both the Corning and Olivetti alliances aimed to deliver "more bang for the buck." They made it possible for Corning to leverage its technology investments while minimizing the cost of reaching new markets. They made it possible for Olivetti to minimize R&D investments while leveraging its marketing expertise and distribution infrastructure. Table 9-2 summarizes the trade-

TABLE 9-2 *Trade-offs Facing Firms at the Center of an Alliance Portfolio*

STRATEGIC BENEFITS	DIFFICULTIES AND LIMITATIONS
• Reach out toward more opportunities than limited resources would allow.	• Difficult to invest/divest selectively into/from individual alliances, in particular with limited resources.
• Maximize asset cospecialization for new business creation.	• Difficult to select "right" partner early, then held hostage to existing partner.
• Maximize leverage of core competencies across application domains and geographies.	• Easy to be stretched too thin. How "core" are core competencies?
• Maintain excellence of contributions and competencies.	• Risk of losing nodal "star position."
• Learn across alliances and cross fertilize.	• Tough to manage the organizational complexity of a nodal position.
• Maintain "most valued" links between separate partners.	• Need to keep partners separate.
• Use the cumulative "weight" of multiple partners to one's own advantage.	• Difficult to maintain a strategically united and purposive portfolio.

offs faced by nodal firms like Corning and Olivetti that position themselves at the center of a portfolio of alliances.

Several Partners, Several Alliances: The Alliance Web

Rather than preserve the separateness of their alliances—the Corning approach—other companies have explicitly acknowledged the multilateral nature of their alliance webs and attempted to make the most of them. As a general rule, reducing the independence of the partners in an alliance makes the job of managing the alliance more difficult. The experience of the European aerospace industry is instructive on this point.

Both Aérospatiale and DASA viewed themselves, somewhat incorrectly, as nodal firms in their alliance portfolios. Unfortunately, the core competencies and core technologies of these firms had lesser and lesser applicability to a broad base of alliances as the technological demands of their businesses became increasingly different. At the same time, the collaborative programs in which these companies engaged, such as Airbus, were evolving toward greater and greater cospecialization and toward integration into permanent intercompany entities. Also, the competencies of their partners were becoming more important and relevant to the respective divisions of each partner; in other words, the people designing and making helicopters had more to learn from each other than from people in their own firms who were involved in space systems or missiles.

In the end, the parent companies—Aérospatiale, DASA, British Aerospace, and Alenia—found themselves moving away from the Corning-like logic they had (wrongly) thought possible and toward a financial logic in which their roles resembled those of holding companies with minority equity positions in many specialized transnational ventures. This is much different from the industrial model of core technologies and core competencies, and it may well suffer from the same weaknesses as the GEC approach in the 1980s.

Aérospatiale and British Aerospace still compete in several important markets even as they cooperate in others. This created some strain in the various alliances between these companies. Over time, this mix of cooperation and competition between the same groups is prob-ably untenable. As time goes by, the European Aerospace industry is likely to restructure itself into a single or a few competitive coalitions as conflicts between alliances get resolved. Further, as the existing par-ent companies confine themselves more and more to the role of hold-ing company, they may learn to tolerate different relationships in the businesses in which they hold investments. British Aerospace, whose management is perhaps the furthest among its peers along this move toward financial holding company, may find it easier to keep its busi-nesses strategically separate. This makes it quite feasible for British Aerospace to cooperate with Aérospatiale in civilian airplanes (both Airbus and commuter planes) and with Aérospatiale's archenemy and domestic nemesis, MATRA, in the missile and satellite fields.

FIGURE 9-2 *Major Elements of Fujitsu's Alliance Web*

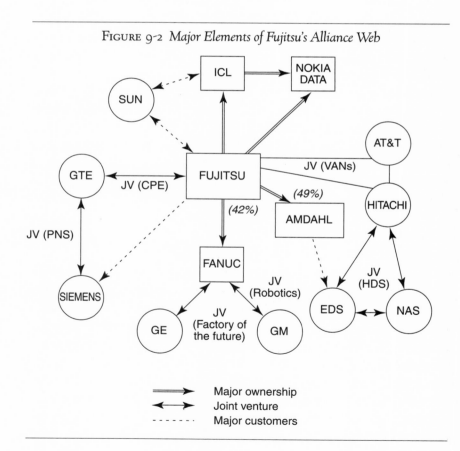

In contrast with European aerospace companies, some companies we have observed actually thrive on the ambiguity of the alliance webs they have assembled, using them to build competitive coalitions. Fujitsu provides an example. Figure 9-2 depicts the relationships between the major elements of the alliance web Fujitsu created in the 1980s to exploit opportunities in the computer business.

Fujitsu used its nodal position to extract various advantages. The first of these were economies of scale and scope. Although Fujitsu alone was far smaller than IBM in mainframes, its web—which included Amdhal, ICL, and other partners—achieved half of IBM's size in mainframe development and production, making it the world's second or third largest mainframe "company."

The alliance web also allowed Fujitsu to capitalize on cross-learning from many market segments and geographical locations. Via ICL, for instance, it learned about pace-setting retailing applications in Europe. From Amdahl it learned about the needs of major computer service companies, such as EDS. Thanks to its relationships with GTE and Siemens, it understood the needs of telecommunications service operators.

Using its alliance, Fujitsu was able to compete vigorously against IBM without having to bear the full brunt of its competitive reactions. For example, when IBM competed strongly on price against ICL in the United Kingdom, Fujitsu suffered only to the tune of its 20 percent share in ICL's equity, leaving the other shareholders to absorb the rest of IBM's assault.

EVOLUTIONS IN COMPETITION

Alliance webs may be nothing more than a transitional phase in an evolutionary process that begins with stand-alone firms and in some cases ends in the competitive coalitions discussed in Chapter 3. (See Figure 9-3.) Initially, companies compete as independent entities. Networks and multilateral alliances are created in response to common threats, the need for joint work, or some other cause. Information and learning networks generally precede joint action alliances. Information networks may in fact spawn focused alliances between members who have discovered enough common ground to collaborate at higher levels of commitment and expectation. To a large

FIGURE 9-3 *A Likely Evolution of Alliance Webs*

| Independent
Competitors | Emerging Information
and Action Networks | Multilateral
Alliances | Competitive
Coalitions |

extent, this explains the European Community's ESPRIT program. A network of European scientists would facilitate the emergence of webs of specific alliances within the EEC. Once scientists from European companies came to know each other and work together, it was reasoned, they would be more likely to develop alliances among themselves than with peers in Japan or the United States.

Multilateral alliances in which firms are both collaborators and competitors tend to evolve into more stable competitive coalitions. Where uncertainty and complexity are not particularly high, the transition to more stable competitive coalitions may be rapid. The automobile industry, for example, has quickly evolved toward stable competitive coalitions.[19] So has the mainframe segment of the computer industry. Coalitions have also formed in microelectronics, where two rival alliances of a relatively stable nature have emerged and endured for a while around Intel and Motorola.

The evolutionary process may be slower in industries or industry segments that contain higher uncertainty and complexity. The minicomputer industry provides an interesting example of this slower process. There the open standards triggered by UNIX, and by customer resistance to proprietary standards (that would protect the individual supplier's monopoly power), has changed the nature of competition. The impulse to form alliances in this more open industry is decidedly weaker. Further, in industries where technology development takes place very quickly, existing networks may slow down adoption of new technologies and ultimately turn against the network members.

The clustering of networks and webs into more stable competitive coalitions is typically a solution to conflicts between partners and a result of the trust built through repeated ties and long-lasting alliances. Aérospatiale's managers involved in alliances with DASA, for instance, saw their continued competition in commuter planes as a sore spot capable of ruining the trust and cooperative spirit the two companies had already built. They saw a broader coalition as a logical way to eliminate this problem but could not agree on its terms.

DYNAMIC NETWORKS

Not all firms have an interest in stabilizing their coalitions. Sun Microsystems, for example, believes that it can learn more rapidly than its competitors and bring innovations to market more quickly on its own. Thus it is less interested in stability than in maintaining a dynamic network of partners that can quickly adopt its technology. In the view of its management, Sun benefits from the *acceleration* of competition, not stability. Microsoft's management may hold this view even more strongly than Sun and see it confirmed by Windows NT's success against UNIX.

Dynamic networks like Sun's can also be used to catch up with those who have inched ahead. Here alliances are used as virtual learning networks in which each alliance contributes to the competence base of the firm. This extends the learning ladder approach we advocated in the preceding chapter to multiple alliances. The German aerospace industry followed this approach when it rebuilt from the devastation of World War II. Beginning in the early 1960s, German aerospace firms engaged in a series of alliances in which they learned from each new partner. Two firms in particular, Messerschmitt Bolkow Blom (MBB) and Dornier (now largely merged into Daimler-Benz Aerospace), used skills learned in one alliance to gain strength and position in the next. Specific technologies appropriated in one alliance were used as bargaining chips to gain a better partner role and a stronger say in the alliance that followed. Figure 9-4 summarizes the progress of these firms over time, showing how MBB and Dornier took more and more important roles in each alliance, literally climbing the learning ladder.

In each alliance, the partner who is trying to catch up can coax other partners into transferring the technology essential to the success of the overall project. For instance, in the 1990s, Daimler-Benz

FIGURE 9-4 *The Alliance Learning Ladder*

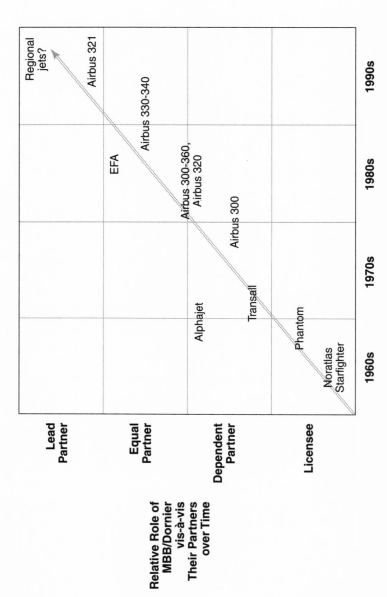

Source: *Interavia, Flight, Aviation Week* (various issues).

FIGURE 9-5 *Merck's AIDS Research Network*

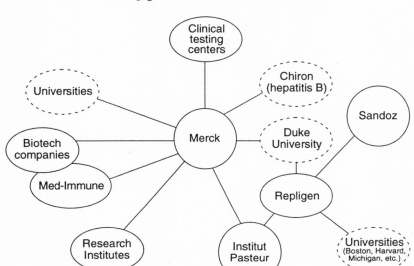

Aerospace was helped (grudgingly) by GEC-Marconi in the development of the digital fly-by-wire control system of the European
Fighter Aircraft (EFA 2000), one of the relatively few core aerospace
technologies it had not yet mastered. It was thus possible for the
weaker partner to use the dynamic alliance network to improve its
own position vis-à-vis the leaders.

Dynamic networks can also be used to create options in situations
of high uncertainty. The networks formed in the 1990s to develop
and commercialize digital videodisk (DVD) technology were probably responses to this motive. While everyone saw the digital
videodisk as a key technology for future consumer electronics, the
direction its development would take remained uncertain. To an
extent, the DVD networks are option networks: industry participants
will use them to take options on the development of alternate industry futures. Matsushita, for instance, kept a foot in both the Time
Warner–Toshiba and the Philips–Sony coalitions. The AIDS network
formed by Merck (Figure 9-5) serves a similar function. That network
of relationships should position Merck as a leader in AIDS preven-
tion and therapy when the relevant discoveries are made.

Building the network when the uncertainties are high, as Merck has, may actually increase the odds that discoveries will be made by network members. Having made commitments and built linkages early, Merck is poised to move quickly as discoveries are made.

Conclusion

As firms shift from single alliances, with two or a few partners, to broader networks, or to portfolios of related alliances, or even to webs of relationships, the goals and value creation motives for partnering remain the same. Co-option, cospecialization, and learning still drive the partners. However, as the number of partners and of alliance relationships increases, the strategic and managerial issues we discussed in previous chapters become even more challenging: value creation and value capture must be available to each and every participant; strategic compatibility is harder to achieve and sustain. Further, the need for cooperation, or its feasibility, may not be so obvious to all partners a priori, which calls for more deliberate network-building activities. Although interpartner gaps may occur less frequently than in other alliances, since firms in a network tend to be more similar, the fact that they usually are competitors is a constant threat to continued cooperation.

Despite these many difficulties, multilateral relationships bring obvious advantages to their members: new capabilities and stronger competitive advantage, influence that extends beyond what each member could accomplish alone, opportunities for accelerated learning. Nodal firms extend their reach and leverage their capabilities, other members gain from the collective strength and benefit from the nodal firm's leadership.

10

❖

BUILDING COLLABORATIVE ADVANTAGE

When we look at the many companies that have formed alliances, and then look at the outcomes, we are struck by how different they are. Some companies have benefited enormously from their alliances, while the experience of others has been rocky. What explains these differences?

Previous chapters of this book have addressed the question of success and failure through the mechanisms of alliance design, configuration, governance, partner selection, division of work and benefits, and so forth. This chapter shifts the focus from the alliance to the partnering firms themselves. What characteristics make a firm fit to enter an alliance? What organizational traits enhance its ability to collaborate successfully with others? Is there such a thing as "alliance readiness"? Our answers to these questions are somewhat paradoxical and, to an extent, may be sobering for managers who enter alliances with sanguine expectations. As we will show, the very factors that prompt some companies to join an alliance are likely to undermine its success. At the same time, many of the capabilities that lead to successful alliance management are the same that support good internal management. Success in alliances often stems from the same factors that drive good management, in particular successful collaboration and integration between units of the same firm.

Preconditions for Success

Successful alliances are more likely when managers and their firms enter them with "the right stuff"—that is, appropriate personal attitudes and organizational habits. The assumptions held by managers, and how those managers work and interact, precondition their success or failure as managers of alliances. If they see their alliances in the context of a future-driven strategic architecture, not as mere remedies to past failures, they are more likely to succeed. If they sense keenly the limits of their own resources and are possessed by an ambition that stretches beyond these resources, they will be more driven to leverage their alliances effectively and will strive to get the most from them.

Culture, too, is a precondition for alliance success. Corporate values, and the extent to which employees are encouraged to balance cooperation and competition, strongly influence alliance outcomes. If the culture of a firm supports a mix of collaboration and competitiveness, if employees are encouraged to be imaginative and creative in how they create value, and if they feel comfortable in making their commitments and delivering on them, the preconditions for success will have been met.

Open communications, experience of effective teamwork, and steadfastness of shared purpose are also aspects of alliance readiness. The quality of communication within the partner organization, the experience of its employees in managing interunit collaboration and in working in teams within the firm, and the ability to maintain management continuity over long periods of time are observable traits in successful partner firms.

STRATEGIC ARCHITECTURE

"If you do not know where you are going, all roads will take you there," is a time-honored warning. (Or, as the French would say, "If you are a good Catholic, all roads lead to Rome.") Effective alliances are approached with a clear strategic intent and an architecture for turning that intent into reality.

Strategic architecture provides a dynamic model of how efforts at building capabilities and gaining strategic market positions interact over time. It provides an overarching strategic context for the choice of individual alliances and for the strategic goals they are assigned. Why enter a particular alliance? Why join with certain partners? These are difficult questions to answer without a clear sense of where one wants to go and therefore of where a particular alliance fits in along the way.

Too clear a sense of direction, too tightly set an itinerary may, however, make for an uninteresting and unrewarding journey. As many of the cases in this book have confirmed, the rewards of alliances are often partly serendipitous. This fact raises an interesting dilemma: Without a clear strategic architecture, there is a lack of purpose and focus; yet defining that architecture too precisely may blind one to opportunities that cannot be anticipated. Alliances may be used as "feelers" to help define and sharpen a firm's strategic architecture, a perspective consistent with the use of alliances as options.

Still, absent an ambitious future-oriented strategic architecture, a firm's alliance strategy is likely to be reactive and incremental. Too often firms fall back on the tried and tested, the "no-brainer" alliance: industry consolidation, standards setting for known products, capacity rationalization, and the like. These alliances are often successful but seldom create unassailable advantage for their partners. They are usually "remedying" or defensive alliances that plug gaping holes in a firm's range of capabilities and positions. They may remedy past mistakes, but they seldom put their partners out front in the race for the future.

Firms that are truly "alliance ready" view alliances as a tool for actively discovering or creating the future and overcoming resource disadvantages. They are willing to accept the difficulties of interfirm collaboration, since collaboration helps them accomplish otherwise unfeasible objectives. Simply picking the low-hanging fruit is not on their agenda.

A useful strategic architecture has a number of features. First, it is driven by a rich and original understanding of the opportunity set available to the firm, not by industry recipes and conventional wisdom. Second, managers who create the strategy understand the "profit engine" that drives their business and its underlying assumptions. Their understanding goes far beyond the obvious ("What products to sell for how much") to a broader, almost ecological context ("What niche do we occupy? How do we contribute to the success of others? Why are we successful?"). They understand intuitively that they are part of a broader set of intercompany and often interindustry interdependencies and rivalries. They know they are part of a business ecosystem that they are unlikely to master or control on their own. Yet they are clear on just where and how they intend to drive competitive innovations and on what new capabilities they will require to do so. Using that awareness, they build a space for collaborative relationships into their strategic architecture. Thus, they are prepared to partner.

It is a mistake to think that the kind of high-level strategic scheming we have just described is the sole province of managers in dynamic, fast-paced industries. This is not the case. Opportunities for high growth and profitability exist in virtually every industry. Even the most lackluster industry contains companies that are creative, dynamic competitors by any measure, the "average" performance of companies in that industry notwithstanding.[1] The true barriers to opportunity creation are not in the marketplace but in the minds of company executives.

So when we see a company whose managers are oriented toward the creation of competitive advantage in emerging arenas, who think in terms of core competencies rather than discrete businesses, who

TABLE 10-1 *Qualities of Firms That Are and Are Not Alliance-Ready*

UNPREPARED	PREPARED
• Protective	• Creative
• Imitative	• Innovative
• Focused on core business	• Focused on core competencies
• Product oriented	• Functionally oriented
• Focused on linear goals	• Focused on nonlinear goals
• Customer-led	• Beyond customers
• Focused on maximizing hit rate	• Faster learning
• Define failure as money lost	• Define failure as money forgone

aim to deliver superior value to customers, we see a company that is "alliance ready" in one or more important respects. Table 10-1 lists a number of the mindset characteristics of those firms which are alliance-ready and those which are not.

RELATIVE WEALTH

We have observed that rich companies seldom make effective and dedicated partners. Their ample resource endowments are to blame. They are driven neither to form alliances nor to get the best from them. Like old China, rich firms are inclined to see themselves as complete universes, lacking for nothing. "What could foreigners possibly have to contribute?" they ask. Although this is obviously no longer true—witness their managers' answers to the question, at the beginning of this book, about whether they need alliances—deep down the splendid isolation mindset endures. Whether or not one sees oneself as rich or poor is a function of the ratio of one's ambitions and opportunities over one's resources; it is not of objective measure.

Resource-poor, ambition-rich firms, often small and rapidly growing firms with strategic windows of limited duration, in contrast to rich and lazy ones, are always painfully aware of their resource constraints and must, on a regular basis, find ways to complement, leverage, and stretch what they have. If they are poor in resources but "rich" in ambition and opportunities, they tend to join forces with others. Notice this was a key motive of the poorer partner in just about all the examples we described in this book.

This affinity for using allies to create and access opportunities and to leverage resources is often driven by the desire to retain family control of a company or to take advantage of a growing set of opportunities; these factors were at work in the alliances of Corning and Fleming, two of the more systematic users of alliances we observed in our research. The affinity for partnering is also driven by historical and cultural traditions of "doing more with less" and of using interdependencies to one's advantage—two factors that may account for the extensive use of alliances by Japanese companies.

The distinctions between rich and poor companies may also influence the decision to go with an alliance versus an acquisition. Alliances are favored by the avid but cautious learner who uses resources sparingly, places multiple bets, and makes a big commitment only when a positive outcome is reasonably certain. This profile is more typical among resource-poor firms. They can afford neither to make big mistakes nor to buy their way out of them. They must deploy their resources with care and intelligence, always asking, "What have I learned?" before taking the next step.

Acquisitions, on the other hand, are the favored tool of the rich. Rich firms use their superior resources to remedy shortfalls in strategic foresight. "We should have begun developing this technology ten years ago," they will confess, "but since we did not, we'll just buy a company that has the technology." The mindset of acquisitions is therefore radically different from the mindset of using alliances strategically.

Alliances are not universally preferable to acquisitions. Each has its place. Both small acquisitions and alliances leverage firm resources, particularly for a large company. Acquisitions may be the best course when a competitor is moving faster or when the acquired company needs to be actively rescued. But the mindset of the shrewd users of alliances is much different than that of the active acquirer. The former has a keen sense of its relative poverty but harbors ambitions that go far beyond its current resources and capabilities. The active acquirer sees itself and its ambitions much differently.

BALANCE OF COOPERATION AND COMPETITION

In Chapter 2 we discussed how the ability to serve self-interest through mutually beneficial cooperation is at the heart of constructive alliance development. Both national and corporate cultures may foster or inhibit this ability. Cultures that balance the needs of the group with the independence of the individual—affirming duties as well as rights—may well have an advantage here. In contrast, cultures that affirm the primacy of the individual may find the combining of competition and collaboration more difficult. Time and time again we have heard American and some European managers lament the alleged superior negotiating and implementation skills of their Asian partners, who show a better balance between individual competitiveness and group belonging.

Corporate cultures are not bound by national cultural disadvantages when it comes to blending competition and collaboration. They can set their own standards and ingrain their own habits. Unfortunately, most corporate cultures have set standards and ingrained habits that work against the behaviors that alliances require. Over the decades, corporate control systems have trained managers to be uncollaborative, pitting managers in contests over careers and resource allocation. Destaffing, delayering, and downsizing have intensified these rivalries and made cooperation even more difficult. It is not surprising, therefore, that highly competitive managers cannot easily switch to a collaborative posture.

Training in the skills of negotiation and cooperation can help. So too can new individual measurement processes, such as "all-round" feedback, reward systems that recognize and encourage mutually supportive activities, and the early involvement of managers and professionals in collaborative projects. Training, measurement, rewards, and practice *can* build partnering skills and behaviors.

Competition and collaboration are the yin and the yang of alliance readiness. Though they traditionally represent opposing poles of organization culture, managers must find ways to bring them into coexistence. When this is accomplished, the organization gains the benefits of constructive tension and trust among employees. Table 10-2 lists the principal traits associated with competition and collaboration.

COMMITMENT AND FLEXIBILITY OF EMPLOYEES

Individual commitment of all involved parties is an obvious requirement for the success of any alliance. Cooperating firms need to address the interests of the managers and technical personnel they assign to alliances. These people also want to know: "What's in it for me?" The alliance-ready firm answers this question to their satisfaction. Many managers may initially see appointment to an alliance as a career sidetrack. The alliance-savvy company will help employ-

TABLE 10-2 *Traits Associated with Competitive and Collaborative Behavior*

COMPETITION	COLLABORATION
• Isolation	• Belonging
• Unit autonomy	• Interdependence
• Ownership	• Sharing
• Local focus	• Global focus
• Fixed priorities	• Flexibility
• Maintenance	• Development

ees understand not only the broad strategic logic behind the alliance but also the personal benefits they can draw from the experience.

Individual commitment is also a function of personal comfort and self-confidence. If the individuals assigned to the alliance are already uncomfortable in their roles, fearful in their working relationships, or worried about their future career, they are likely to limit their commitment to the alliance and to present themselves as less than predictable and dependable to the alliance partner.

The degrees to which one is at ease in one's own organization and to which one has effective and trusting working relationships with colleagues are good indicators of how one will fare in an alliance. Only managers whose "home base" is safe, who can venture into a relationship with the partner without worrying about their backs, should be appointed to the interface between partner organizations. Only managers whose personal interests are aligned with the success of the alliance should participate in the process. In general, this suggests that an alliance should attract the very best among a company's employees if it is to succeed. An alliance is no place for second stringers.

CAPACITY FOR CONSTRUCTIVE DIALOGUE

Alliances require learning, reassessment, and readjustment over time. This in turn calls for constructive dialogue and a cooperative working environment, both precursors to the well-made decision. Research on interunit cooperation in complex corporations has made it possible to identify those attributes of internal dialogue which foster cooperation.[2] Our observations suggest that these attributes—described below—also foster cooperation between partners in a strategic alliance.

1. A *multiple advocacy process* brings different perspectives to bear on sources of tension affecting a decision that has ramifications for both partners. The decision-making process should be informed by analytical data, improved problem definition through ongoing dialogue, and the search for a mutually beneficial solution.

2. A *flexible power structure* allows managers at the interface to challenge the existing positions in each partner's organization and to search for what makes the best sense for the alliance, based on forbearance and a long-term perspective on the collaboration process rather than each partner's hierarchies and political pecking order.

3. *A legitimacy to dissent* makes it possible for partners to perceive dissent not as political opportunism or mistaken aggressiveness but as well-rooted, legitimate disagreement motivated by each partner's interest in the long-term success of the alliance.

4. *A discipline* of *"due process"* based on open and honest communications allows partners to reach joint decisions they will be committed to implement.

Here, too, we observe companies are unable to lend these attributes to an alliance unless they already have them on their own.

Enabling Conditions for Alliance Management

The previous section discussed how the internal workings and culture of organizations make their managers more or less "alliance-ready." The quality of management processes in the partner organizations plays a significant role in preparing managers to be effective in alliance situations. In this section, we add to these preconditions a series of key priorities that should be part of the alliance organizational context in each partner's organization.

QUALITY OF COMMUNICATION

Alliance performance suffers when communication *between* partners is lacking. It also suffers when the people and functions *within* the partner firms fail to communicate. Rapid and effective communication is essential. A firm largely without barriers to vertical and horizontal communication is more alliance-ready than a firm that finds internal communication difficult. Good communication supports many of the skills and behavior that a firm needs when it joins an alliance. Good communication:

- distributes leadership and decision making.
- weakens the effects of functional "silos."
- speeds the resolution of issues.
- fosters mutual understanding and trust.

ACCUMULATION OF EXPERIENCE

Firms that pursue alliances strategically make the most of them when lessons learned inform their other activities. This organizational learning is a key factor in long-term success. We mentioned earlier the role of Fujitsu's cooperation office in using its accumulated experience to facilitate cooperation with ICL and other partners. This is the exception. Most companies fail to capitalize on their experience from alliance to alliance.

The best preparation for learning from alliances is skill in *intrafirm* learning. If a company can capture and share learning within its own boundaries, it is naturally better prepared for working in an alliance. Intrafirm learning can take many forms: project post-mortems, the strategic movement of personnel between projects and business units, and so forth.

Beyond the specific methods used to foster learning, the ability to consider failure objectively and to refrain from immediate and indiscriminate personalization of failure is also central to learning from experience; it allows partners to take positive and constructive action in alliance crises rather than lose themselves in "Death Valley." For failure to be considered objectively, risks must be understood and assessed, uncertainties recognized, and the odds turning against a sound decision distinguished from stupid blunders. Unfortunately, most firms find it easier to "shoot the managers" than to look for the true causes of difficulties.

ENCOURAGEMENT OF CONTINUITY

Continuity of personnel can help build understanding, self-confidence, and trust between alliance managers. Yet many corporations undermine continuity through rotation and promotion policies. Some companies, for example, limit the tenure of managers in any given position, including positions in their alliances.

When an alliance is large relative to the size of its partners, rotations may be beneficial. Rotations in the GE–SNECMA alliance, for example, successfully built a cadre of managers who shared firsthand experience and a high level of understanding of the alliance. The result was a "snowballing" of commitment and support for the alliance within each partner organization.

The problem of discontinuity is substantial when partner organizations are large relative to the size of the alliance. We have observed this in the case of AT&T and its alliances. Here lack of continuity caused by rotations has had detrimental effects on the ability of partners to maintain a trusting relationship. Within AT&T overall, the alliance relationship enjoyed only limited priority. The management of AT&T's computer division was in a state of flux, leading to many reassignments and shifts in responsibilities, each of which led the alliance to fall back on interinstitutional trust and prevented interpersonal trust from developing and taking hold.

EXECUTIVE OVERSIGHT

Alliances require constant attention. Like small aircraft in turbulent skies, they are pushed off course by wind currents and heading errors. As fuel is consumed, their handling characteristics change. A good pilot flies his plane to its destination by means of small, frequent adjustments and periodic navigational checks. He doesn't simply set it on autopilot and then take a nap.[3] In this sense, senior executives of companies such as Corning are master pilots. They have abundant piloting experience, and they give their alliances plenty of attention.

Others are less methodical. They tend to overlook strategic incompatibilities that can break alliances apart at the seams. They underinvest in day-to-day management. And they put too much reliance on formal contracts and governance agreements, overlooking the informal relationships and agreements that ultimately define how the alliance works.

Summary

As alliance candidates, not all companies are created equal. Some have the "right stuff," others do not. In most cases, their experiences and the cultures they develop as independent businesses create their readiness for collaboration. Companies that fail in alliances may do so for reasons that have more to do with internal deficiencies than with the alliance itself. Or, as Pogo once said: "We have met the enemy, and it is us!" This suggests that companies that intend to

play the alliance game should first take a fitness test, asking themselves:

- Do we have a strategic architecture? Do our people understand it?

- Are we ambition rich and resource poor, or the reverse?

- Are our managers driven to do more with limited resources?

- Do people here know how to collaborate? Does our system of
  rewards encourage collaboration or pit one employee against another?

- Are we capable of commitment?

- Can our employees respond quickly when the game changes?

- Do we communicate well?

- Do we learn as a group?

- Do our policies encourage continuity?

- Do our managers have the steadfastness of purpose to provide
  continual oversight of their projects?

How would your company stand up to this fitness test? What about
your existing or prospective partner?

Assuming that a company is weak in some areas, a program of
fitness development should complement, if not precede, entry into
the alliance game. As we suggested at the beginning of this chapter,
there is a terrible irony in the fact that companies enter alliances
because they are unfit to race for the world or for the future alone.
Unfortunately, that lack of fitness causes them to fail in alliances.
Conversely, though, strategically ambitious and organizationally fit
companies put alliances to extremely effective strategic use and
thrive on growing webs of alliances.

APPENDIX:
ASSESSING A STRATEGIC
ALLIANCE

T HIS APPENDIX highlights important questions managers should address as they plan, design, enter, and manage a strategic alliance over time. It focuses on the issues presented in the main text, and the sequence of questions roughly follows the flow of the argument presented there: (1) assessing value creation potential and partner compatibility, (2) determining the design of the alliance, (3) starting and maintaining the cooperation process, (4) managing the alliance's value creation and value capture over time, and (5) assessing the alliance in light of the other relationships the partner maintains in related areas. (See Table A-1.) The questions remain at the strategic and organizational levels that characterize the whole text; for contractual and legal design, more specialized sources and advice should be sought.

While this appendix may seem limited in that it raises questions rather than providing answers, our experience with alliances suggests that asking the right questions is half the work. Bear in mind that the appendix is not meant to be read sequentially and as distinct from the main text but to provide a structured checklist to help the reader apply the insights gained in reading the main text to the specific alliance situation the reader may be facing.

Obviously, therefore, not all sections of the appendix will be equally relevant to all readers. At any point in time, for a given alliance, only a few questions from the very rich menu provided here are likely to be critical. This checklist may also provide a vehicle for focusing and structuring the dialogue between partners and within one's own organization.

TABLE A-1 *Key Topics*

1. Validating the Alliance's Strategic Foundations
   - Assessing value creation and capture potential (Chapters 1 and 2)
   - Assessing interpartner compatibility (Chapter 4)

2. Designing the Alliance
   - Valuing contributions (Chapters 3 and 5)
   - Setting the alliance scope (Chapters 3 and 5)
   - Understanding the joint task demands and designing the interface (Chapters 3 and 5)
   - Defining and measuring progress (Chapter 3)
   - Anticipating longevity (Chapter 3)

3. Getting Started
   - Understanding and bridging initial gaps between partners (Chapter 6)
   - Establishing the interpartner learning agenda (Chapter 7)

4. Managing for Value Creation and Value Capture over Time (Chapters 7 and 8)

5. Assessing the Alliance's Interdependence with Other Relationships (Chapter 9)

Validating the Alliance's Strategic Foundations

The central purpose of this first step in the analysis is multifold: to discover, establish, and validate a robust value creation logic for the alliance and to ensure that the partners (current or potential) are likely to be, and to remain, strategically compatible.

A set of broad questions establishes the value creation profile of the alliance, based on the arguments developed in Chapters 1 and 2. Here we assume that the reader will already be involved in, or at least be considering, a strategic alliance.

Beyond value creation and value capture, the current and future strategic compatibility between partners is another fundamental enabling condition for alliance success. The second set of questions, based on the argument developed in Chapter 4, probes at the strategic compatibility between partners.

ASSESSING VALUE CREATION AND CAPTURE POTENTIAL

1. What will each partner gain from the alliance?

2. What are the various ways in which the alliance will create value?
   - Gaining stronger competitive capabilities through co-option of partners.
   - Leveraging cospecialized resources between partners to create and exploit new opportunities.
   - Gaining competence—both to remedy skill deficits and to develop new competencies for the future—through learning and internalizing from the alliance and the alliance partners.
   - Other (to be specified for each alliance).

3. Is the alliance to provide value primarily in one way or in several ways?

For value creation through co-option

1. Do you need to build critical mass?
   - Defensively (in your existing markets)?
   - Offensively (to penetrate new markets)?

   What are the key dimensions of critical mass?
   - Scale in operations (manufacturing, R&D, processing, logistics, and the like)?
   - Share of customer attention, customer access?
   - Density of coverage locally for service and competitive advantage?
   - Reach of coverage globally?
   - Brand, reputation, corporate image, credibility?

2. Do you need to build a nodal position?
   - To what extent does the value of your product (or service) to a customer increase as a function of how many other customers use it (network externalities)?

- To what extent does the value of your product (or service) to a customer increase as a function of the wide availability of complementary standardized products (for example, software products for a personal computer)?

3. Do you observe/expect several rival coalitions being built to pro-vide competing services? Is there a race between coalitions to ally with the most critical providers of complementary products, market access, unique "gateway" technologies, or infrastructures?

4. How strong is the sense of urgency? (Do you face a race between rival coalitions being built in activities characterized by high net-work externalities?) Do you participate in a "winner takes all" race?

5. If you try to build a nodal position, how do you make yourself attractive to partners? What uniqueness do you bring? How will-ing are you to share the benefits of a nodal position? How do you assuage potential fears of dependence on the part of partners?

6. If you join a coalition without being a nodal player, what are the benefits and risks? How do you avoid becoming overly depen-dent on the nodal player?

7. Is co-option likely to make competition take place in your areas of strength, or not? (If co-option takes competition into your areas of weakness, you may, obviously, want to reconsider.)

8. Do you have the "right" set of partners in the coalition? Strong enough and complementary? Able to surround incum-bents and leaders? Not so strong that they will dominate and dwarf you?

9. Who is likely to gain and who is likely to lose from the emer-gence of competitive coalitions? Why? How?

For value creation through cospecialization

1. Do you need complementary, cospecialized resources to access new markets and/or create new business development opportunities?

2. Do you need complementary cospecialized skills and technolo-gies to develop, build, and sell your products?

3. Are there opportunities to create new businesses that require combining and melding skills and experiences from multiple companies?

4. Can access to the complementary cospecialized resources be achieved more easily and simply through means other than an alliance (for instance, buying technological licenses, obtaining subcontractors' or distributors' contracts)?

5. What makes the alliance superior to alternatives?
   - A partner making unique contributions (such as embedded competencies, government relations, and "insider" status) that cannot be traded easily between companies?
   - A partner making unique contributions that cannot be substituted? (For example, there is no alternative partner and/or no alternative source for the contribution.)
   - A partner making unique contributions that cannot be developed or replicated independently within a reasonable time frame?

For value creation through learning and internalization

1. Do you suffer from skill gaps?
   - If so, are these missing skills likely to be collective, tacit, organizationally embedded—that is, do you need to copractice them with a more experienced company, or can you purchase these skills by hiring the right people or licensing the appropriate technologies?

2. Given your position in the race for the future, what new capabilities and skills do you need to harness?

3. Do your partner companies possess these capabilities and skills?
   - Will your partners be willing to share them with you?
   - Are you comfortable depending on a partner? Or do you need to learn these capabilities and skills yourself if you don't want your bargaining power in the alliance to become weak and your position thus precarious?
   - If the required capabilities and skills are "new to the world," how much can you benefit from developing them jointly with partners (for example, in an R&D collaboration program)?
   - As you plan your competence strategies and technology road maps for the future, can you consider a sequence of alliances with different partners allowing you to access, learn, and internalize the range of required capabilities and skills over time?

ASSESSING INTERPARTNER COMPATIBILITY

Understanding each other's positions and ambitions

1. How well do you understand the respective, and relative, competitive positions of the partners vis-à-vis the alliance's activities?

2. Do you understand the strategic stakes of your partners in the alliance?

3. Are the partners really in different competitive spaces (for instance, applying similar competencies to different industries)? Or are the partners market rivals?

4. Are the partners likely to converge toward the same competitive space outside the alliance and hence risk becoming market rivals?

5. If partners are market rivals in the same industry, how can one characterize the status of each in the industry: leader, challenger, laggard, newcomer?

6. How well do you understand the strategic ambitions of the various partners? Which partner wants to use the alliance to improve its status in the industry? Which is content with the status quo? Which may consider the alliance to be a means of phased exit?

7. Is there a risk that you misread the strategic ambitions of your partners because you implicitly assume they are like you?

8. Do you consider the alliance from your partners' standpoint, given their stakes, ambitions, and positions?

Assessing compatibility

1. How compatible are the relative competitive positions of the various partners, actual or potential, in the alliance?

2. How compatible are their strategic ambitions?
   - Are they similarly positioned, sharing the same ambition and common enemies?
   - Are their positions and/or ambitions different but compatible (in the alliance)?
   - How acceptable is (mutual) dependence?

3. Are the partners sufficiently differentiated and making suffi-

ciently unique and sustainable contributions for the alliance to endure? And to create value for all partners?

4. Do they have reasons to be equally committed to the alliance?

5. Is compatibility between partners likely to improve or to deteriorate over time?

6. If you are a leading firm in an alliance, are you sure you do not show misplaced hubris and arrogance in dismissing weaker partners? Might you not be surprised by their ambitions? Do you risk mistaking momentum for energy and drive? Are you willing to help your partners improve their competitive position?

7. If you are a newcomer or challenger, how realistic are your ambitions? Where do you accept continued dependence on your partners? Where do you challenge it? Are the areas where you challenge dependence likely to be acceptable to your partners?

8. What quid pro quo are you prepared to provide to make your ambitions in the alliance more palatable to partners?

Designing the Alliance

This section begins with a set of questions on the parameters that should guide alliance design, roughly paralleling the outline of Chapter 3: valuing contributions, understanding the strategic and economic scopes of the alliance and setting its operational scope, understanding the joint task demands, defining and setting measurements of alliance progress, and anticipating likely longevity.

This section also incorporates more specific questions about design that stem from our discussion of governance and interface design in Chapter 5.

VALUING CONTRIBUTIONS

1. How clearly can you connect alliance results to partners' contributions?
   - Do the partners make contributions that are difficult to value ex

ante (such as local "insider" relationships or competencies being applied to a new opportunity that requires their adaptation)?

- Can you isolate the contributions made by each partner to the success of the alliance, or is there causal ambiguity between the partners' contributions and alliance success?
- If contributions are hard to value ex ante and their role in alliance success is difficult to assess, can you build into the alliance design provisions for reevaluating contributions over time and for reapportioning benefits between partners?
- Can you blend a priori evaluations of contributions (for example, a "50-50" joint venture, assuming contributions are equal) with a posteriori flexibility (for example, provisions that allow dividends from the joint venture to be shared according to criteria other than the shares of equity)?

2. To what extent are partners accruing costs and benefits outside the alliance?
   - How clearly can you identify costs and benefits outside the formal scope of the alliance for each of the partners?
   - Does your approach to value creation take into account a comprehensive range of alliance costs and benefits (direct and indirect, economic and strategic, tangible and intangible), not merely a simple input-output accounting?
   - Does your assessment of the benefits of the alliance clearly distinguish the value each partner draws separately from the value created jointly?
   - Do you understand the full extent of the "trade," explicit and implicit, between the partners? (For example, what is explicitly understood between partners as a cospecialization alliance, and seen only as such by a partner, may offer considerable opportunities to learn surreptitiously for another partner in the alliance that sees the "trade" more broadly and less explicitly.)
   - What are the nature and the terms of the "trade" taking place between partners?
   - Do you have reliable external benchmarks to value the trade between partners? (For instance, is there any form of market price for some of what is exchanged between partners?)
   - Do you observe, or infer, the presence of strong asymmetries between partners in how interdependent (versus "stand alone") the activities of the alliance are with each partner's operations?

- If the alliance is very interdependent with the activities of only one partner, have you reflected the differences in the alliance design?

3. How do you discover the actual value sought by each partner?
   - Have you set a climate of openness in the negotiation process (for instance, by revealing your true interests rather than taking bargaining positions)?
   - Do you carefully monitor partner behavior for possible unexpected departure from the behavior that declared goals would lead one to expect?
   - Do you understand the forms, arenas, and stakes of potential rivalry in the alliance, between your partners and yourself?
   - How comfortable are you with self-interest being served by cooperation, hence being dependent on mutual interest?
   - Do you have a comprehensive enough perspective on alliance costs and benefits to place specific tension areas in a broader context and address them from that broader perspective?

4. How do you handle shifts in the relative value of partners' contributions over time?
   - Do you think of the alliance as an evolving, flexible relationship?
   - How comfortable are you and your partners with being unable to fully plan the alliance at its inception or to encapsulate it fully in detailed initial agreements?
   - Are you considering the alliance as a likely series of commitments made over time that will be reassessed periodically?
   - Are you comfortable with the prospect of bargaining recurring over time, reflecting changes in the value of respective contributions?
   - Are you willing and able to balance the need for continuity and longevity (assuming the alliance creates value over time) with the need to constantly keep score on benefits?
   - Are you comfortable with the possibility of increasing commitments (which are likely to become increasingly irreversible) to the alliance over time as a key to value creation?

SETTING THE ALLIANCE SCOPE

1. How clearly do you understand the strategic scope of the alliance for yourself? What unintended strategic outcomes could the alliance bring about?

2. How clearly do you perceive your partners' strategic scope? Do you have a clear picture of that scope, or is the true strategic significance of the alliance for the partners hard to fathom?

3. Do you understand what underlying assumptions need to hold true for your partners to remain strategically committed to the alliance and to its success?

4. Are differences in the respective strategic scopes the partners each assign to the alliance likely to become sources of conflict?

5. To what degree are the actions of each partner likely to be contingent on a broader strategic context?

6. How compatible are the economic scopes of the alliance for each partner (given the valuation questions raised in the previous section)?

7. Are you setting the operational scope of the alliance, as well as its governance structure, so as to minimize "trade frictions" between partners?

UNDERSTANDING THE JOINT TASK DEMANDS

1. Do you understand how different value creation logics might require tasks to be jointly performed by the partners in a more or less interdependent way (co-option usually calling for the least, cospecialization typically for more, and learning and internalization for the most task interdependence)?

2. If the alliance value creation requires complex interactions between partners, do the alliance design and the process you put in place measure up to the task?

3. Are you ready to devote the amount of attention and effort to the alliance that will be necessary for value creation and capture?

4. Are you willing to review and readjust the governance and day-to-day processes of the alliance implementation periodically?

5. Does the form given to the alliance match the needs for joint optimization under uncertainty, task integration, and speedy decision making?

6. Is the design of your interface capable of handling the task demands?

7. Are you striving both to decrease the task demands and to improve the interface?

8. Do you build bridges between partners at multiple levels?

9. Are you sensitive enough to the need for coordination within your own organization and between the various people and sub-units involved in the interface with the partner organization?

10. To what extent do you need to exercise control? How do you exercise control and influence? Is that need for control strong enough to justify trade-offs against efficient task performance?

DEFINING AND MEASURING PROGRESS

1. Are the criteria you select and use to measure success fully consistent with the value creation expectations you hold and the value creation logics you follow? In particular, do your measurements reflect the full scope of the benefits sought? Or are some benefits ignored in your measures of alliance success?

2. Is the balance between using the alliance to develop options and achieving commitment to the alliance captured in your measurement? Does it correspond to the nature of alliance objectives?

3. How do you assess the loss of strategic autonomy that nearly always results from a cospecialization (and often from a co-option) alliance? Conversely, how do you measure the gain in future strategic autonomy that normally results from successful learning and internalization through an alliance?

4. Does the way that you measure success and assess contributions give partners the incentives to excel in the alliance?

5. Do you distinguish in your assessment of progress the value creation perspective (efficiency), the value capture perspective (benefits for you), and the strategic perspective (risk of dependence versus gain in bargaining power)?

6. Are the partners using compatible criteria to measure progress?

ANTICIPATING LONGEVITY

1. Is your expectation of the alliance's duration realistically anchored in its value creation logic?

2. What are the critical assumptions (about markets, technologies,

the environment, and partners' strategic contexts) that need to hold true for the alliance to keep creating value?

3. Have you designed into the alliance ways to periodically reassess whether these assumptions still hold true?

Getting Started

Questions in this section stem from the arguments developed in Chapters 6 and 7. They can help you address two basic, but critical, questions: First, how wide are the gaps between partners at the start of cooperation, and how can they be bridged effectively? Second, what do the partners need to learn about each other, the alliance, and its context to be able to improve the effectiveness of their cooperation over time and to create and extract the full value of their alliance?

In this section, questions are aimed sequentially, first at each of the interpartner gaps discussed in Chapter 6, and then at elements of the learning agenda discussed in Chapter 7.

UNDERSTANDING AND BRIDGING INITIAL GAPS BETWEEN PARTNERS

How favorable is the initial context of collaboration? Does the frame gap get in the way of collaboration?
Do partners have compatible frames (definitions, perspectives, rules, assumptions) of the alliance?

1. Is there a risk that you are applying an inappropriate frame to the alliance (for instance, an acquisition frame to a partnership of equals)?

2. Is your framing incompatible with that of your partners (for instance, you see the alliance as a step toward a takeover, they see it as a temporary cooperative agreement)?

3. Does everyone in your own organization who is to be involved in the alliance share the same frame? Are these inconsistencies between functions, geographical units, or levels in the hierarchy?

4. Do you carry obsolete frames or frames borrowed from an ear-

lier experience, which may not be transferable? Do you see your partners doing the same?

To bridge the frame gaps you may have identified above:

1. Do you try to see the alliance through the eyes of your partners?
2. Do you share past experiences with alliances with your partners?
3. Do you give partners feedback as to why you believe they joined the alliance, what you perceive to be their motives? Do you discuss discrepancies between stated motives and behavior? Do you resolve misunderstandings?
4. How well do you communicate about the alliance internally to ensure that everyone involved shares a common and accurate frame?

Is the expectation gap likely to lead to disappointment?
How realistic are your expectations and those of your partners?

1. Are the negotiation terms of the alliance likely to have led to overly optimistic or ambitious expectations?
2. Is there a risk that you and your partner oversold the merits of the alliance to each other?

To bridge the expectation gap:

1. How well have you assessed and validated the alliance's value creation logic?
2. Have you involved those who will be responsible for implementing the alliance in the negotiation process? Have they accepted the stated expectations as their own?
3. Are you preparing your managers for the possibility of an expectation downfall?

How wide is the organizational context gap?
How dissimilar are you and your partner organizations in the ways you make decisions and perform work? (See Table 6-2.)

1. Do differences in the size of your company as compared with that of your partners make collaboration difficult because of

- different speeds or styles of decision making?
- different pace and rhythm of strategizing and planning?
- different ways of handling data?

2. Are any of the differences between you and your partners in how work gets done likely to make joint work in the alliance hard to perform?

3. Are these differences likely to make you uncomfortable about working together? Might this, in turn, prevent learning?

To bridge the organizational context gap:

1. Have you recognized the importance of organizational and cultural compatibility in the design of your alliance? How?

2. Can you appoint to the alliance managers who have had experience working in different kinds of cultures (national, organizational, and so on).

3. Did you make an effort to learn how partner organizations really operate?

4. Can you refrain from making premature judgments about the partner's ways of working?

5. Have you planned for "gatekeepers" and buffers in the design of the partnership interface?

6. Do you and your partners create space and time (for instance, in joint workshops and seminars) for members of the partner organizations to share and understand their respective organizational contexts?

7. Do partners exchange enough personnel or is the relationship kept at "arm's length"?

8. Are your managers comfortable with the level of interaction with their partners or is it too little or too much?

Do you suffer from a confidence gap?
As they enter the partnership, do your managers and specialists feel secure enough in their position with your company so that they will feel free to adjust to the partner's ways of working and to adapt their own behavior in order to make the alliance work?

1. Is the alliance itself seen as a personal threat, for instance, to anyone's job?

2. Is mutual dependence accepted by members of the partner organizations?

3. Are any members of your organization or your partners likely to see the need for the alliance as an admission of failure?

To bridge the confidence gap:

1. How well understood are the likely personal consequences of alliance success, and failure, for everyone involved?

2. Are potential fears contained?

3. Is the value creation profile of the alliance understood and shared by all at the personal level?

4. Are there risks that individual managers and specialists will lose from the alliance?

How feasible is the planned content of the alliance?
Do you face a skill gap?

1. Are your partners' skills very different from yours?

2. Do your partners have areas of competence that you don't understand, and vice versa?

3. How strongly do the organization, business processes, and work practices of your partners reflect the nature of their skill base? What about in your company?

4. How tightly interdependent and intertwined are the various areas of skills, both for your partners and for your organization?

To bridge the skill gap:

1. Can you codify the partners' skills and your own, so they become more easily understandable?

2. Is such codification just a "representation" of the skills (which would suffice if you merely need to juxtapose skills) or an "operationalization" (which is required for process integration)?

3. What tools (such as software design tools) support the partners' respective skills?

Do you face a task definition gap?

1. How precisely are you able to define and accomplish the alliance tasks?

To bridge the task definition gap:

1. Do you make task (re)definition an interactive process in your design, or merely a one-shot affair?
2. Is the advantage of engaging first in fast feedback tasks, which allows learning, reflected in the design of the alliance?
3. Do you learn from the feedback of performing tasks together?
4. Can you start by tackling relatively small tasks that are likely to succeed and use the learning to address more ambitious and difficult tasks later on?

How well did you start the process of collaboration?

1. Did the negotiation process between partners promote mutual goodwill or mistrust?
2. Did you gain or lose trust in your partner during negotiations?
3. Are the various parties satisfied with the negotiation outcomes?

Do you suffer from an enduring information gap?
Do partners share information openly or do they maintain enduring "information asymmetry" between them?

1. How is information shared: through unilateral disclosures? quid pro quo? constrained release?
2. Do partners trust each other with key information?
3. Do partners create joint new information (market studies, for instance) or just exchange existing information?
4. What are the arrangements concerning intellectual property rights? Do they involve open sharing between the partners or separate ownership? How do they balance the need for partners to share information with the need to prevent leakage of valuable information to third parties?

To bridge the information gap:

1. Can you build norms of reciprocity into the sharing of information? Can you use these norms to foster sharing?
2. Can you foster sharing and joint protection of intellectual property rights?

Do you suffer from a time gap?

1. Is the schedule of costs and benefits likely to be significantly different between the partners, thus creating a time gap between them?
2. Does one partner incur significant costs early, with benefits deferred until much later?
3. Is there a significant difference between the relatively certain nature of short-term costs and benefits and the uncertain nature of long-term costs and benefits?

To bridge the time gap:

1. Do milestones and scorecards for the alliance reflect the expected schedules of costs and benefits for each partner?
2. How do you ensure score keeping cumulatively over the life of the alliance?
3. What safeguards do you put in place against the temptation to "defect" on the part of the partner who gets benefits early?
4. Can you realistically expect the partners to collaborate in further alliances over time beyond this one?

ESTABLISHING THE INTERPARTNER LEARNING AGENDA

How do you plan to learn, as partners, about the environment of the alliance? (The *what* to learn is specific to each alliance, the *how* to learn it is generic; questions therefore focus on the *how*.)

1. Do you use new data common to all your partners rather than your own?
2. Do you clarify and debate assumptions with your partners?
3. Do you share the *whys* of your positions with your partners?

4. Do you contain perceived personal risks for the managers involved?

5. Are you patient enough?

6. Do you actively seek convergence of your perspectives on the environment? Or do you just assume convergence will occur?

About the alliance tasks

1. Is the planned level of interaction between partners likely to meet the needs of the task?

2. Do you facilitate joint task learning between partners?

3. Do you make the knowledge to be shared to perform the task as explicit as possible?

4. What is the "bandwidth" of communication between the partners? Is it broad enough to meet the needs of the alliance tasks?

5. Do you limit the number of sites, groups, and teams involved in interaction but make that interaction intense and in-depth?

6. Do you strive to improve the likelihood that alliance implementers will perform the alliance tasks as well as they can?

About the cooperative process

1. Do you understand how your partners approach the cooperation process?

2. Do you understand whether your operating procedures are conducive to a successful cooperation process?

3. Do you understand what makes the partner(s) give their best?

4. Does anyone involved step outside the process for a better view of it? (Or is everyone very much in the thick of it?)

5. Do you let objective, outside parties observe the process?

6. Do you make unilateral commitments? Are such commitments reciprocated?

7. Do you work to resolve misunderstandings as soon as their presence is detected? (Or are they occasionally left to grow and fester?)

About a partner's skills

1. How much do you need to learn about a partner's skills to combine them with your own?

2. How much did you know or find out about a partner's skills before even forming the alliance?

3. Do you understand how each partner's skills, organization, and procedures interact?

4. How likely is it that your skill bases will be compatible?

About goals and expectations

1. How clear are partners' goals? Are the stated goals likely to represent the full agenda?

2. Do you observe partners in order to detect behaviors inconsistent with shared expectations (which might reveal the presence of a hidden agenda)?

3. Do you observe related actions by partners outside the scope of the alliance that might give you clues about unrevealed objectives?

4. Do you analyze how partners may cumulatively use other separate but related alliances to gain bargaining strength in their alliance with you?

5. In your exchanges, do you discuss your respective interests rather than take bargaining positions? Or are partners' true interests unknown to you?

Managing for Value Creation and Value Capture over Time

The questions in this section are designed to help you assess an ongoing alliance along three dimensions: (1) how much further value is it likely to create, (2) whether that value is being shared equitably between partners, and (3) given uncertainties and change, whether partners are able and willing to make needed adjustments in the way they work together. The questions are not intended to help you address the value creation issue in substance but to help you determine whether the quality of the cooperation process between partners is improving or deteriorating over time and, therefore—other things being equal—whether the odds of success are increasing or not.

Questions 9–14 address the issues of balance and equity in the relationship between partners. They will help you analyze how much the alliance balance between partners matters, what influences it, and how interpartner skill learning may be used to restore that balance.

As the collaboration progresses, partners should keep asking three evaluative questions to decide on next steps:

- How much value remains to be created, at a minimum? (Use the measurement yardsticks described above in "Designing the Alliance," under "Defining and Measuring Progress.")
- Is that value likely to be captured equitably by each partner?
- Given uncertainties and the need for change, how capable and willing to make adjustments are you, and your partners, likely to be?

Is your learning sufficient to enable you to answer the above questions? In particular, can you answer the third positively? Or are you running into a crisis? (See Table 7-1 for a list of symptoms).

1. In your monitoring of progress, do you consider the quality of the process, not just the results?

2. Are you observing shifts in the nature of individual participation in the alliance? Do involved managers and functional specialists shift from interinstitutional to interpersonal trust?

3. Are they willing to shed the constraints of organizationally prescribed roles?

4. Are you and your partners willing to make adjustments to the alliance interface and governance processes to improve efficiency?

5. Are you and your partners willing to make greater, more irreversible commitments? (See Figure 7-5.)

6. What is the basis for the uniqueness of each partner's contribution?

7. Is the uniqueness of each partner's contribution being maintained?

8. What determines the relative pace of skill learning between partners?
   - How strong is each partner's intent to learn? Strategically? Practically?
   - How transparent (to the other partners) is each partner's contribution?
   - Are you managing transparency?
     - Are you concerned with making yourself less transparent?
     - Do the interface design, and the interface process, limit transparency? In whose favor? In a balanced way?
     - How well do you understand the value of your skills to a partner?
     - How deeply embedded are the skills you contribute to the alliance?
     - Can you collaborate successfully without process integration, and thus without having to reveal your skills?
     - How receptive are you and your partners to new skills?

9. Is mutual dependence shifting between partners, one (or some) becoming more dependent, others less so?

10. Is one partner making a more specialized contribution to the alliance (for instance, providing assets or developing skills that would have no use outside of the alliance)?

11. Is cospecialization intensive enough to make the partners mutually dependent to the extent that balance is assumed? Or, on the contrary, are concerns for asymmetric cospecialization preventing cospecialization from taking place?

12. As your alliance evolves, is the balance between partners reasonably well maintained? (See Figure 8-1.)

13. What are the various "scales" on which balance is achieved in your alliance? What tips each scale? Which scales carry more weight? Are the weights on the various scales additive, or do a few determine the overall balance in the alliance?

14. Have you successfully completed one (or several) learning reevaluation and adjustment cycle? Have your commitments and expectations grown from cycle to cycle?

Assessing the Alliance's Interdependence with Other Relationships

Questions in this last section focus on a set of issues that go beyond assessing a single alliance to address the interdependencies among multiple alliances.

1. Is the alliance the only one, or is it part of a web of alliances between the same partners?

2. To what extent can decisions be made autonomously by partners on the alliance's own merits, or to what extent do other alliances interfere?

3. If the alliance is part of a broader network, what is the nature of the interdependencies between the alliance and other relationships?

4. What is the structure—planned or emergent, explicit or implicit—of the network?

5. How is the network maintained?

6. What is your role in the network? Your alliance partners' role?

7. Do the network interdependencies create a risk of unjustified dependence on the partners? Is your specific alliance hostage to other relationships? Which ones?

8. If the alliance is embedded in a network, how robust is the network and how strong is the commitment of the members? (See Table 9-1.)

❖

NOTES

INTRODUCTION

1. Statistics on strategic alliances are notoriously unreliable, since definition and reporting vary across industries and data bases. However, for statistical evidence, readers may consult the following: Deigan Morris and M. Hergert, "Trends in International Collaborative Agreements," *Columbia Journal of World Business* 22, no. 2 (1987): 15–21; Herbert I. Fusfeld and C. S. Haklisch, *Industrial Productivity and International Cooperation* (Oxford and New York: Pergamon Press, 1982); John R. Harbison and P. Pekar, "A Practical Guide to Alliances: Leapfrogging the Learning Curve," in *Series of Viewpoints on Alliances* (Los Angeles: Booz•Allen and Hamilton, 1993); John R. Harbison and P. Pekar, "Cross-Border Alliances in the Age of Collaboration," in *Series of Viewpoints on Alliances* (Los Angeles: Booz•Allen and Hamilton, 1997); John Hagedoorn, "Understand the Rationale of Strategic Technology Partnering: Interorganizational Modes of Cooperation and Sectoral Differences," *Strategic Management Journal* 14 (1993): 371–385; and Joel Bleeke and D. Ernst, eds., *Collaborating to Compete: Using Strategic Alliances and Acquisitions in the Global Marketplace* (New York: John Wiley & Sons, 1993).

CHAPTER 1

1. An actual network is not even required to create network economies. What creates "network economies," as defined by economists, is the mere existence of complementary, standardized goods that must interface, such as video tape recorders and tapes. This complementarity means that

the value to each user of using the goods or services increases with the number of users, creating increasing returns to diffusion.

2. For more information on Iridium, see "Iridium Inc.," *Industry Week*, December 19, 1994, 51–54.

3. H. Landis Gabel, *Competitive Strategies for Product Standards: The Strategic Use of Compatibility Standards for Competitive Advantage* (New York: McGraw-Hill, 1987); and Adam H. Brandenburger and Barry J. Nalebuf, *Co-Opetition* (New York: Currency/Doubleday, 1996).

4. Kathryn Rudie Harrigan, *Managing for Joint Venture Success* (Lexington, Mass.: Lexington Books, 1986); and Jean-François Hennart, "A Transaction Cost Theory of Equity Joint Ventures," *Strategic Management Journal* 9, no. 4 (1988): 361–374.

5. Jason Christopher Spender, G. Slowinski, G. S. Farris, and F. Hull, "Handling the Uncertainty in R&D Alliances," *Advances in Global High-Technology Management* 6 (1996): 55–70.

6. Paul S. Adler, B. Goldoftas, and D. I. Levine, "Ergonomics, Employee Involvement and the Toyota Production System: A Case Study of NUMMI's 1993 Model Introduction," *Industrial and Labor Relations Review* 50, no. 3 (April 1997): 416–437; and Clair Brown and M. Reich, "When Does Union-Management Cooperation Work? A Look at NUMMI and GM-Van Nuys," *California Management Review* 31, no. 4 (1989): 26–44.

7. For details on the Ciba-Geigy–Alza relationship, see INSEAD case studies by Reinhard Angelmar and Yves Doz, "Ciba-Geigy/Alza Case Series: Condensed" (including "Advanced Drug Delivery Systems: Alza and Ciba-Geigy"; "Alza Corporation"; and "Ciba-Geigy Limited: Pharmaceutical Division"), 1988, condensed 1994; "Ciba-Geigy/Alza Case Series" (including "Advanced Drug Delivery Systems: Alza and Ciba Geigy" A–F; "Alza Corporation" A and B; and "Ciba-Geigy Limited: Pharmaceutical Division" A–C), 1988, rev. 1992–1993.

8. Henry Mintzberg, *The Rise and Fall of Strategic Planning* (New York: Prentice Hall, 1994); and Philippe Haspeslagh and D. B. Jemison, *Managing Acquisitions: Creating Value Through Corporate Renewal* (New York: Free Press, 1991).

9. Gary Hamel, Yves L. Doz, and C. K. Prahalad, "Collaborate with Your Competitors—and Win," *Harvard Business Review*, January–February 1989, 133–139.

10. Fuji-Xerox's TQM program was borrowed from Fuji and led Fuji-Xerox to win the Deming prize; it was subsequently adopted by Xerox to win the Baldrige Award and the EFQM Prize. More important, it led to tremendously improved quality.

11. For details on the evolution of the relationship between Fuji and Xerox, see Krista McQuade and B. Gomes-Casseres, "Xerox and Fuji Xerox," Harvard Business School case #9-391-156, 1991, rev. 1992.
12. Ranjay Gulati, "Does Familiarity Breed Trust? The Implications of Repeated Ties for Contractual Choice in Alliances," *Academy of Management Journal* 38, no. 1 (February 1995): 85–112.
13. Ranjay Gulati, T. Khanna, and N. Nohria, "Unilateral Commitments and the Importance of Process in Alliances," *Sloan Management Review* 35, no. 3 (Spring 1994): 61–70.
14. Peter S. Ring, "Fragile Trust and Resilient Trust and Their Roles in Cooperative Interorganizational Relationships," in *Proceedings of the International Association of Business and Society, Fifth Annual Conference,* ed. S. Wartick and D. Collins (Hilton Head, S.C., March 17–20 1994), 107–113.
15. This threat subsided in early 1996 when DASA ended its support of Fokker, which then went bankrupt. DASA's move was seen by Aérospatiale as a peace signal. The threat increased again in 1997 with DASA's alliance with MATRA and British Aerospace in missiles and satellites.
16. Gary Hamel, "Competition for Competence and Inter-Partner Learning Within International Strategic Alliances," *Strategic Management Journal* 12 (1991): 83–103.
17. See Henry Kissinger, *Diplomacy* (New York: Simon & Schuster, 1994).

CHAPTER 2

1. After a few years, the relationship faltered and the alliance was dissolved.
2. For a summary of the "winner take all" approach, see Brian Arthur, "Increasing Returns and the New World of Business," *Harvard Business Review*, July–August 1996, 100–109.
3. David B. Yoffie, *Competing in the Age of Digital Convergence* (Boston: Harvard Business School Press, 1997).
4. Henry W. Chesbrough and D. J. Teece, "When Is Virtual Virtuous? Organizing for Innovation," *Harvard Business Review*, January–February 1996, 65–74.
5. Yves Doz, "General Electric and SNECMA" A–C, INSEAD case study, 1990, 1996.
6. Competitor co-option bolsters one's own competitive position by enlisting the participation of weaker competitors into one's coalition, as Fujitsu did with Amdahl, ICL, Siemens, and others. Complementer co-option makes one firm more attractive, both as a supplier and as a partner, than others since it enjoys privileged, often exclusive, access to complementary goods.

7. See H. Landis Gabel and O. Cadot, "High Definition Television in Europe," INSEAD case study, 1993. See also "The U.S. Wins One in High-Tech TV," *Fortune*, April 8, 1991, 50–54.

8. This is the "empty box syndrome" experienced by many acquirers in the investment banking industry. In more than a few instances, the star bankers and financial engineers walked away from the acquired firm, leaving its purchaser with an expensive, but empty, box. The same is often true of acquisitions of research-based companies by large groups.

9. The case of the former number four U.S. auto producer, American Motors (AMC), offers an example of a failed alliance. In the late 1970s, AMC teamed up with the French car maker, Renault, itself a financially troubled company with innovative but poorly made products ill-suited to the U.S. market. Nor was Renault in a position to bring AMC the skills it needed most: quality management and effective product development. Renault sold its controlling stake in AMC, at great loss, to Chrysler in 1987, leading to AMC's disappearance. (Chrysler continued to develop and manufacture AMC's old Jeep product line quite successfully and inherited a few outstanding French managers who contributed to Chrysler's recovery.) AMC had entered into a merger with a company from which it had little to learn, and which suffered from many of the same skill gaps as did AMC. In the meantime, the other three U.S. car makers had built a much better basis for skill complementation, and much better channels for plugging their skill gaps, through alliances with their respective Japanese partners.

CHAPTER 3

1. Gary Hamel, "Competition for Competence and Interpartner Learning Within International Strategic Alliances," *Strategic Management Journal* 12 (1991): 83–103.

2. Yves Doz, P. S. Ring, S. Lenway, and T. Murtha, "Pixtech," INSEAD case study, Loyola Marymount University, University of Minnesota, 1997.

3. Philips and Sony had, however, won the equally important standard battle for CDs and CD-ROMs.

4. Technology from Matsushita allowed the development of the single-sided high-capacity disk that overcame the disadvantage associated with the dual-sided technology of the coalition's first product proposal. (The dual-sided disk would have had to be turned over in the middle of a movie.)

5. Once the coalition becomes successful, these competitors may have no choice but to join, in particular when network externalities are strong and working against them. Joining a successful coalition late, however, prevents them from obtaining terms as favorable as those they would have negotiated had they joined early. These competitors typically join only when defeated.

6. Ingemar Dierickx and K. Cool, "Asset Stock Accumulation and Sustainability of Competitive Advantage," *Management Science* 35 (1989) 1504–1510.

7. SNECMA was the only French maker of powerful jet engines (Turbomeca, another French jet engine company, made only smaller turbines, mostly for helicopters and training and commuter planes) and the only European company other than Rolls-Royce that could develop such engines on its own.

8. See Jean-François Hennart, "A Transaction Cost Theory of Equity Joint Ventures," *Strategic Management Journal* 9, no. 4 (1988): 361–374. See also Oliver E. Williamson, "Credible Commitments: Using Hostages to Support Exchange," *American Economic Review* 73, no. 4 (1983): 519–540.

9. "The Partners," *Business Week*, February 10, 1992, 38–43; "How Ford and Mazda Shared the Driver's Seat," *Business Week*, March 26, 1990, 68–69; and Michael Y. Yoshino and U. S. Rangan, *Strategic Alliances: An Entrepreneurial Approach to Globalization* (Boston: Harvard Business School Press, 1995).

10. Barring this wider scope, there was concern that SNECMA would push the sales of the joint products only, while GE would push those it made on its own, possibly straining the relationship. There was also concern that airlines and plane makers would not see the alliance as "neutral" to their choices of aircraft types. Of course, the fact that SNECMA's participation was not the same across the whole product range could still lead to suspicions that each partner would push the engines in which it had the larger or more profitable share.

11. Ashish Nanda and C. A. Bartlett, "Corning Incorporated: A Network of Alliances," Harvard Business School case #9-391-102, 1990, rev. 1992.

12. Ciba-Geigy's management was aware that imposing too broad an operational scope on the alliance might reduce Alza's freewheeling innovativeness and entrepreneurship by dissolving its originality into a big company's bureaucracy.

13. Whether it had learned everything it needed to learn from Honda, Rover had learned a great deal. Over the course of its fifteen-year alliance, Rover's productivity increased fourfold, its quality improved by a factor of ten, and its development cycle times and costs were cut in half.

CHAPTER 4

1. One must define "leadership" in terms close enough to the object of
   the alliance to be meaningful; too broad a definition can be misleading. For example, GM may be a "leader" in the auto industry in
   terms of size, but it may have a lot to learn from Toyota, the competence leader in lean manufacturing. In the personal computer business, IBM and Compaq may be leaders from the standpoint of end-
   product volume, but they are very dependent on Intel and Microsoft,
   the true industry leaders.
2. David C. Mowery and N. Rosenberg, "The Japanese Commercial Aircraft Industry Since 1945: Government Policy, Technical Development,
   and Industrial Structure," Stanford, Calif., 1985 working paper, and
   Thomas W. Roehl and J. F. Truitt, "Stormy Open Marriages are Better:
   Evidence from U.S., Japanese and French Cooperative Ventures in Commercial Aircraft," *Columbia Journal of World Business* (Summer 1987): 87–95.
3. For an illustration, see the case study of Italtel in William H. David-
   son and J. R. de la Torre, *Managing the Global Corporation: Case Studies in
   Strategy and Management* (New York: McGraw-Hill, 1989).
4. Peter Grindley, D. C. Mowery, and B. Silverman, "SEMATECH and
   Collaborative Research: Lessons in the Design of High-Technology Consortia," *Journal of Policy Analysis and Management* 13, no. 4 (Fall 1994):
   723–758; and Larry D. Browning, J. M. Beyer, and J. D. Shetler, "Building
   Cooperation in a Competitive Industry: SEMATECH and the Semiconductor Industry," *Academy of Management Journal* 38, no. 1 (1995): 113–151.
5. Siemens, in fact, disappointed Corning by not becoming the world
   leader in telecom transmission and cable systems, while Corning was
   and still is the technology leader in optical fibers.
6. Gary Hamel, Y. Doz, and C. K. Prahalad, "Collaborate with Your
   Competitors—and Win," *Harvard Business Review*, January–February
   1989, 133–139; Gary Hamel, "Competition for Competence and Inter-
   Partner Learning Within International Strategic Alliances," *Strategic
   Management Journal* 12 (1991): 83–103; Robert B. Reich and E. D. Mankin,
   "Joint Ventures with Japan Give Away Our Future," *Harvard Business
   Review*, March–April 1986, 78–86; and Dominique Turcq, "La Tunique
   de Nessus: Les Stratégies d'Accords Internationaux des Entreprises
   Japonaises," working paper, Groupe ESCP, Paris, 1985.
7. Krista McQuade and B. Gomes-Casseres, "Xerox and Fuji Xerox,"
   Harvard Business School case #9-391-156, 1991, rev. 1992.
8. The negotiated sale of a high-speed train system by GEC-Alsthom,
   the European electrical equipment firm, to South Korea involved an
   alliance with South Korean construction and engineering firms. The

terms of that alliance would lead to at least 50 percent of the value of the system being manufactured locally, an extensive technology transfer to the Koreans, and a licensing agreement giving the Koreans the right to market the GEC-Alsthom product (or their own derivatives) to any market outside Europe. Potentially, this arrangement will put the Koreans in competition with GEC-Alsthom's own product. The European company was so eager to establish itself in a demanding non-European market that it accepted these terms, knowing they might be setting up a future competitor.

CHAPTER 5

1. Yves Doz, "Eurovynil Corporation (A) and (B)," INSEAD-CEDEP case study, 1991, rev. 1992.
2. Although a similar risk exists for supplier relationships (witness the dependence of PC makers on Intel and Microsoft), this risk seems less tangible when the dependence is for a market or a key component than when it is literally for another nonstandardized "part" of the same product, and in particular when partners feel that they have given up some core technologies or competencies in the cospecialization pattern.
3. A second, related valuation issue arises in government-funded cooperative programs, in which weaker partners are assisted by their governments' demands for "juste retour," that is, for workshares that match their governments' shares of program financing. An overly rigid application of this principle prevents programs from moving ahead, particularly when the required technologies are too demanding to lend themselves to politically imposed sharing. Even in the absence of government pressures, the partners may want to ensure that the balance of contributions is in line with the balance of revenues, as was done in the initial worksharing agreement between GE and SNECMA. Such an approach, however, may tempt each partner to overstate the value of its contribution. Partners that are knowledgeable about each other's contributions will not allow such overestimation; conversely, partners whose contributions are more differentiated will have more difficulty assessing the real value or the cost of each other's contributions.
4. They are also constrained by labor laws and fiscal measures. The absence of a legal European company status, and differences in fiscal policies between European countries, for instance, remain major hindrances to pan-European alliances.
5. For a summary discussion, see Christine Oliver, "Determinants of Interorganizational Relationships: Integration and Future Directions," *Academy of Management Review* 15, no. 2 (1990): 241–265.

6. The classified nature of GE technologies would have made joint development or manufacturing unacceptable to the U.S. government.

7. Many such alliances falter, as did the alliance of Publicis and FCB in advertising. In that case, the alliance adopted the more decentralized structures and management systems that characterized Publicis in Europe, rather than the transnational network approach that had characterized FCB. In the eyes of FCB's management, this undermined the very logic for value creation—to better serve FCB's global customers, particularly those that were globalizing their brands and their promotion! As clients such as Nestlé and Levi Strauss were shifting toward managing themselves as global networks, the alliance was shifting in the opposite direction. As the alliance lost clients, its partners lost patience and filed for a breakup. Similar difficulties now undermine many airline alliances. Despite their proponents' claims to the contrary, these alliances seldom create real value for airline passengers. Service standards and brand images remain too different for seamless service to work in practice, and code sharing (the practice of numbering the same flight under various airlines' names) is often seen by passengers as a deception.

8. Kyonori Sakakibara, "R&D Cooperative Among Competitors: A Case Study of the VLSI Semiconductor Research Project in Japan," *Journal of Engineering and Technology Management* 10 (1993): 393–407.

9. "Iridium Inc.," *Industry Week*, December 19, 1994, 51–54.

10. Gary Hamel, "Competitive Collaboration: Learning, Power and Dependence in International Strategic Alliances" (Ph.D. diss., University of Michigan, 1990).

CHAPTER 6

1. For a general discussion of the term "organizational context" as we use it here, see Joseph L. Bower, *Managing the Resource Allocation Process* (Boston: Harvard Business School Division of Research, 1970; Boston: Harvard Business School Press, 1986).

2. Although the possibility of such contracts was part of the initial agreements, Ciba-Geigy did not expect they would materialize. In any case, Ciba-Geigy would have to vet them one by one. This was a clear case in which Alza's and Ciba-Geigy's private expectations clashed and where the design of the alliance, which stipulated that Alza could initiate third-party deals subject to prior approval by Ciba-Geigy, did not avoid conflicts.

3. Peter S. Ring, "Fragile Trust and Resilient Trust and Their Roles in Cooperative Interorganizational Relationships," *Proceedings of the International Association of Business and Society, Fifth Annual Conference*, ed. S.

Wartick and D. Collins (Hilton Head, S.C., March 17–20 1994), 107–113; Peter S. Ring and A. H. Van de Ven, "Developmental Processes in Cooperative Interorganizational Relationships," *Academy of Management Review* 19 (1994): 90–118; and Nagesh Kumar, "The Power of Trust in Manufacturer-Retailer Relationships," *Harvard Business Review,* November–December 1996, 92–106.

4. Larry Hirschhorn and T. Gilmore, "The New Boundaries of the 'Boundaryless' Company," *Harvard Business Review*, May–June 1992, 104–115.

5. This is an example of the problem we examined in our discussion (Chapter 1) of the danger of carrying over the mind-set and assumptions from traditional joint ventures into the newer types of alliances.

6. In alliances that lead to relatively autonomous joint ventures—in particular, multipartner R&D collaboratives—it may be useful to let the frame define itself rather than to try imposing a frame. This may sidestep the risk of discrepant, inappropriate, or improperly shared frames.

7. Interestingly, the reciprocal flow of personnel from Xerox to Fuji-Xerox has totaled only about 150, despite the fact that Fuji-Xerox has become increasingly more important to Xerox as a source of products, and learning, and as a window on Japanese competition in the photocopier and office automation industries.

8. Ranjay Gulati, "Social Structure and Alliance Formation Patterns: A Longitudinal Analysis," *Administrative Science Quarterly* 40, no. 4 (December 1995): 619–652.

9. Ranjay Gulati, T. Khanna, and N. Nohria, "Unilateral Commitments and the Importance of Process in Alliances," *Sloan Management Review* 35, no. 3 (Spring 1994): 61–70.

CHAPTER 7

1. In this respect, the contrast between the TTS and OROS projects in the Ciba-Geigy–Alza relationship is striking. While the TTS teams at Alza would organize parties for visiting Ciba-Geigy scientists, and often have them stay at their houses, the OROS team would cancel its usual Friday night beer bash when Ciba-Geigy representatives were in town, and everyone would go home early.

2. Peter S. Ring and G. Rands, "Sensemaking, Understanding, and Committing: Emergent Transaction Processes in the Evolution of 3M's Microgravity Research Program," in *Research on the Management of Innovation: The Minnesota Studies,* ed. Andrew H. Van de Ven, H. Angle, and M. S. Poole (New York: Ballinger/Harper Row, 1989), 337–366.

CHAPTER 8

1. Jean-François Hennart, "A Transaction Cost Theory of Equity Joint Ventures," *Strategic Management Journal* 9, no. 4 (July–August 1988): 361–374.

2. Two major new military programs, called respectively "Tiger" and NH90, were expected to account for the bulk of Eurocopter's activities in the mid- to late 1990s, and the respective national contributions to development costs were set as a function of expected orders.

3. Farok J. Contractor and P. Lorange, "Why Should Firms Cooperate? The Strategy and Economics Basis for Cooperative Ventures," in *Cooperative Strategies in International Business*, ed. F. P. Contractor and P. Lorange (Lexington, Mass.: D. C. Heath and Company/Lexington, 1988); and Franklin R. Root, "Some Taxonomies of International Cooperative Arrangements," ibid.

4. Richard W. Moxon, T. W. Roehl, and J. F. Truitt, "International Cooperative Ventures in the Commercial Aircraft Industry: Gains, Sure, But What's My Share?" ibid.

5. Because a partner's ambition and range of complementary capabilities may be difficult to ascertain, and because there may be no easy way of calculating the cost to a partner of acquiring particular skills in the absence of the partnership, it is difficult to determine the strategic worth of one's own skills. How firms deal with this problem is an issue for research.

6. William G. Ouchi, "Markets, Bureaucracies and Clans," *Administrative Science Quarterly* 25 (1980): 129–141.

7. Richard B. Peterson and J. Y. Shimada, "Sources of Management Problems in Japanese-American Joint Ventures," *Academy of Management Review* 3 (1978): 796–804.

8. Richard B. Peterson and H. F. Schwind, "A Comparative Study of Personnel Problems in International Companies and Joint Ventures in Japan," *Journal of International Business Studies* 8, no. 1 (1977): 45–55.

9. Alan A. Altshuler et al., *The Future of the Automobile* (Cambridge, Mass.: MIT Press, 1984).

10. Peter J. Killing, "Understanding Alliances: The Role of Task and Organizational Complexity," chap. 3 in Contractor and Lorange, *Cooperative Strategies*.

11. Kathryn R. Harrigan, *Managing for Joint Venture Success* (Lexington, Mass.: Lexington Books, 1986).

12. Christopher A. Bartlett and S. Ghoshal, *Transnational Management: Text, Cases and Readings in Cross-Border Management* (Homewood, Ill.: Irwin, 1992).

13. Yves Doz, "Technology Partnerships Between Larger and Smaller Firms: Some Critical Issues," in Contractor and Lorange, *Cooperative Strategies.*

CHAPTER 9

1. Ronald S. Burt, *Structural Holes: The Social Structure of Competition* (Cambridge, Mass.: Harvard University Press, 1992).
2. Mitchell P. Koza, "Nexia International," INSEAD case study forthcoming in J. R. de la Torre, Y. Doz, and T. Devinney, *Managing the Global Corporation* (Homewood, Ill.: Irwin).
3. Peter Grindley, D. C. Mowery, and B. Silverman, "SEMATECH and Collaborative Research: Lessons in the Design of High-Technology Consortia," *Journal of Policy Analysis and Management* 13, no. 4 (Fall 1994): 723–758.
4. Actually, the initial goal was to share manufacturing technology expertise directly between the various semiconductor manufacturers. The fact that their manufacturing skills differed widely, however, made such sharing unfeasible; concentrating on improving the supplier base provided a fallback position to SEMATECH participants, one that all but three of the original partners endorsed. (Those three dropped out, partly because of their discomfort with SEMATECH's new focus.)
5. Thomas P. Murtha, J. W. Spencer, and S. A. Lenway, "Moving Targets: National Industrial Strategies and Embedded Innovation in the Global Flat Panel Display Industry," *Advances in Strategic Management,* vol. 13 (Greenwich, Conn.: JAI Press, 1996), 245–279.
6. Jürgen Häusler, H. Hans-Willy, and S. Lütz, "Contingencies of Innovative Networks: A Case Study of Successful Interfirm R&D Collaboration," *Research Policy* 23 (1994): 47–66.
7. Yves Doz and O. Baburoglu, "From Competition to Collaboration: The Emergence and Evolution of R&D Cooperatives" (Paper presented at the 4th International Conference on Multi Organizational Partnerships and Cooperative Strategy, Balliol College, Oxford, July 1997).
8. Häusler, Hans-Willy, and Lütz, "Contingencies of Innovative Networks."
9. Barbara Gray, *Collaborating: Finding Common Ground for Multiparty Problems* (San Francisco: Jossey-Bass, 1989).
10. Kyonori Sakakibara, "From Imitation to Innovation: The Very Large Scale Integrated (VLSI) Semiconductor Project in Japan," working paper #1490-83, Sloan School, MIT, Cambridge, Mass., October 1983; and Joe Bower, "The Microelectronics and Computer Technology Corporation," Harvard Business School case #9-383-067, 1982.

11. Larry D. Browning, J. M. Beyer, and J. C. Shetler, "Building Coopera-tion in a Competitive Industry: Sematech and the Semiconductor Industry," *Academy of Management Journal* 38, no. 1 (1995): 113–151.

12. Local banks in Illinois, for instance, collaborated to develop informa-tion technology systems jointly, under the leadership of Information Technology Consultants.

13. James L. Heskett, "Benetton (A) and (B)," Harvard Business School, cases #9-685-014 (rev. 11/85) and #9-685-020 (1985).

14. Raghu Garud and A. Kumaraswamy, "Changing Competitive Dynamics in Network Industries: An Exploration of Sun Microsystems' Open Systems Strategy," *Strategic Management Journal* 14 (1993): 351–369.

15. David Sheff, *Game Over: Nintendo's Battle to Dominate an Industry* (Lon-don: Hodder & Stoughton, 1993).

16. Ashish Nanda and C. A. Bartlett, "Corning Incorporated: A Network of Alliances." Harvard Business School case #9-391-102, 1990, rev. 8/12/92.

17. Quoted in "Corning Glass Work: International (A)," Harvard Busi-ness School case #9-3-79-051, 1978.

18. Olivetti experienced greater problems of consistency in its alliances than did Corning. The fact that Olivetti was not an overwhelmingly strong company relative to its partners, even in marketing, made its relationships with some partners difficult. Some treated Olivetti sim-ply as an OEM customer; others bypassed it, as Canon did when it sold its photocopiers in direct competition with those produced through its joint venture with Olivetti in Europe.

19. The large European assemblers (Peugeot, Renault, Volkswagen, and Fiat) worked selectively together but did not attempt to build strong global coalitions. The failure of some heralded grand alliances in that industry, such as the one between Renault and Volvo, may have had a sobering effect on potential partners in other alliances. See Nitin Nohria and C. Garcia-Pont, "Global Strategic Linkages and Industry Structure," *Strategic Management Journal* 12 (1991): 105–124.

Chapter 10

1. A 1995 Mercer Management Consulting study of Fortune 1000 com-panies in twelve major industries indicated that each industry con-tained one or several "hot" companies—even industries thought to be moribund, such as metals and textiles. The greatest variation was not, according to the study, between industries, but between companies within each industry. See Dwight L. Gertz and P. A. Joao Baptista, *Grow to Be Great: Breaking the Downsizing Cycle* (New York: Free Press, 1995).

2. C. K. Prahalad and Y. Doz, *The Multinational Mission: Balancing Local Demands and Global Vision* (New York: Free Press, 1987), chap. 11, "Managing Interdependencies Across Businesses," and chap. 12, "Creating Strategic 296apability: Toward an Ideal DMNC Organization."
3. For a full development of the analogy between piloting and organizational management, see George Labovitz and Victor Rosansky, *The Power of Alignment* (New York: John Wiley & Sons, 1997).

INDEX

ABOUT THE AUTHORS

Yves L. Doz is the Timken Professor of Global Technology and Innovation at INSEAD. From 1987 to 1994, he was director of INSEAD's Management of Technology and Innovation program, a multidisciplinary effort involving about twenty faculty members and researchers. Between 1990 and 1995, he was associate dean for R&D. He has also served on the faculty of the Harvard Business School and held visiting appointments at Stanford University and at Aoyama Gakuin University in Japan.

Professor Doz has worked on multinational aircraft programs and has consulted for many multinational corporations on global strategies, organization, strategic alliances, and competitive revitalization. His research on the strategy and organization of multinational companies, specifically in high-technology industries, has led to numerous publications, including four books. He is the co-author of a forthcoming Harvard Business School Press book, *The Metanationals: Competing Globally in the Knowledge Economy*. Professor Doz can be reached at yves.doz@insead.fr

Gary Hamel is founder and chairman of Strategos, a company dedicated to helping its clients get to the future first; Visiting Professor of Strategic and International Management at the London Business School; and the Thomas S. Murphy Distinguished Research Fellow at Harvard University Graduate School of Business Administration. Additionally, Hamel serves on the board of directors of the Strategic Management Society. *The Economist* calls Dr. Hamel "the world's reigning strategy guru," and Peter Senge views him as "the most influential thinker on strategy in the western world." As the author of concepts such as strategic intent, core competence, corporate imagination, strategic architecture, and industry foresight, he has fundamentally changed the focus and content of strategy in many of the world's most successful companies.

Gary Hamel has published eight articles in the *Harvard Business Review*, seven with co-author C. K. Prahalad. Hamel's article, "Strategy as Revolution," won the 1996 McKinsey Award for Article of the Year, Hamel's third McKinsey Award. His most recent article, "Strategy Innovation and the Quest for Value," appeared in the *Sloan Management Review*. His book, *Competing for the Future* (Harvard Business School Press), has been hailed by *The Economist, London Financial Times, Washington Post*, and many other journals as one of the decade's most influential business books, and by *BusinessWeek* as the "Best Management Book of the Year." It has been translated into fifteen languages and released in paperback.

Professor Hamel resides in Woodside, California, and can be reached at strategosnet.com or gh@strategosnet.com